The Chinese Worker

Chinese lumber-yard workers using a crane built by the workers themselves (China Reconstructs, *vol. 22, no. 11 [November 1973], inside back cover*)

The Chinese Worker

Charles Hoffmann

State University of New York Press

Albany 1974

For Shirley, Richard, Brian—
and all the others I love—
without whom the making of this book would
have had little meaning or purpose.

First published in 1974 by
State University of New York Press
99 Washington Avenue, Albany, New York 12210
Second Printing 1975
© 1974 State University of New York

Library of Congress Cataloging in Publication Data

Hoffmann, Charles, 1921–
  The Chinese worker.

  Includes bibliographical references.
  1. Labor and laboring classes—China.   2. Labor
policy—China.   I. Title.
HD8676.5.H6   301.44'42'0951   74-3053
ISBN 0-87395-238-3
ISBN 0-87395-239-1 (microfiche)

Preface

This book is an attempt to put today's Chinese worker into context; to see his or her work activities against the background of the revolutionary changes which Chairman Mao and his party followers have wrought and also to see how that same worker's condition is modified as Mao and his followers press toward equalizing the workers' and the peasants' environments. As an economist, I am also interested in how China's leaders deal with issues of training, allocating, motivating, and managing labor as well as shaping the dimensions of workers' welfare: their level of living and quality of life. On these issues I am especially curious to determine whether the labor institutions which have been utilized or reshaped to help achieve the regime's desired results follow the patterns of such institutions in the capitalist world or the Soviet Union or take on a different character that breaks with the psychological and philosophical assumptions upon which labor markets and incentive mechanisms function both in western capitalist countries and the USSR.

The completion of this work has been facilitated by the productive assistance and generous cooperation of a number of colleagues and friends, and valuable material support has been rendered through a variety of institutions. I am happy to acknowledge this assistance and to express my gratitude for it.

The Center for Chinese Studies at the University of California, Berkeley, is like a second home for me and even after these many years of enjoying its facilities and staff its warm welcome is still felt. Chalmers Johnson, Jack Service, C.P. Chen, Jo Pearson, and many others, some of whom are no longer directly connected with the center, have always been most helpful, and my feeling of belonging there that has developed has been a significant factor in making my work more enjoyable and fruitful. The specific material help forthcoming from the center has also been a major contribution to my work. In particular I am appreciative of the conscientious and effective aid given me by Frank Huang during the 1969–70 academic year while I was a visiting research scholar at the center. He uncovered much new and important primary material for me. Chalmers Johnson generously made Frank's invaluable research services available for the year, and I am grateful to both of them.

While this book was in various stages of development I benefited from comments and suggestions made by Gordon Bennett, William Hamovitch, Joyce Kallgren, Jim Nickum, Carl Riskin, Bill Snead, and Anne Thurston who read parts or all of an earlier draft. Their support, individually and collectively, was of great value to me.

My research trip to Hong Kong during the winter of 1970 was financed in a major way by a grant in aid from the Graduate School of the State University of New York at Stony Brook. I appreciate the support that Dean Herbert Weisinger gave to this venture.

Over the course of the years while this book was in process I enjoyed the use of materials from libraries of the following institutions: State University of New York at Stony Brook; University of California, Berkeley; the Hoover Institution, Palo Alto, Calif.; Columbia University (University Library as well as East Asian Institute Library), and the Universities Service Centre, Kowloon, Hong Kong.

While I was in Hong Kong I was assisted in a variety of ways by Eric Axilrod, L.F. Goodstadt, William Hsu, Talbot Huey, Stanley Karnow, Liu Doo Sung, Colina MacDougall, Guy Searls, and D.R.A. Spankie. I am grateful to them as well as to others who helped to make my stay in Hong Kong productive.

My recent visit to the People's Republic of China afforded me an opportunity to check on some of the information in this book. I am indebted to Ward Morehouse, Director of the Center for International Programs and Comparative Studies of the New York State Education Department, leader of our study group, and Jack Chen, formerly consultant to the Center, for this valuable opportunity. I also benefited from the observations and analyses of the other ten members of the group.

The typing and processing of a book easily becomes a source of frustration, irritation, and annoyance. The fact that such feelings have been at an absolute minimum is testimony to the cooly capable and devoted way in which Betty Hill, my secretary, has steered the book through its various stages. For her such performance is routine. For my good fortune and her wonderful assistance I am deeply thankful.

Brian, Richard, and Shirley Hoffmann helped to process the manuscript in various ways, lightening my burden.

Contents

Contents
viii

Tables

Tables

Abbreviations

The following abbreviations appear throughout the text.

ACCTU All-China Congress of Trade-Unions

ACFTU All-China Federation of Trade-Unions

CCP Chinese Communist Party

FFYP The First Five-Year Plan (1953–1957)

GLF The Great Leap Forward (1958–1960)

GPCR The Great Proletarian Cultural Revolution (1966–1968)

NPC National People's Congress

PLA People's Liberation Army

PRC People's Republic of China

SC State Council

WFTU World Federation of Trade-Unions

One

Introduction

The broad dual economic objectives of the Chinese Communist Party (CCP) to industrialize and to socialize the means of production and the work force have been accepted as generally compatible and reinforcing until recent years. Sharp differences had arisen, however, over their exact meaning and the strategy, time horizon, and priority for their realization. These were among the issues which formed the heart of the struggle within the CCP and crystallized into the sharp division between the Maoists and their Liuist adversaries, which led to the Great Proletarian Cultural Revolution (GPCR) from 1966 to 1968. They were issues that focused on economic questions but involved also major political, social, and philosophical considerations. As the division developed, the Maoists became increasingly aware that the rate of industrialization and modernization might be retarded by extended efforts to collectivize man and his organizational structures. That awareness subsumed the conviction that where a choice between the two goals was forced, socialization of man and structures took precedence.

In this context the changing course which the Chinese economy has taken since 1949 has affected significantly the conditions of life and labor of China's varied workers, reflecting both ideological-strategic struggles and economic vicissitudes. While the party has struggled over such concerns as rapid development of heavy industry, agricultural mechanization versus collectivization, investment policy for agriculture, material versus social incentives, laborpower allocation, and the like; the Chinese worker has found that the models he or she has been called upon to emulate and the quantity, variety, and type of rewards he or she has received have changed greatly. The rapid change, the zig zags and swings of policy, and the disarray that have been salient features of China's recent history have affected deeply the life and labor of the worker.

China's Economic Problem

The fundamental economic problem that the Chinese revolution has to meet is to shape China's given material endowments and economic institutions to fit the requirements of a modern industrial society. In broad societal terms this has meant a deep social revolution in many ways much more far reaching than those of France and Russia, one which demands the most profound modifications not only of structured institutions and relationships but also of individual attitudes, values, and consciousness: a great continuing cultural revolution.

The relationships among labor, land, and capital have to be modified drastically though not too precipitously as institutional constraints are reshaped for the new functions thrust upon them. The great pool of crude labor, being utilized mainly in centuries-old fashion, has to be harnessed to generate greater output, including capital, to shape productive processes in modern, more fruitful ways. At the same time the varied advantages of indigenous methods of production are not to be rejected until the new processes and those manipulating them are sufficiently advanced to allow easy assimilation of the handicrafts that reflect Chinese craftsmanship at its best.

China's factor endowment is quite poor. There is a great scarcity of capital in all forms. Certainly the nation's supply of modern machinery and equipment, concentrated in a few enclaves, is rather limited; but also its roads, canals, irrigation systems, reservoirs, etcetera are inadequate given the wide expanse of the country which is third in total land area among the other countries of the world. This large land mass, in its present stage, is not readily usable for cultivation. The 12 or so percent of the land which is arable (in the United States 60 percent of the land mass is cultivable) has been so long denuded that constant renewal through organic and inorganic fertilization—a kind of constant capital inflow—is mandatory. The relatively rich mineral reserves of China depend for their effective exploitation on very large quantities of that same scarce factor, capital.

Similarly, the quite abundant raw labor power of China (with a population of about seven hundred ninety million growing by over ten million each year) must rely on heavy capital inputs in the form of education, training, health service, and recreation before its potential may be released. China's vast peasant work force of up to about three hundred fifty million people who are skilled in the ancient ways of tilling the soil and who often work sporadically has been ill prepared to carry out the technical revolution implied in modernization and industrialization. Its nonagricultural labor force though now numbering about fifty-five million—roughly two thirds of the total work force in the United States—is one eighth or so of the total agricultural and nonagricultural work force. Among this large group are many millions who are not skilled beyond the requirements of ancient handicraft activity and are in many ways poorly prepared to make major contributions to the development of modern industrial modes of production. These millions of workers are part of a recent modern industrial tradition whose canons of behavior in mines, factories, and other enterprises are more in tune with capitalist development than with the revolutionary aspirations and discipline of the CCP.

The present unhappy endowment mix in China retards movement toward modernization and industrialization. Capital accumulation, so necessary for rapid economic growth, must come from what is abundant: hundreds of millions of peasant workdays. (In the experience of the United States, the relative and almost unlimited abundance of virginal land with scarcities in capital and labor was an easier relationship out of which to fashion steady growth.) Abundant labor must be converted into capital by producing enough food for all China, first, and then by utilizing surplus in labor or kind to forge or buy abroad the factories, machinery, transportation networks, electric power, and market complexes that define modern industrial society.

As do so many emerging countries, China has to contend not only with this poor endowment mix, but also with institutional constraints arising from her traditional and imperialist heritages. The system of land tenure and technology in China is one in which traditional techniques and small-scale cultivation have persisted despite the world-wide technological revolutions. Fragmented and absentee land ownership militated against important changes in technique and the size of a farm so that Chinese agriculture has fallen greatly behind rapid world technological advances.

The introduction of modern products and industrial enterprise to China was achieved by various foreign interventions through which the interests of foreign mercantile and industrial groups and their Chinese agents were advanced. The resulting light industry which predominated was located in certain coastal cities, and the internal communications and transportation networks followed the paths of foreign commercial and industrial needs. The result was an economic dualism in which agriculture languished at its traditonal subsistence level while certain very limited areas of China enjoyed the impacts of the commercial and industrial revolutions. The people outside commercial-industrial enclaves reaped very little benefit (indeed, they suffered heavy costs) from the one-sided innovation that emanated from beyond the middle kingdom, because they were little involved in the various economic channels through which modern trade and industry carried on its daily activities.

In the great rural labor pool whose members traditionally plied their ancient skills in cultivation of the land, a tremendous potential for capital accumulation existed. Millions of peasants contributed little, if anything, to the substantial but inadequate output of grains. During certain seasons, when laborpower requirements slackened under the lash of the natural elements, additional millions generally were idle or made uncoordinated attempts to engage themselves in some useful activity. Other millions of people in the countryside, the women and children, contributed only in small measure to the main occupation of the farm which was cultivating the grain that, at China's level of existence, was so precious. Labor input on the farms, sometimes even during the peak seasons, was far below the potential which was implicit in the demographic configuration of China's 80 to 85 percent rural inhabitants. Paradoxically, at peak cultivation periods labor shortages often arose.

If the hundreds of millions of peasants struggling to make ends meet could be mobilized within a different framework in which the new technology was coordinated with better organized laborpower, the increased quantity and quality of inputs not only would make possible the adequate feeding of China's vast millions on the farms and in the cities but also would enable both excess production and saved laborpower to be transformed into an ever-growing mass of sorely needed capital. Construction of dams, roads, canals, reservoirs, and the like, crude as they might be, would increase capital, improving agricultural production with less labor input, and reduce the peasant's subjection to the elements. Land reclamation, terracing, and other forms of preservation and extension (such as forestation and stocking lakes and ponds with fish) would also enrich the arsenal of agricultural capital. The gathering of organic wastes as well as the production of inorganic fertilizers would reinvigorate the soil so that its natural richness would yield more. Saved laborpower could also be employed in the crude yet valuable production and servicing of new tools and simple machines and put to use in producing handicraft and other consumer goods for domestic and foreign sale.

Chinese Economic Development since 1949

The fundamental economic problems described above have had to be faced squarely by China's leaders. The CCP's response to the challenges of rapid socialist economic development necessarily has gone through several phases, with zig zags and pendulumlike swings in policy. Each phase embodied varying policy prescriptions that have shaped the path of the People's Republic of China (PRC), and certain of these phases may be identified with particular periods.

The first four years, through 1952, was a period of conscious rehabilitation of the economy to prewar levels with widespread land reform followed by a slow beginning of agricultural cooperativization and industrial socialization. The problem of inflation was met directly with a battery of fiscal and monetary measures, increased production, measures to reduce hoarding, stimulation of saving, etcetera.

During the next period, from 1953 to 1957, the first Five-Year Plan (FFYP) was put into motion, though its full scope and objectives were not completely worked out until 1955. In this phase the leaders of the PRC imitated the Soviet development model, which emphasized heavy industry and relied heavily on Soviet products and technicians with solid success at least in quantitative terms as physical output rose sharply in the modern sector. In the indigenous sector, however, gains were much less impressive: agricultural output, for example, barely equaled population growth. Socialization of industry proceeded at its planned, measured pace with little difficulty, while the cooperativization of agriculture progressed slowly as planned but was suddenly accelerated in 1955 so that by the end of 1956 most Chinese farms had been collectivized earlier than scheduled in a form similar to the Soviet *Kolkhoz*. Throughout this period, motivation of peasant and worker was developed through heavy emphasis on and rationalization of income maximization mechanisms, while nonmaterial or social schemes were modestly introduced and nurtured.

In the next period, 1958 to 1960, the leaders of the CCP veered away from the Soviet model and the high priority given to heavy industry with capital formation which was to come mainly from agriculture. Their innovative efforts were advanced in the Great Leap Forward (GLF) and the spreading of the rural people's commune, an encompassing, autonomous socioeconomic administrative unit aimed at a revolutionary transformation of the countryside as a prerequisite for sustained economic development. This experimental effort to break through the cycle of poverty was aimed at unleashing vast amounts of creative efforts in the rural areas through macro decentralization of operational and organizational controls within the broader framework of a unified set of CCP policies (microcentralization in the commune was a dysfunctional factor). Based on the assumption that the peasants' revolutionary fervor was at a high level, which proved to be a misjudgment of gigantic consequences, the leaders of the party expected bountiful harvests and relied heavily on nonmaterial or social incentives as well as organizational acumen to motivate and guide the masses of peasants in herculean efforts to raise the *worst* part of the economy, agriculture, to ever higher levels. The initial economic results were quite impressive: even after downward revision due to cadres' exaggerated reports, total grain output rose between 20 and 30 percent from 1957 (a very good year) to 1958. In industry, the quantitative gains were even more impressive: factory production soared by about 30 percent during 1958, and steel production of varying quality shot up by about 50 percent (from 5.35 to 8 million tons) in the same year. But the disarray caused by the varying impacts of the commune, including poor management and planning, and by three years of extremely bad weather resulting in sharp declines in agriculture and then in industry, brought the GLF to an almost disastrous conclusion.[1]

In the period from 1961 to 1965 the damage wrought by the ramifying dislocations of the GLF was repaired, and the commitment to placing agriculture at the center of any development strategy was more tightly sealed. The economy recovered slowly as incentive policy swung to its opposite extreme: material incentives were reemphasized on communes and in the factories. The commune itself had been reorganized after its first traumatic impact so that authority over production and payment was transferred first from the commune to the production brigade and then down further to the basic unit, the production team. Industrial output was reordered to provide important machinery and fertilizers for agriculture. The mandate, "Take agriculture as the foundation and industry as the leading factor," first enunciated by Mao Tse-tung in 1959,[2] was stressed repeatedly as the fundamental principle underlying China's efforts to modernize. The improvement of the economic situation throughout this period was accompanied by Mao's growing serious concern over the widening influence of "capitalistic" practices (spreading private farming, overemphasis on wages and other material emoluments, and the widening development of rural markets) as the Maoists intensified proletarian propaganda in the Socialist Education Movement without the desired results.

The next period, 1966 to 1968, was the Great Proletarian Cultural Revolution (GPCR), a tremendous effort to make the common conscience both socialist and revolutionary, during which policy swung to another extreme, and there was widespread conflict over control of the CCP and how Chinese economic and political development was to be guided. Though the lines and issues were quite blurred as the GPCR followed varying courses (with no one avowedly anti-Maoist), at its heart the struggle was to reshape the CCP and fulfill an unequivocal commitment to the Maoist revolutionary strategy for transforming China. Class struggle took precedence over industrialization and modernization. Chairman Mao had concluded that the party mechanism, defined eventually as a group around Liu Shao-ch'i which relied more on the Soviet experience and forms, was giving aid and comfort to all those in agriculture and industry who were developing and institutionalizing individualistic values and practices. Since the problem was not the mode of production—socialist economic forms such as the commune and state enterprise already had been set up—but was rather in the minds of men, revolutionization of the party and the people was urgently needed to avoid going the "revisionist" route of the USSR. During the GPCR the sharp conflicts occurring throughout China, often involving bloodshed but never degenerating into outright civil war, affected industrial activity and foreign trade adversely. For the Maoists this was a price that had to be paid: capitalistic consciousness had to be eradicated. In the countryside, the effects of the GPCR on production were contained. Overall, though, the GPCR did slow down and reverse somewhat the recovery of the period from 1961 to 1965.

The most recent phase of postcultural revolution has been one of political reconstruction of the CCP, containment of extreme revolutionary elements, continuing class struggle to exorcise negative attitudes, and the measured formulation and implementation of economic institutions consistent with the Maoist vision of the revolutionary society. Political mending of the shattered CCP has been given perforce the highest priority. The economic policies that define the Maoist strategy of development, though slow in emerging, have become much clearer. The priority assigned to agriculture has not only been reaffirmed, it has been heightened as the communes themselves have been directed to accumulate more capital for use on the farms and in rural industrial and service activity. The infusion of capital from the modern industrial sector has taken the shape of not only machines, tools, and fertilizer but also a variety of workers transferred down from cities and towns to the communes to convert their laborpower into goods and services which were to assist in improving the quality of rural life and work and to have their socialist consciousness raised by the peasants and commune living.

Major Economic Issues since 1949

To help understand China's situation, we focus on major economic difficulties which precipitated sharp conflicts among CCP leaders and resulted in changed policy prescriptions of great moment. In the 1950s such problems seemed to be resolved by the CCP fairly harmoniously until the GLF; then policy conflict intensifed, and during the 1960s sharper reactions were generated as some leaders continued to use Soviet experience as their main guide while Mao drew upon the CCP's collective experience, including the Yenan period, and new forms to meet the issues.

The question of stark demographic reality which the size and growth of China's population pose has always been one of major policy. Whether the population of China is seven hundred ninety million or fifty million more or less, and whether it increases each year by 1.5 percent or by 2.0 percent makes little difference in comprehending the enormity of the problem. Unless agricultural output is increased each year on average by an amount at least equal to the food needs of the larger population, grave consequences will result. The signal importance of agricultural output and, in human terms, of the over six hundred million peasants in every policy question cannot be overstated.[3]

In the middle fifties, a campaign was mounted to restrict population growth through mass education and production of birth control devices. This campaign was abruptly stopped once the GLF began in 1958 when leaders denounced population control for purposes of "solving the population problem" as anti-Marxist. In 1959 official policy was prescribed softly and succinctly: "We insist on family planning, but generally speaking we think it is a good thing to have a large population."[4] During the sixties official policy again advanced population control, this time calling on medical and public health workers to carry the burden.

Another major issue, always a central problem in Communist economies, is the difficulty of significantly improving agricultural output in a sustained fashion. For China this has been perhaps *the* key issue. For, as suggested above, if capital is to be generated in large and continuous amounts, it must arise from the surpluses of a still primitive agriculture.

During the fifties, while agriculture was being collectivized with attendant disruption, its output lagged considerably behind the general growth of the economy and eventually with the sharp declines after 1959 forced a halt on that general growth. Contributing to the generally slack conditions on the farms was the very limited success in disseminating the technical know-how essential to robust and continuous farm production. During the sixties, after the recovery from the impact of the GLF, efforts in these directions were pushed vigorously and with considerable success as grain output rose each year by more than the rate of population growth. This pattern has continued into the seventies.

Closely connected to the agricultural issue but transcending it ideologically is the persistence of individualistic practices throughout the economy. Variously denounced are "profits in command," "bourgeois speculation," "distributing and eating up everything," "capitalist style," "economism," and "bourgeois selfishness," which are all remnants of China's past that must be eradicated. This issue is central to the attempts to heighten "class struggle," to cultivate and reinforce proper revolutionary attitudes of workers and peasants toward their work, to get them to forego consuming large proportions of increased output necessary for rapid capital accumulation, and to develop the basic qualities of "communist man."

Another troublesome problem that vexed the authorities was the widening disparity in income between peasants and industrial workers during the FFYP and after, a gap which not only was fraught with political dangers but also generated problems of labor misallocation. The obvious political dangers were the undermined peasant morale and the establishment of vested interest in income differentials among workers and between workers and peasants. With incomes moving apart during the middle and late fifties, peasants moved into the cities in swollen numbers and added to the 1940s' legacy of unemployment.

In implementing industrial policy another knotty question arose and has persisted since the early fifties: Following the Soviet example, should all industry, including traditional handicraft activity, be put in the modern mold; or should the dualistic development of modern industry and the most primitive handicrafts be perpetuated? In other words, Should capital-intensive techniques be emphasized in all industry with labor-intensive ones downgraded? In the economic reality of China the question is made more complicated by the fact that handicraft pursuits include not one, but a wide array of economic activities of varying technical complexity. This means that a host of laborpower and raw material allocation judgments and policies have to be flexibly applied in varying patterns throughout the country.

The Maoist Economic Model

One can perceive a set of first approximations of how Mao and the CCP leaders are proceeding and expect to surmount the many difficulties outlined above and to achieve their objectives of industrialization and socialization within a revolutionary socialist context through uniting city and countryside, worker and peasant, rather than lifting one on the shoulders of the other, through egalitarian rather than elitist policies. This "Maoist Economic Model" cannot be found in one tract or in even a few official statements, but its reality is now clearer, having emerged over the last fifteen years as Chairman Mao has become increasingly involved in questions of economic policy.

The model must be viewed cautiously; abstraction of guidelines to social action from often chaotic and seemingly unrelated events necessarily conveys a tidiness which should not be mistaken for reality. Furthermore, the consistency and continuity which may be inferred from a model of this sort can be quite misleading. Mao and the "Maoists," whoever they may be, have not followed the model consistently over the last two decades. Just as Mao has opposed aspects of the model at various times, Liu Shao-ch'i and his followers similarly have not always opposed the main points of this model and have supported parts of it over time. Of course, the dialectical approach that Mao uses analytically foreshadows pendulum swings of policy in the implementation of policy and should be recalled as policies are evaluated.

Goals

The dual economic objectives of the party are the rapid attainment of modern revolutionary industrialization within a framework of planning and the socialization of all enterprise and people. With political considerations taking precedence over economics, the Chinese expect to surpass Western capacities, eventually raising the people's level of living substantially if not in the same qualitative manner as the West. The attainment of high technical, scientific, and industrial levels through superior Chinese organization, planning, and motivation is viewed by the CCP as mainly a means to shape communism using the time horizon for success as a function of the degree of revolutionary consciousness among the masses.

The second objective, socialization, deals more with an ultimate, non-economic end: a certain kind of Communist person as well as an important material means for achieving both goals. The socialization of the means of production is both a means and an end, a *means* for unleashing the revolutionary forces necessary for the rapid achievement of technical successes and the fundamental change in man's consciousness and also an *end* in ultimately becoming the mode of production sustaining a new person. The notion of human socialization or revolutionization is an important concomitant of material socialization in the Maoist view. Mao, in his attack on Soviet "revisionism" and on vestiges of the old society in China today, even after the socialist mode of production has been implemented, has stressed the urgent need to continue fighting against old individualistic attitudes and practices which are still widespread among all Chinese regardless of class. The more immediate realization of rapid growth has to be managed with a transitional human motivating mechanism which would both lead to large immediate results and lay the foundation for the long-run collectivist ideal of a selfless, socially productive Communist human being. During the sixties Mao came to the realization that the goal of shaping such a collectivist society with Communist consciousness might be advanced sometimes only at the cost of slower industrialization and modernization. The GPCR and its aftermath demonstrate that he sees socialization and class struggle as the sine qua non of his ideal society. To push industrialization without an adequately socialized society is to follow the "revisionist" road.[5]

Thus socialization of the people means the active cultivation of "socialist" behavior through widespread education and propaganda as well as changed working conditions and institutions. The Soviet "revisionists," Maoists maintain, allowed "bourgeois" traits and behavior to take hold again on the presumed, deterministic faith that once the mode of production was transformed, and the capitalist class had been abolished, the masses would naturally grow more thoroughly socialist and egalitarian. For Mao, the class struggle is ever continuous and must be vigorously waged, since strong traits of individualism still linger in men's minds: "After . . . the socialist transformation of the ownership of the means of production, there are still classes and class struggle, the struggle between the proletariat and the bourgeoisie and between the socialist road and the capitalist road, there is the danger of capitalist restoration, and [therefore] the proletariat must continue the revolution." Furthermore, "it is man's social being that determines his thinking. Once the correct ideas characteristic of the advanced class are grasped by the masses, these ideas turn into a material force which changes society and changes the world." [6] The fundamental question in the Marxist context, according to Lin Piao, is, "If we fail to make revolution in the superstructure, fail to arouse the broad masses, . . . fail to criticize the revisionist line, fail to expose the handful of renegades, enemy agents, capitalist-roaders in power and counter-revolutionaries and fail to consolidate the leadership of the proletariat, how can we further consolidate the socialist economic base and further develop the socialist productive forces?" [7]

Though the dual objectives of the party, industrialization and socialization, are not necessarily contradictory, tensions between them can and have arisen, trade-offs between them may be required, and a conscious dialectical swing in policy stressing one and then the other may be followed. Slower industrialization, for example, may be necessary, following doctrinal dictates, to reinforce proper attitudes or weed out reasserted "bourgeois" traits. The GPCR may be viewed as a vast upheaval in which its significant ideological goals were promoted at even the cost of lost industrial production. The constant attack against "production in command" or "production comes first" is an implicit reiteration at a particular juncture in time that long-run social and political considerations must take priority over rapid industrialization. When socialization has been pushed close to or past acceptable limits, then a return to considerations of industrialization will occur moderating policies developed during the period of emphasis on socialization.

The Italian novelist and intellectual, Alberto Moravia, who visited China during the GPCR, interprets Mao's vision.

> . . . the ground has been prepared [by the cultural revolution] for a universal revolutionary ideology that tomorrow perhaps may be able to compete with the Soviet ideology. More important still, the foundations may also have been laid for an egalitarian and technological society in which social advancement does not come through consumption as the result of profit as in the United States, or through prosperity as the prize of power as in Russia, but through diversity and the quality of technical capabilities—a technocracy consisting of diversely qualified cadres and working masses in which everyone is provided with the necessary but not the superfluous. . . .

One might ask: once technological progress has been achieved, once the civilization of automation has triumphed, what will happen to the immense capital produced through so much work and so many privations? The answer might be this. It will be applied first to the uses of free time, toward culture, education, and the development of man; and then perhaps to scientific undertakings—the conquest of outer space . . . a futuristic science-fiction civilization inhabited by the peasant, his humanity intact, not by the damaged, amputated, prejudice-ridden petit bourgeois.[8]

Institutional Arrangements

In reaching the goals of industrialization with planning and socialization, the present leaders of the CCP have a clear image of how ideology is to be served by remolding and organizing economic, political, and social institutions. This view unveils a clear-cut path for the development of basic economic institutions and their supporting scientific-technological agencies as well as the correct psychological bearing for individuals in all such units.

The institutional arrangements of property, its ownership, and distribution of its fruits are restructured along lines already familiar in Soviet types of economies, modified by the more profound dualistic nature of Chinese economic activity and the revolutionary view that the market must be replaced as the key allocative institution. Social ownership of the means of production in either the state enterprise or the cooperative form, as they exist in Eastern Europe, is mandated. Where new means of production issue from state capital, or where large means were expropriated at the time of the takeover, the organization permits ready central control, and the state enterprise form prevails. The amalgamation of agricultural and smaller industrial holdings as well as various wholesaling and retailing establishments has developed the second form: cooperative ownership by the merging owners. In the very long run, as cooperative units grow and graduate from the handicraft-indigenous stage and are merged eventually into larger and larger units with the feasibility of wider managerial operations, they, too, would take on the form of state enterprises, or ownership of the whole people.

As this socialization occurs, some kinds of private enterprise and "bourgeois motivation" are permitted. The tolerance of such private pursuit and income maximization is considered necessary until the level and distribution of output, revolutionary fervor, and the development of new incentive mechanisms make possible their eradication. On the communes small private plots are allowed, and vegetables, fruit, dairy and meat products (from family-owned chickens, pigs, cows) produced there are consumed or sold in rural markets. Former capitalists, who received a fixed return on their industrial holdings until the GPCR, carry on usually in managerial capacities in enterprises which had been transformed from private to joint state-private to state enterprises. Overseas Chinese still receive fixed returns on capital invested in Chinese enterprises. And in all sectors of the economy, labor input is motivated by the socialist principle of payment according to the quantity and quality of output. In fact, graded time-wage payments, though of narrowing range, are the basis of remuneration and piece rates are still used in some factories.

Socialist production is to be bolstered and advanced by firm commitment to the utilization of science and technology. Scientific and technical institutes set up by and supported by the government are tied to industry, agriculture, and the educational network. All people are given a scientific orientation as part of their education and party and mass organizations instill and reinforce this commitment: a true "socialist enterprise is where three great revolutionary movements—class struggle, the struggle for production and scientific experiment—are carried out." [9]

Organization of the Economy

The economy is organized according to classic Marxist principles modified by the experience of the CCP and the particular needs dictated by Chinese reality. Industrialization and socialization are coordinated by broad, loose socioeconomic planning with longer range plans such as the five-year plans and the twelve- and twenty-year agricultural plans which set major objectives to which more short-run specifications may be consistently related. Varying from Soviet practice, the Maoists would shape their plans more flexibly and allow greater experimentation and decentralization. The elements of local spontaneity and initiative are recognized as quite important factors. In fact, the FFYP and subsequent plans move away from the more comprehensive, specific blueprints of the Soviet type. Planning is to be based on many socioeconomic considerations rather than mainly on profit indicators.

Our national economic planning must serve this great political goal [building a great socialist country] and should proceed from the needs . . . of the domestic and international class struggle and our country's socialist construction. . . . we use the law of value [profit] as a tool in planning and business accounting but *we are steadfastly opposed to making it the basis for regulating production or working out our plans. . . .* the modern revisionists . . . exaggerate theoretically the role of value, and want to use it to regulate and control social production.[10]

In this planning context, the Maoists have consciously put prices in the service of their economic and ideological policies, neutralized them, and used direct controls such as rationing when necessary. They have been much concerned that market distribution with price acting as the rationer might lead to inequitable distribution of consumer goods. Agricultural prices have been used to stimulate peasant output. Industrial prices have been kept high and recouped through returned profits, a simpler method than that of using low prices, lower costs, and subsidies, as is done in the USSR.[11]

For the Maoists the size and diversity of China as well as revolutionary imperatives mandate a radical departure from the Soviet pattern of making decisions at the center. Their interpretation of the Marxist idea of democratic centralism calls for continuous, dynamic economic interchange between center and base and optimization of performance and development. At the center the CCP would focus clearly on major objectives and the broad strategy to be pursued; at the base, initiative and spontaneity would be necessary to overcome a wide variety of historical, physical, traditional, and personal impediments. (The "center" applies to provincial, municipal, and county control as well as that from Peking.) The involvement of the masses, led by party cadres on commune production teams or factory work squads, would be the means by which the tactics of production, remuneration, innovation, education, and so forth, would be developed subject to party validation. Interaction between the center and the base would allow for spontaneous mass- and cadre-initiated movements to be encouraged and reinforced or discouraged and deterred. Policies propounded at the center would sometimes be subject to some modification (ruling out fundamental socialist policies such as socialization) by negative or other mass responses as transmitted through the organizational hierarchies. This duality is a characteristic element of Maoist outlook and policy, and it allows differential emphasis of either opposite at different points in time.

Democratic centralism for the Maoists is a fundamental means to effect mass participation in economic as well as political and social spheres. Within the framework of the dictatorship of the party, active involvement of China's people is to be institutionalized for ideological as well as operational reasons. Mao has stated, "If we are to make the Party strong, we must practice democratic centralism to stimulate the initiative of the whole membership." The "democratic style of work" advocated by Mao is "to forge close ties with . . . and consult [with] the masses when problems crop up." This involves "letting all people have their say" in order to "concentrate on correct ideas, fully arouse the revolutionary initiative of the masses, . . . and bring about a new upsurge in socialist construction. . . . we must be all the more modest and prudent, guard against arrogance and impetuosity, consult the masses when problems crop up, be good at inspiring the masses to criticize and discuss. . . ." [12]

Operationally this general ideological mandate calls for three guidelines: (1) allowing everyone to have his say; (2) consulting repeatedly on important matters; and (3) paying attention to the views of the few since they are sometimes correct: *While no infringement upon the party committee's collective leadership can be tolerated, it is necessary to adhere to the principle of division of work and responsibility. Decisions on all important questions . . . are made by the party committee through collective discussion. . . . By so doing, the party committee not only develops the initiative of each member, but also frees itself of the burden of routine business. . . ."* [13]

Within this strategic-tactical framework of feedback the Maoist group, since the end of the FFYP, have been shaping and refining a strategy for economic development which is presumably better suited to Chinese conditions than is the Soviet policy of forced industrialization with retarded agricultural and consumer goods development. Ideology aside, this strategy of uneven growth had proved inappropriate for China, whose primitive agricultural system does not permit building industry from the capital squeezed out of farms and peasants. The Maoist strategy, tested in the crucible of adversity, places agriculture *and* the peasant at the center. Industry leads in technology and modernization and provides agriculture with the essentials to raise its output and yield the capital which has been elicited from more efficient allocation and utilization of the peasant millions for its further technical and mechanical advance. Heavy industry is to develop rapidly and to support agriculture either directly or indirectly: steel, fertilizers, tools, machines for the countryside, other products for export. The farm and the factory are to unite to spur economic development.

The economy as a whole, under this strategy, is to develop in a "planned and proportionate" way somewhat autarkically. This is necessary for ideological and economic reasons: unbalanced growth generates wide differentials in payment, and this undercuts egalitarian ideals and fosters bottlenecks and back-ups which affect agriculture adversely, further complicating human as well as technical problems. Such uneven development foreshadows either a more onerous load for the peasant masses and indigenous sectors of the economy or a heavy dependence on foreign sources of supply, both of which clash with the Maoist emphasis on the importance of the peasant and Chinese self-reliance. "Proportionate" development means that non-agricultural growth is determined by the food and industrial raw materials output of agriculture.[14]

Structure of the Economy

In the strategy of balanced or proportionate growth where agriculture is given priority, the CCP leaders have reorganized and redirected the different sectors of the economy to meet varied tasks. The result is a changed structure for the economy in which rapid industrialization, socialization, planning, and commune activity have all been coordinated toward the fulfillment of important Maoist intermediate and ultimate goals in which a radical change in man's consciousness plays a major role.

Relationships among the various sectors of the economy are to be radically modified to eradicate three major differences which reflect material as well as psychological inequality and which stand in the way of the realization of communism. These differences still exist between industry and agriculture, between town and country, and between mental and manual labor. Their elimination would set the stage for the economy to begin a sustained growth.[15]

In agriculture as in other sectors Mao's emphasis on the prime importance of man and the proper organization and indoctrination of him—the way he and the land are to be related—is manifest. Mao's model insists that for China at that time in the fifties collectivization and its smooth operation had to precede wide-scale extension of mechanization and technological improvement. Not that no mechanization or technological application ought to occur before complete collectivization, but rather that the introduction of the most advanced mechanized equipment and agricultural technology must await the fuller organizational, technical, and psychological development of the collective. Only then can the most advanced methods be transmuted into effective instruments for realizing prime economic goals. As the collective is developed, introduction of simple mechanical devices and elementary technology is to be encouraged. Even tractors may be introduced at strategic points. While gradual introduction of technology and mechanical aids takes place, light industry is also to be nurtured within the collective's framework to support and generate tools, machines, irrigation aids, stronger seed strains, fertilizer.

The critical issue of collectivization preceding advanced mechanization has divided the Maoists from the Liuists. The Maoist stand is based on the judgment that major economic and ideological benefits will accrue from extended agricultural collectivization now at an early stage of development. In the middle of July 1955, while discussing various problems of agricultural cooperation and setting the stage for accelerated collectivization on the farms, Mao clearly set forth his view that cooperativization must come first: "With conditions as they are . . . cooperation must precede the use of big machinery. . . . the method we are using in the socialist transformation of agriculture is one of step-by-step advance . . . this social transformation [cooperativization] will continue to be the main feature of the transformation of the countryside, while technical transformation will take second place; the number of big farm machines will certainly increase, but not to any great extent . . . economic conditions being what they are, the technical transformation will take longer than the social." Mao's phased, deliberate approach was aimed at making the cooperative advancement of agriculture solid and lasting: "These steps make it possible for the peasants gradually to raise their socialist consciousness . . . and . . . change their mode of life, thus lessening any feeling of any abrupt change." [16]

Industry's role in this model is more complex than being the "leading factor" implies. The same prescription for the advanced sector is not necessarily an apt one for the indigenous segment; the two sectors ought to develop along the lines of their inherent strengths. For modern industry the prescription is fairly clear: develop advanced techniques; gear these to the needs of agriculture; use the most capital-intensive methods of any of the main sectors of the economy; refine methods and products, improving over-all quality. There is also a call to move away from plant specialization with an autarkic policy of *comprehensive utilization* in which the manufacture of items related to the plant's principal product is developed from all available materials and with the regular work force.

As for the indigenous segment of industry: labor-intensive techniques are indicated. To use more advanced machines and methods would be wasteful. Instead indigenous industrial activity must be developed by drawing on abundant though primitive labor and material resources that

Workers in the modern Fushun Excavator Plant (China Pictorial, 1, 1973, p. 8)

Introduction
19

are not used by the modern industrial sector. If this is successful, modern industry will obtain useful products from the indigenous sector while that sector meets some product needs of agriculture and peasants who are consumers. Extension of indigenous industry also affords an excellent opportunity for rural workers to upgrade their agricultural and industrial skills.

This policy, called *Walking on Two Legs,* embodies prescriptions bearing on autarky, industrial location, ecology, national minorities, and national defense as well as a main thrust of utilizing China's particular factor endowment in economical ways.

> While speeding up economic construction, we must . . . step up construction for national defense. . . . Every region . . . should also proceed from war preparations, and act in accordance with Chairman Mao's directive that local areas should devise means of setting up an independent industrial system and that first the cooperative zones and then the many provinces should . . . institute relatively independent though different industrial systems. We must devote attention to a rational geographic distribution of industry [and] enhance the capacity to assemble industrial products locally. . . . Development of industry in the interior may also make it possible to further arouse the activism of the people of various nationalities . . . to change the backward state of industry in the national minority areas . . . and to strengthen the great unity among various nationalities.
>
> Development of industry in the interior is primary, but attention must be given to industrial construction in coastal areas. If we make full use of the equipment and technical forces of industry in coastal areas, we can provide more advanced techniques and equipment for the development of industry in the interior, cultivate a greater technical force, accumulate more capital, and foster rapid development of industrial construction in the interior.[17]

Walking on Two Legs is defined and developed further as "the simultaneous development of industry and agriculture and that of heavy and light industry, with priority given to . . . heavy industry; the simultaneous development of [modern] industries . . . and of local industries; and the simultaneous application of foreign and indigenous methods for production . . . with overall planning and the proper division of labor and coordination." [18]

The many advantages to be realized have also been catalogued.

Large and medium-sized and small enterprises advance one another and create favorable conditions for one another. . . . It is comparatively easy to raise funds for setting up medium-size and small enterprises . . . because they are small in scale and do not need much capital. [They are developed] to give full play to the existing industrial capabilities of localities and to make full use of discarded, obsolete, or unutilized equipment. . . . small enterprises can take full advantage of various scattered, limited, local resources so that they can produce with what is locally available and sell their products in local markets in order to cut down shipping costs. . . . the sum total of all small enterprises constitute a tremendous force; . . . the masses are enabled to master the technical know-how in the course of production and achieve greater, faster, better, and more economic results in developing . . . technicians. [This policy] arouses the revolutionary spirit of self-reliance, . . . fully exploits local manpower, . . . makes full use of discarded materials of large enterprises and turns the discarded into the treasured. . . . Shortages . . . may be alleviated.[19]

Thus an integrated notion of using crude local resources and laborpower where labor-intensive activity predominates along with modern capital-intensive techniques emerges.

Concern about ecological problems of human and industrial pollution has reinforced efforts to utilize labor in reducing health hazards and in recycling waste materials to supply both indigenous and modern industry with raw materials. In cities and countryside labor has been mobilized to raise public health levels by eliminating insects, cleaning up many polluted waterways, providing proper disposal of human waste, expanding urban sewerage and treatment facilities, and transporting wastes for use in irrigation and fertilization on communes. Industrial wastes, often disposed of at sea and elsewhere at appreciable cost, are being recycled. Following the slogan Transforming 'Scrap' into 'Treasure,' workers have converted a wide variety of waste products into useful, if sometimes crude, raw materials: sulfuric acid waste into crude iron; slags into pig iron and nonferrous metals, powder bricks, cement, and carbon steel; sugar cane, slag and waste liquids into pulp sheet, cap paper, wrapping paper, adhesives, alcohol, and insecticides; scrap steel plate into small transformers. Afforestation has been widely pushed and reclamation of land from lakes, rivers, and wasteland has also been an important means of expanding the scarce area of cultivable land.[20]

The organization of the process of capital formation and its distribution among various economic activities demands careful conception and execution if converting surplus labor into capital is to be fruitful in hastening modernization. During the fifties when capital was accumulated centrally, agriculture received relatively meager capital investment through the national budget. Under the more fully developed Maoist model, agriculture is slated for much heavier capital investment. That investment, however, is to come principally from the commune and its component parts. The greater investment is made more feasible by modified tax and laborpower policies. Agricultural tax rates have remained fundamentally the same, and prices paid for agricultural products have been raised so that as grain and other farm production have risen, the amounts available for capital investment have been greater. In addition, through transferring labor to the communes from the cities a larger and more versatile labor force can be drawn upon to expand rural capital improvements. The broad investment policy is devised at the center to improve capital availablity at the farm level. The responsibility is lodged there for carrying out the actual allocation of labor to specific capital formation projects which are programmed locally.

For modern industry, capital formation comes mainly from the industrial profits realized each year. The basic policy for the types of capital improvement that will be undertaken comes from the center, but the implementation is heavily on the shoulders of the groups who are accountable for decision making in the factories.

The importance of agriculture and human beings is reiterated in the significant role that utilization of laborpower plays in development policy. The earlier channeling of "excess" labor into the cities for use by industry, following the Soviet model, had only complicated matters, for the Soviet practice was ill suited to the conditions of China. Reversal of that policy has become a prime necessity to avert swelling urban unemployment and wasted labor. Administrative assignment remains a key instrument in funneling labor to required locations. This, rather than the wage system, is now the mainstay of labor allocation unlike the situation in market economies or even in the Soviet Union.

Moving laborpower to various locations is one aspect of labor mobility; another aspect is facilitating movement vertically to jobs of different skill requirements. Toward the end of developing needed skills, the educational system has been radically changed and is geared to vocational training and cultivation of skills. Aside from general education, vocational training is a joint responsibility of the operating units (the factories and communes) and the education sector, and they have been closely linked in the post-GPCR period. The Maoist model calls for the "joining of theory and practice" in this area: spare time or after work, part study-part work, and more radical training formats are put forth to train and season workers of all kinds and on all levels.

Because of the unemployment problem in the cities and the need for large amounts of capital formation, the Maoists call for a massive shift of millions of excess urban workers, employed as well as unemployed, to the countryside for utilization in various commune activities. In the cities, the labor essential for whatever industrial growth is planned there can be obtained readily from the natural population growth of the over one hundred million urban dwellers. In the countryside, the influx of urban labor of various kinds is to be an infusion of additional laborpower available for peak farming needs as well as an investment in human capital through the initiation of various social welfare programs, including health as well as educational and cultural services, and the stimulation of sideline service and consumer goods production.

The transferred urban dwellers include industrial workers of all types, former peasants who had moved to the cities, cadres of various levels, teachers and students, medical and paramedical personnel, and other intellectuals. Units of the People's Liberation Army (PLA) are also deployed for economic purposes and retired PLA personnel are sent to rural locations. The PLA has played a principal role in the economic development of Tibet and Sinkiang. Assimilated into communes and other local and regional economic enterprises, these varied additional workers are expected to help generate greater production. In peak farming periods they contribute to the greater output which is necessary to feed the new workers and to provide capital improvement of the communes. They also man the newly developed industrial activities which produce consumer goods and services as well as fertilizer, steel, tools, simple machines, and the services necessary to maintain and repair the equipment of the communes. The city is thus joined to the countryside to maximize economic growth.

Role of Human Beings

A most prominent element in the Maoist model is the manner in which human beings are to be motivated and changed. The success of the entire scheme for achieving communism hinges on the aptness of the Maoist insight into human nature to diagnose how people can be changed and to implement that diagnosis effectively. In the Maoist view the principles governing human nature are universal and egalitarian and have been uncovered by Marxism-Leninism as interpreted and informed by Mao Tse-Tung thought. To achieve modernization and socialization through planning, all Chinese, in the long run, must be raised not simply to the level of the elite, but to the level of the new Communist man. As one observer puts it, China is to "build on the worst" not on the "best," as have the advanced countries including the USSR.[21] In the short run, people must be motivated to generate high levels of output, but in a way that lays the foundation for complete social motivation under the communism of the future. Individualistic motivational mechanisms have to be kept in check, and social mechanisms, must be developed without undercutting production. Mao has expressed these high expectations for the Chinese masses: "Of all things in the world, people are the most precious. Under the leadership of the Communist Party, as long as there are people, every kind of miracle can be performed. . . . The Chinese people have high aspirations, they have ability, and they will certainly catch up with and surpass advanced world levels in the not too distant future."[22]

For the Maoist the major stumbling block to modernization and communization is the stubborn persistence of narrow individualism. A constant "class struggle" must be waged to eradicate such behavior through the continuous inculcation of revolutionary values and attitudes. Individualism includes various aspects of selfishness: putting individual gain above the group welfare, "departmentalism" (caring for one's own unit to the neglect of the larger community), "anarchism" (following individual impulses without regard for the group), and "profits in command" (basing economic decisions on immediate profit expectations without regard for impacts on other parts of the economy and society). Class struggle against undesirable practices will lead to practices more in tune with the socialist mode and the ideal of a proletarian human being: "When one unit has a problem help pours in from all sides. Every one takes it as an honor to help and cooperate with others and displays the communist style, insuring the building of socialism with greater, faster, better and more economical results."[23]

In restructuring the Chinese incentive system from its earlier, individualistic forms, the Maoists have reiterated the necessity and efficacy of basing the motivational mechanisms on revolutionary fervor, with a minimum of attention on individual material inducement. Material incentive is not abolished but used as the basis for differential rewards not so much for the quantity of labor input as for the attitude attending that input. The standards and evaluations for compensation are socialized. Distribution is carried out by the small group in which the individual participates rather than by administrators at higher levels. Material incentives in Chinese industry continue to operate in a context of social insurance and welfare with living levels rising, though the pay differentials between the varying industrial skills as well as those between industrial workers and salaried workers (technicians, engineers, managers) have been more and more telescoped since the GPCR. (Recently a greater emphasis on material incentives has grown.)

The Tachai incentive system, developed in a Shansi commune brigade, is the national model mechanism for harnessing the revolutionary spirit in the service of heightened class consciousness and rising socialist production. Under this system, which is far from being universally used, peasants receive work points based on periodic self- and group evaluations with the peasant's personal and civic qualities rather than his output taking precedence: "The criteria for receiving a high evaluation are high skills, an abundance of enthusiasm for work, support by the masses, honesty, and a high degree of class consciousness." In producing more, the peasant or worker is to be fired not by the desire to produce more alone, but by the desire to produce more for the good of his class and society: working cooperatively and for the masses is more important than producing more. The combination of the two, correct attitude and cooperative endeavor, is the ideal to be achieved.[24]

The Tachai model brigade has its industrial analog in the Tach'ing oil workers. All workers are exhorted to "learn from Tach'ing," a "red-banner pacesetter on China's industrial front." The general principle to be followed is to "grasp revolution and spur production." Five specific principles to implement this canon are set forth in the constitution of the Anshan Iron and Steel Company and provide the guideline for realizing the Tachai or Tach'ing spirit:

Keep politics firmly in command; strengthen party leadership; launch vigorous mass movements; institute the system of cadre participation to productive labor and worker participation in management, of reform of irrational and outdated rules and regulations, and of close co-operation among cadres, workers and technicians; and go full steam ahead with the technical revolution.[25]

Toward the end of cultivating proper collective attitudes and values, the regime constantly projects national models of exemplary behavior for peasants, workers, teams, communes, factories, etcetera, and exhorts individuals and units to emulate the models. Such projections become the images which are expected to inform the revolutionary emulation campaigns through which individuals and units reshape themselves, "grasping revolution" to "spur production." Enhanced production is expected to follow from correct revolutionary consciousness to fulfill people's material and cultural needs.

While each person's performance as a producer is being shaped in an incentive system stressing social more than individual considerations, other principal characteristics of division of labor are to be modified and then replaced. Narrow specialization of function, individualization in motivation and performance, and centralized decision making and coordination of production (within the unit as well as the integrated industrial structure) are slated for radical modification. For the Maoists these qualities not only are integral to "bourgeois" industrial functioning, but they also obstruct functionally the development of proletarian attitudes which are prerequisite to unfettered socialist development toward communism.

For the Maoist group, the configuration of narrow specialization, individual motivation and operation, and centralized decision making produces alienation and anarchy of production which retard the unit's total output and deaden creativity. Over the years the CCP has swung back and forth in its emphasis on the importance of being "red" (having proper attitudes) and expert (being technically specialized and adept), though the ideal is to have the two combined in one model person. More recently, in the Tachai model, "redness" has been stressed in cultivating a more generalized peasant, worker, or cadre, and the interchanging of roles on communes, both temporary and permanent, reflects the growing importance of a labor force still skilled yet flexible enough to take on new tasks in a rapidly changing economic environment and allowing the union of peasants and city workers to develop the entire economy together. This laborpower principle is paralleled in an industrial policy termed *comprehensive utilization* in which the usual plant specialization is modified so that actual production is diversified: a steel plant produces steel, but also machines; a coal mining enterprise mines coal, but also produces chemicals. This represents a breaking away from the classic economic principle of specialization.[26]

The cultivation of egalitarian attitudes and values is another major characteristic of the model and is a key element in coordinating the labor force for maximum output. For the overall development plan to succeed, in Mao's view, the peasant and the rural areas must be given principal roles. Therefore the urban-rural gap in material recompense as well as in status must be narrowed. The reliance on the peasant to raise the material level of the society is at the core of the Maoist strategy. Bringing workers and cadres permanently to the countryside and assigning them general duties as well as utilizing their special skills considerably lowers the level of their income and status. The successful modernization and development of China, then, becomes a task for all, and its successful execution would be the first revolution carried out by the mass rather than by an elite.

Mao and the CCP leaders thus expect to realize their long-term goals through revolutionizing people's consciousness; through the shaping of "Communist man." For Mao that person must be shaped now if communism is ever to be attained.

> . . . the party organization should be composed of the advanced elements of the proletariat; it should be a vigorous vanguard organization capable of leading the proletariat and the revolutionary masses in the fight against the class enemy . . . and in continuing the revolution under the dictatorship of the proletariat." [27]

The ideal party member is the stuff out of which the ideal communist is made; he motivates nonmembers through his exemplary attitude and behavior, and he must meet five requirements: "study and apply Marxism-Leninism-Mao Tsetung Thought in a living way," advance "the world," be capable of "uniting with the great majority, including those who have wrongly opposed them," "consult with the masses," and effectively make "criticism and self-criticism." [28]

It is in this context of the Maoist model and the unfolding of Chinese economic development that we wish to look at the worker to see what his position has been, what it is, and what it is likely to be. In this context, too, many fundamental questions pose themselves about the worker and his role in developing Chinese society: What occupations does he engage in? In what numbers? How have they changed? What has been the role of indigenous or handicraft industry? How has it changed?

We are interested in the industrial labor force's profile and its changing pattern, and the economist is always curious about how such a large and developing group is moved into jobs and locations, influenced by either the market or social design. How is Chinese labor allocated? By wages? By assignment? Or by a combination? In other words, what is the structure and function of the wages and incentive system? And in a socialist economy what role do the trade-unions play? How does the Chinese trade-union fit into our image of trade-unions? How does it contribute economically and socially in China? How has the conflict of interest in trade-unions been handled? How harmonious have worker-management relations been in China? What avenues if any have been open to allow workers to air grievances with hope of reasonable resolution? What official view has been taken of labor disputes? How have they been handled?

A major question involves the quality of industrial workers' lives and working conditions. Different aspects of this question emerge: What is the worker's level of living like? How has it changed? What is the quality of that level of living? What is the overall material and cultural situation of the Chinese worker compared to his counterpart earlier in the century? How does it compare to the Chinese peasant today? What are the prospects for the worker in tomorrow's China?

We now turn to the task of answering these questions.

Two

Employing the Chinese Worker

Though the Chinese worker stands in the shadow of the peasant, he nevertheless occupies a key position in the industrialization-modernization process to which Mao and his followers are committed. In the long run workers and peasants will become indistinguishable. In the present period of transition, while the differences between workers and peasants are being reduced, the worker's skills, work input, and quality of performance are important elements in the regime's strategy for material growth and social transformation.

This chapter outlines the structure of the nonfarm work force, the unemployment problem, and the worker's productivity in various industrial sectors. This ought to provide both a framework for understanding a variety of labor institutions to be viewed later and an agenda of significant problems facing the entire economy.

In our survey of the Chinese worker the definition underlying the quantitative data to be analyzed is embodied in the term *nonagriculturally employed* which refers to employed staff and workers in state enterprises and in cooperatives, paid workers in street enterprises, workers in private economic activity, and individual workers (i.e., self-employed). Thus, those laboring in extractive pursuits such as the work on state farms and communes, and forestry (except for fishermen) are excluded. Our term means all those working in modern and traditional sectors of the economy: industry, construction, trade, transportation and communications, finance, education, health and cultural affairs, and a similar variety of pursuits of an indigenous cast.[1]

We use this term not only because it is convenient, since data on the work force are built on this definition, but mainly because given the Marxist and egalitarian commitments of the Maoist regime the doctrinal notions the leaders have are reflected in our concept. Thus, the term *worker* excludes, in addition to those already noted, students and military personnel working part time, household laborers, rich peasants, landlords, practitioners of "superstitions," those in religious orders, and those labeled "criminal or quasi-criminal." The inclusions as well as the exclusions satisfy the Maoist ideological set. Included are not only blue-collar workers, but a range of white-collar and professional personnel: engineering-technical staff, managerial, administrative, and clerical personnel. Given the clear homage to egalitarian values as well as the notion of imposing manual labor on all staff members, the comprehensiveness of the term *worker* is consistent with the social reality we are dealing with. In an opposite vein, exclusion of those whose class position is clear cut and not likely to be reversed, such as those who remain as landlords and capitalists, accords with ideological definition.

At present there is a distinction between *worker* and *peasant* which is understandable due to the fundamentally different conditions of the two, but this is diminishing because of the peasant's widening responsibility for industrial operations in commune sideline activity. Over time, the distinction between worker and peasant will become less marked as the work they do and their relationship to the production agency become quite similar. In the interim, however, the difference between the two is more than a literary convenience reflecting as it does important variations in the conditions of work and life.

The projected Maoist goal of erasing the differences between workers and peasants rests upon the objective of transforming the conditions of work and life in the countryside. This goal has several dimensions which are reflected in proposed modifications of the organization of work and in the status and role of tomorrow's Communist man. Most workers carry out their operations in state enterprises (though many work in cooperatives), while peasants pursue their tasks within the commune structure, a form of cooperative or collective rather than the state enterprise type of ownership, and still engage in "capitalist" practices in their exploitation of their private plots for vegetable and animal products. At the same time, workers, especially in modern industry, function under conditions of complex division of labor with specialization of operations, while peasants function with a growing set of specialized chores. The more versatile commune laborer, wherever he carries out his work responsibilities, will be doing very much the same thing as the worker once the private plot is eliminated and the state enterprise form is universally adhered to. The new, ideal, skilled but versatile worker in the countryside will represent the hundreds of millions of commune members upon which the Maoist continuing revolution depends.

As the role and status of worker and peasant merge, the ideological and practical distinctions are expected to disappear. If the conditions of work are identical, generally speaking, and if the pay schedules—telescoped for all types of workers, as has been happening in recent years for technical and professional staff—are narrowed, then another salient difference will have been erased. Further, as the egalitarian ideals of all doing some manual work and all participating in the decision making of the basic economic unit are realized in the plant and on the soil, the term *worker* will apply equally to what are now *peasant* and *worker*.

Age-Sex Distribution of the Population

Analysis of the available data on the age and sex distribution of the Chinese population during the 1950s reveals a population that seems to be getting younger and thus is likely to sustain high levels of growth unless countermeasures are taken. The slight decline from 1953 to 1958 in the

Table 2.1

*Estimated Age and Sex Distribution
of the Chinese Population, 1953 and 1958*

Age	1953 Percentage			1958 Percentage		
	Both Sexes	Male	Female	Both Sexes	Male	Female
0 4 years	16.6	16.6	16.6	17.0	16.9	17.0
5–14 years	23.1	23.0	23.2	24.3	24.3	24.3
15–24 years	18.5	18.6	18.5	17.8	17.8	17.8
25–34 years	14.5	14.7	14.4	13.9	14.1	13.8
35–44 years	11.0	11.2	10.8	10.8	10.9	10.6
45–54 years	8.0	8.1	7.9	7.8	7.9	7.7
55–64 years	5.1	4.9	5.2	5.1	5.0	5.2
65–74 years	2.5	2.3	2.6	2.5	2.4	2.7
75 and over	0.7	0.6	0.8	0.8	0.7	0.9
All Ages	100.0	100.0	100.0	100.0	100.0	100.0

Source: John S. Aird, *The Size, Composition, and Growth of the Population of Mainland China* U.S. Bureau of the Census, International Population Statistics Reports, Series P-90. No. 15 (Washington, D.C.: Government Printing Office, 1961), p. 83.

Table 2.2

*Age Distribution of Workers
in Public Sector, Industry,
and Capital Construction, 1955*

Age	Percentage
Under 18	1.0
18–25	38.3
26–35	35.9
36–45	17.1
46–50	4.3
51–55	2.2
56–60	.9
Over 60	.3
	100.0

Source: "The Number, Structure, and Distribution of Workers and Staff in the Whole Country in 1955, "T'ung-chi kung-tso [statistical work], no. 23 (1956), pp. 28–30; cited in Christopher Howe, *Employment and Economic Growth in Urban China: 1949–1957* (Cambridge: Cambridge University Press, 1971), p. 61.

sex ratios favoring males over females is another reinforcing factor in the upward trend of population. The relatively high and growing proportions of people in the group through age fourteen assures a labor force growing at a rate higher than that of the overall growth rate of population.[2]

Table 2.1 presents an estimate of the population's distribution by age and sex for 1953 and 1958 in which a trend toward a younger population is suggested. During this period the proportion of the population under age fifteen increased from 39.7 percent to 41.3 percent. The median age of the population in 1953 was about twenty years and seven months, and by 1958 it declined to about nineteen years and nine months. The increased proportion of the population under fifteen moved up on a par for males and females. Those who were forty-five years of age and over remained the same proportion of the population in 1958 as in 1953.

The male-female ratio overall favors males. In 1958 that ratio was 103.3 males per 100 females, a decline of four points since 1953. The favorable male ratio runs the range from birth to age fifty-nine; then the ratio favors females markedly, running from 97.5 males to 71.7 males per 100 females. In the period from 1953 to 1958 the imbalance at both ends of the age continuum has been somewhat redressed as old practices of infanticide have been erased and retirement and health care provisions have been extended.[3]

The youthful nature of the nonfarm work force is reiterated in table 2.2 which shows figures on national age composition. The very high proportion of workers under forty-six—over 92 percent—reflects the bulging population at younger ages that table 2.1 records. The low percentage of workers under eighteen is due to the fact that large numbers of these young people were unsuccessful in getting jobs in the public sector.[4]

The Changing Structure of the Employed Work Force

I have broken this review into two parts: first, a survey of the period from 1949 to the end of the GLF; and then, a look at the period from 1962 to 1972. Even though the Soviet model was rejected by the end of the FFYP, and the GLF represented a veering away from that model to a new direction, the impact of the first strategy had such momentum that carried it, especially in the nonagricultural sectors, for several years. The dislocations and dysfunction of the GLF also affected industry adversely. There was a significant contraction in the total of workers employed as the drop in agricultural output reduced greatly the levels of nonagricultural pursuits. The period starting in 1962 is one in which the policies of an indigenous growth model were beginning to have some positive effect both on agriculture and the other sectors: recovery moved along at a fair pace and the reallocation of labor resources proceeded.

1949–1961

This time span covers three distinct periods: 1949 through 52, recovery and rehabilitation; 1953 through 1957, the FFYP; and 1958 through 61, the GLF and its breakdown. But the data on the nonagricultural work force, in table 2.3, must be viewed within the context of preparation for implementation of the Soviet model, its actual implementation, and the conse-

Table 2.3

Nonagricultural Employment, 1949–1958

(In Thousands of Workers)

Branch of the Economy and Component	1949	1950	1951	1952	1953	1954	1955	1956	1957	1958
All Branches and Components	26,267	30,314	34,730	36,752	39,116	39,750	38,864	39,366	39,667	56,117
MODERN [1] Total	7,977	10,166	12,705	15,656	18,069	18,588	18,861	23,939	23,921	44,223
Material production branches	5,176	6,163	8,066	10,298	12,172	12,701	12,852	17,203	17,280	37,470
Industry	3,059	3,386	4,379	5,263	6,121	6,370	6,121	7,480	7,907	22,984
Water conservancy	61	80	108	134	198	266	261	409	340	1,360
Capital construction	200	400	600	1,048	2,170	2,100	1,935	2,951	1,910	5,336
Transport, posts, telecommunications	634	799	964	1,129	1,238	1,347	1,426	1,564	1,878	2,955
Trade, and food and drink industry	1,222	1,498	2,015	2,724	2,445	2,618	3,109	4,799	5,245	4,835
Nonproductive branches	2,801	4,003	4,639	5,358	5,897	5,887	6,009	6,736	6,641	6,753
Finance, banking, and insurance	...	...	...	346	377	384	384	417	400	300
State education, medicine and public health, and cultural affairs	1,176	...	...	2,392	2,607	2,715	2,824	3,211	3,211	3,811

Branch	1949	1950	1951	1952	1953	1954	1955	1956	1957	1958
utilities	...	...	...	41	69	96	123	133	133	150
Meteorology	1	1	2	3	3	4	6	12	15	28
TRADITIONAL [1] Total	18,290	20,148	22,025	21,096	21,047	21,162	20,003	15,427	15,746	11,894
Material production branches	17,309	19,159	20,937	19,902	19,782	19,609	18,406	13,605	13,673	9,698
Handicrafts and carrier services	5,855	7,229	7,258	7,364	7,789	8,910	8,202	5,780	6,560	1,465
Salt extraction	500	500	500	500	500	500	500	500	500	700
Fishing	800	1,200	1,268	1,336	1,404	1,472	1,540	1,500	1,500	2,000
Transport, posts, telecommunications	3,526	3,526	3,526	3,526	3,526	3,526	3,450	2,539	2,539	2,868
Trade, and food and drink industry	6,628	6,704	8,385	7,176	6,563	5,201	4,714	3,286	2,574	2,665
Nonproductive branches	981	989	1,088	1,194	1,265	1,553	1,597	1,822	2,073	2,196
Finance, banking, and insurance	...	...	...	5	19	248	320	260	221	100
Services	425	417	434	443	452	461	470	479	489	489
Traditional medicine	564	564	654	746	794	844	807	1,083	1,363	1,607

Source: John Philip Emerson, *Nonagricultural Employment in Mainland China: 1949–1958* (Washington, D.C.: U.S. Government Printing Office, 1965), p. 133.

Notes: Figures are year end; ellipses (...) indicate data was not available, and no estimate was made.

[1] Workers and employees in the nonagricultural branches constitute employment in the modern components; persons engaged in nonagricultural occupations and not classified as workers and employees constitute employment in the traditional components.

quences of the model's execution, including the overall continuing shock of the GLF on the work force.

The changing configuration of the work force, starting in 1949, displays the distinctive characteristics of a thrust toward modernization with a strong emphasis on the heavy industrial sector. At the same time, as the traditional branch of the economy shows marked absolute and sharper relative declines, it is clear that by even the end of the period under review that branch still included a significant proportion of workers and was performing a role of importance in overall economic activity. Though explicit statement of a policy of dualistic economic development was not put forth until late in the period under review, given China's backwardness the elimination of indigenous work patterns, if such was ever a policy, could not be achieved for considerable time; and in the end CCP review of development strategy led to the conclusion that China would have to rely heavily upon her great, if backward, native labor resources. To understand better the process of changing the structure of China's work force to facilitate modernization, we must keep uppermost in our minds the dichotomy between the modern and the traditional branches of the economy at the same time as we remember that changes of laborpower in either are interrelated.

A striking generalization emerges from analysis of table 2.3: for the most part the quite remarkable increase in nonagricultural output from 1949 to 1958 occurred with a relatively modest rise in the work force. From 1949 to 1958 nonagricultural output rose by a multiple of at least three to one, while the work force increased by about 116 percent. The increase in workers in 1958, due to the shock campaigns of the GLF, was quite sharp and atypical, and one ought thus to take the 1949 through 1957 span as the Soviet model period. Then the rise in the work force was a very modest 51 percent; for the period of the FFYP (1953–1957) the growth of the work force was an insignificant 5 percent. Part of the increase in the work force from 1949 to 1951 is probably the result of better statistical reporting rather than an actual increase. If this is so, the higher adjusted base figure for 1949 yields a much narrower expansion of the work force to either 1957 or 1958. To the extent that the solid growth in output during the fifties was accomplished with little absolute change in the work force, it was achieved through modifying the mix of that labor force rather than significantly changing the input of laborpower.[5]

The interrelated changes in the distribution of workers among various components of the two branches of the economy and between those two branches themselves assume greatest importance during the FFYP. From 1949 to 1952 the main thrust of recovery and rehabilitation was to channel workers in larger numbers into the going structure of economic activity, traditional as well as modern. The work force grew in both branches at a good pace, though in 1952 in the traditional branch there was a slight decline as the plateau characterizing the FFYP was approached. This period saw the launching of phased socialization throughout the nonagricultural sectors. Once the FFYP was under way its various programmed objectives began to make themselves felt in the structure of the work force in ways that this analysis delineates.

While the objectives of rapid industrialization and modernization were being programmed *à la Russe* in the FFYP, the plan also called for socialization of the industrial as well as the agricultural sectors albeit on different timetables. The phased socialization of industry from private and capitalist activity, to joint state-private activity, and then to socialist enterprise, was an underlying mechanism in the reallocation of workers among the branches and components of the economy. Table 2.4 illustrates the accomplishments of the program from 1949 through 1956 by which time capitalist enterprises were practically eliminated and all industrial enterprises were either socialist or joint state-private in a ratio of two to one. The reallocation of workers during the process of socialization was a constant influence reshaping the structure of the work force to meet the dual goals of socialization and industrialization. For example, the constant decline in the employment of workers in the traditional trade component starting in 1952 was determined in large measure by the accelerating rate of reduction in capitalist enterprise, traditional trade being an area in which small entrepreneurs abounded. Private trade was also declining: it was being transformed into joint state-private enterprise so that as it progressed from one phase to the other, workers were moved from traditional trade to modern trade, which sustained growth in employment in all years through 1957 except for 1953. In parallel fashion, other parts of the work force have changed under the prodding of the socialization process and the FFYP.

Looking at the changing work force structure for the period under review, the obvious becomes apparent: the structure of the work force by 1957 reflected the growing industrialized and modernized nature of the economy. But the pace and the sources of this momentous change (with the traditional branch still of considerable importance) need specification so that how the Chinese worker was affected may be appreciated fully.

The worker was exposed to varying pressures and had to adapt himself to changes of many kinds as he moved into new or different shops under novel organizational systems. Those moving from handicrafts into cooperative industrial plants—from the traditional to the modern branch—were

Table 2.4
Socialist Transformation of Industry, 1949–1956
Percentage Distribution of Gross Output Value of
Industry, Excluding Handicrafts

Year	Socialist Industry	State Capitalist Industry	Joint State-Private Enterprises	Private	Capitalist
1949	34.7	9.5	2.0	7.5	55.8
1950	45.3	17.8	2.9	14.9	36.9
1951	45.9	25.4	4.0	21.4	28.7
1952	56.0	26.9	5.0	21.9	17.1
1953	57.5	28.5	5.7	22.8	14.0
1954	62.8	31.9	12.3	19.6	5.3
1955	67.7	29.3	16.1	13.2	3.0
1956	67.5	32.5	32.5	—[a]	—[a]

Source: People's Republic of China, State Statistical Bureau, *Ten Great Years* (Peking: Foreign Languages Press, 1960), p. 38.
Note: State-capitalist industry subsumes joint state-private enterprises and private enterprises. Privately owned enterprises executed orders and processed goods for the state whereas capitalist industry produced and marketed its products by itself.
[a] Negligible figure.

subject to a different kind of discipline and also were called upon to participate in a new social approach to work tasks and rewards. (In 1958 and early 1959 the new workers in modern industry flowed 70 percent from agriculture and handicrafts and 20 percent from schools, offices, and the armed forces.) Others accustomed to private or capitalistic contexts in their former work where they were worker-entrepreneurs had to work in surroundings that were unfamiliar and to yield to social discipline rather than to self-discipline. Capitalists now working as managers in joint state-private enterprises had to become acclimated to basic decisions either being made or approved by outside authorities other than the market and profit. Many workers with some industrial experience moved into new state enterprises of the most advanced technological conditions and found themselves under a different order of technical and organizational discipline.[6]

The movement of millions of workers within the structure of the work force took a clearly discernible pattern beyond the above generalization. Whatever the span of years analyzed, the growth pattern is clear except for the material component (contributing to material output) of the traditional branch of the economy. The total for the traditional branch also shows contraction throughout the period. The averaging effect of the decline in the traditional material component and its subdivisions, where the absolute numbers of workers involved was quite high, is apparent in the total for all traditional workers. The growth in the entire nonproductive component and its subdivisions was not quite without exception with declines occurring in four years in the two subdivisions of finance and traditional medicine.

The decline in the material component of the traditional branch of the work force is easily understandable in the context of China's industrial thrust under the whip of the FFYP. Among all subdivisions of the material component only one, fishing, shows an almost continuous growth throughout the period. That this activity should grow as the economy was being modernized needs little explanation, since protein food is an invaluable staple. The decline in traditional transportation and trade and related pursuits follows the fiat of the FFYP in which these areas of economic activity were either to be modernized or integrated into the structure of evolving agricultural cooperatives.

The handicrafts situation was a little more complicated, though the same forces and considerations were at work. Handicrafts included three types: subsistence handicrafts, individual handicrafts, and handicraft workshops. The continued high level of employment in handicrafts, though in declining numbers after 1954, was necessitated by the backwardness of this part of the economy and the need to transform gradually at least two of its types into more advanced forms of industrial activity. Table 2.5 indicates the rapid change in handicraft employment as cooperatives were swiftly expanded. The declines that occurred in employment starting in 1956 were due to absorption of handicraft workers into agricultural cooperatives as well as into industrial enterprises so that the change was mainly one of classification. Subsistence handicrafts, the most backward, continued throughout the period and beyond, making up a major proportion of the workers in handicrafts. Individual handicraft activities lent themselves to cooperativization, following lines parallel to those in agriculture, and from that to more advanced industrial operations. Handicraft workshops could most readily be converted into modern industrial workshops. The conversions suggested took time to evolve, and by the middle of the FFYP they began to have an impact on the work force. The

Table 2.5

Development of Handicraft Cooperation, 1952–1956

Year	Total (000)	Workers Employed in Cooperative Handicrafts		Workers Employed in Individual Handicrafts	
		(000)	(%)	(000)	(%)
1952	7,364	228	3.1	7,136	96.9
1953	7,789	301	3.9	7,488	96.1
1954	8,910	1,213	13.6	7,697	86.4
1955	8,202	2,206	26.9	5,996	73.1
1956	6,583	6,039	91.7	544	8.3

Source: State Statistical Bureau, *Ten Great Years,* p. 36.

sharp drop in handicraft employment in 1958 is somewhat illusory and represents the assimilation of many handicraft workers into the commune system. Thus, even though handicraft employment declined relatively by the late fifties, it continued, along with other traditional activities, to play an important role in the evolving Maoist strategy for industrialization as the policy of Walking on Two Legs (simultaneous development of modern and indigenous industry) became more clearly formulated and was revived in the late sixties.[7]

The growth in the nonproductive branches of the traditional segment of the work force was continuous though variable in rate. Since the employment of workers in traditional services was fairly constant throughout the period, and the numbers in traditional finance were quite small; the main influence on the total was traditional medicine which almost tripled over the years. Those working in traditonal medicine were mostly practitioners of the ancient medical art and midwives who operated outside the regular medical and public health organizations. The growth in numbers of these workers was at a modest pace early in the decade, but then, starting in 1956, the pace quickened. The regime had put forth a positive policy for traditional medicine. This quicker pace in the middle fifties was probably a consequence of the official exaltation of traditional medicine and the condemnation of "bourgeois" medical elements late in 1954. Starting in 1958 the further emphasis on traditional medicine in the Walking on Two Legs policy gave added impetus to indigenous practitioners of medical arts.[8]

Traditional services grew slightly each year during the fifties until 1958 when the enormous redirection of labor in the GLF must have especially affected the service component. This work segment was composed of those working in casual roles in barbershops, cleaning and dyeing establishments, hotels, and bathhouses. The nature of the work and the relatively low level of pay, both defining the low status of most of these occupations, made these workers especially attracted to steadier, better paying jobs which might also be held in higher social esteem.[9]

The small but growing numbers of financial workers in the traditional segment were mainly involved in the work of the rural credit cooperatives for which data start in 1952 when that movement began. The changes in numbers of workers are almost mechanically related to the development of rural credit cooperatives, the peak for cooperatives being reached in 1955 after which numbers of cooperatives and financial workers decline. The sharp drop in 1958 resulted from the cooperatives practically being abolished shortly before the people's rural communes were set up.[10]

With very few exceptions employment in the modern part of the economy moved steadily upward as the CCP leadership programmed the modernization and industrialization of China. An increase of 200 percent for the entire modern part from 1949 to 1957 and 454 percent if the period is extended a year attests to the sustained nature of the growth, though we repeat our caveat that data for the earlier years may be incomplete and that the 1958 situation of shock campaigns is a special and short-lived phenomenon. Given industrialization and the marked investment in manufacturing and mining industry during the FFYP, the material production branch increased its employment by considerably more than did the nonproductive branch, growing by 234 percent by 1957 while the nonproductive branch rose by 137 percent. The surge of the former by about 117 percent in 1958 as nonproductive workers increased by only 1.7 percent reflects again the heavy accent on industry in the GLF.

Among nonproductive activities several special situations help to explain the relative slowness in the overall rise in employment in finance, government administration, and mass organizations. The main reason for this slow growth, of course, was the channeling of workers into industry. In finance, workers were involved in state and state-private enterprises specializing in banking, finance, and insurance. The increase of only 16 percent in such workers from 1949 to 1957 and the declines of 4 and 25 percent in 1957 and 1958 reflect two related forces: the centralization and the socialization of financial operations. Financial operations were more and more rationalized as functions were clearly defined, and by 1958, a year of decline in the number of workers to below the 1952 level, the People's Bank was carrying out most of the financial work along with several other large specialized units. While this process was in motion the transformation of private financial enterprises into state-private units prior to their absorption into the centralizing state machine facilitated the movement to fewer units and workers.[11]

The rather slow overall rise in government administration and mass organization employment from 1949 to 1957 and the very sharp decline in the former in 1958 were all born out of the need to funnel more and more workers into the material production branch if industrialization was to meet its planned objectives. In 1954 there was a massive reduction in government administration workers and mass organizations, and in the next year government workers suffered a further reduction in number. Late in 1957 another transfer of cadres took place, and in 1958 decentralization policy coinciding with the establishment of communes led to a massive switch of cadres to other posts. Thus, the restrained growth of nonproductive activities was mainly a consequence of the major thrust toward industrialization and the decentralization aspect of the GLF.[12]

The more robust increases in the number of workers in the material production branch generally and in industry, water conservancy, capital construction, transportation, and trade in particular are completely consonant with the industrialization-modernization objectives of the regime. The very sharp increases for the first three of these sectors in 1958 reflect the conjuncture of FFYP objectives and the first thrusts of the GLF. In the FFYP period, material production and the sectors subsumed under it increased by 68, 50, 154, 82, 66, and 93 percents, respectively. These sectors grew briskly as workers in other parts of the economy were relieved so that they could take on jobs in the modern material branch.

Only transportation, among the various sectors of material production, shows not a single year of decline in numbers of workers. All the others, despite their generally strong growth in employment, suffered a year or .more in which the swelling of workers ceased; capital construction experienced three such years. These seeming aberrations were due to a variety of forces, but in most instances the declines probably resulted from statistical difficulties. In the water conservancy instances the figures are derived from a series whose inferred total may be in error. In other instances interpolations may have spawned underestimates. In one instance, that of capital construction for 1954, the decline is quite probable and reflects somewhat depressed economic conditions late in the year which resulted in reductions in the numbers of workers at the end of the year instead of the customary additions that were ordered in the last quarter of the year.[13]

Unfortunately we do not have a breakdown of employment data for the years 1959 through 1961 to complete our review of the role of the Chinese worker for the entire period from 1949 to 1961. But there are estimates of the total of nonagricultural employment for those years:

1959—54.7 million
1960—52.1 million
1961—45.2 million

These declines from the peak in 1958 were substantial and represent one crude measure of the contraction in economic activity imposed by the setbacks of the GLF. (The drop in employment from 1958 to 1961, almost 21 percent, is only a low first approximation to the unemployment and underemployment that ensued from the GLF, since even in the frenetic days of mass production campaigns in 1958 there were millions of urban unemployed.) The ebb in employment in 1959, 1960, and 1961 must be seen as a direct consequence of the failure of agriculture to generate the sharply increased output which had been anticipated and which was essential to propel industry further along its path of rapid growth. As it was, agriculture could not even provide sufficient ouput to enable industry to maintain its former tempo. Moreover, the shifting away from the Soviet model, even under the best of circumstances, would have forced a considerable redirection of workers into a new employment structure more consistent with the strategy of "agriculture as the foundation, industry as the leading factor."

The changes in economic strategy in the direction of greater help for agriculture and less emphasis on heavy industry per se occurred while the economy changed from a burst of expansion into a sharp contraction. One student of Chinese industrial production, frustrated by the blackout of official statistics on the economy's performance, has pieced together the following index of industrial production which crudely gauges this expansion and contraction:

1957—100
1958—131
1959—166
1960—162–164
1961—104–106

Two facts of importance emerge clearly from these data, imperfect though they be: the expansions in the first two years of the GLF were sharp and in line with earlier industrial growth; and the drop to the trough in 1961, roughly 35 percent, was a decline of significant proportion affecting employment in a traumatic way. (In the agricultural sphere, of course, the contraction in output set in a year earlier and though the decline was 26 percent (less than that in industry), its effect, naturally, was almost disastrous.) [14]

The declines in industrial output starting in 1959 and 1960, depending on the particular industrial activity, were a consequence of two major factors: the drop in agricultural output (food and raw materials) and the sudden withdrawal of Soviet technicians from certain large industrial complexes in the middle of 1960. The first condition meant that many industrial plants had to stop or slow down production either because basic raw materials such as raw cotton were no longer forthcoming in sufficient quantities to sustain production levels, or processed materials such as spun cotton were in short supply due to the drying up of the raw material transformed in an earlier phase of production. The second situation, where operations depended upon Soviet technicians, resulted in shutdowns with workers unemployed, the facility useless in its uncompleted state, or a reduced scale of operations due to the loss of Soviet technical assistance.

Our survey of the numbers of workers in varying nonagricultural activities has dealt with *all* people employed in those pursuits, blue- and white-collar and professional personnel. Some notion of the configuration and development of this group in China is essential not only to complete our sense of who the workers were, what they did, and how they were structured but also to document in more stark detail the powerful commitment of the FFYP strategy to the development of industry and technology. Table 2.6 presents a quantitative breakdown of administrative and technical workers for selected years 1949 to 1961 so that some notion of structure and change may be possible.

Analysis of the data in table 2.6 shows clearly the quite successful development of large numbers of technical and professional personnel over the period 1949 to 1961. This was achieved while the proportions of administrative and technical workers were being completely reversed as the number of technical workers grew significantly faster than the total number of workers and that of workers in the modern sector of the nonagricultural work force. In 1949 administrative personnel comprised 60 percent of the total administrative and technical work force, while the latter numbered only 40 percent; by 1961 the proportions were reversed to 36 to 64 percent, respectively. Administrative workers grew at a lesser pace than technical workers: technical personnel increased almost fourfold in number from 1949 to 1961, while the number of administrative workers

Table 2.6

Administrative and Technical Workers
in China, Selected Years 1949–1961
(In Thousands)

Field	1949	1952	1955	1957	1959	1961
Total	2,993	5,345	6,692	8,091	9,657	9,325
Administrative personnel	1,799	3,302	3,800	4,212	4,500	3,382
Government administration and mass organizations	796	1,461	1,516	1,634	(NA)	(NA)
Other branches of the economy	1,003	1,841	2,284	2,578	(NA)	(NA)
Technical personnel	1,194	2,043	2,892	3,879	5,157	5,943
Engineers and technicians	126	212	626	800	1,000	(NA)
Agricultural specialists	16	68	165	389	872	(NA)
Teachers	834	1,441	1,632	2,116	2,670	2,851
Scientific research personnel	3	8	11	28	36	(NA)
Medical and public health specialists	180	244	370	452	480	(NA)
Cultural affairs specialists	35	70	88	94	99	(NA)

Source: John Philip Emerson, *Administrative and Technical Manpower in the People's Republic of China* International Population Reports, Series P-95, No. 72 (Washington, D.C.: U.S. Department of Commerce, 1973), p. 37.
Notes: Data are year end; NA indicates not available.

rose just over twofold. Administrative workers increased at a rate below that of workers in the modern sector, while technical personnel grew somewhat more rapidly than workers in the modern sector. This was a considerable achievement given the more difficult problem of training such personnel compared to training skilled and semiskilled workers. The response to the more acute scarcity of technical workers reflected the strong commitment in this period to the rapid development of heavy industry with its demands on advanced technology.

The leveling off and decline of the number of administrative workers from 1957 to 1961 (which actually started in 1956 when the total was the same as 1957) reflects concerted efforts to contain and reduce bureaucracy. These efforts started late in the FFYP and were exerted more forcefully during the GLF. Many bureaucrats were transferred down to the countryside. It took a decade of growth for the totals to return to their 1959 peak indicating at least some quantitative containment of administrative costs in real terms.

Technical workers were given a prominent role to play during and after the FFYP in mounting and sustaining rapid technological and industrial growth. The development of what might become a technocratic elite (the regime took this into account in the formulation of the new strategy of the GLF) was not unexpected given Western and Soviet experience, and this posed a problem of major ideological and technical proportions for the regime.

1962–1972

Since the period after 1961 is one with so many momentous changes such as the Socialist Education Movement, the GPCR, and then the political reconstitution of the CCP, all of which involved conflicts over and modifications in fundamental strategy, it is unfortunate that quantitative data are so incomplete. We are forced, therefore, to take pieces of statistical data dropped by CCP spokesmen or reconstructed by foreign students of the Chinese economy, often on tenuous grounds, as the basis for tracing the continuing development of the labor force. The hazards of such a procedure are patent, but some tentative idea of direction and order of magnitude of the growth of the work force can be gleaned from it.

Two sets of estimation, much less solidly constructed than similar sets for the fifties, are the starting point to which is added qualitative information. First, one student of the labor force, whom I have depended upon for my earlier data, has arrived at 45.8 million as an overall figure for nonagricultural employment for 1964 and 14 million as a figure for the total of employed industrial workers for 1965. Next, another student of Chinese industrial production has compiled the following index of industrial production for the period from 1957 through 1968 (1957 is 100) which parallels estimated official data with annual ranges of industrial output.

```
1962—104–108 [150] interpolation
1963—115–121  165
1964—130–138  190
1965—147–159  211
1966—160–175  253
1967—135–150 [217] interpolation
1968—148–167  232
```

In any event, this contour and order of magnitude of Chinese industrial fluctuations, if not the precise annual figures, are confirmed by various other estimates as well as by the inferred official data.[15]

The above production estimates can be projected through 1972. From 1968 industrial production has continued to grow annually by roughly 10 percent or more a year with output in 1972 clearly more than four times that of 1952 and more than double that of 1957. Agriculture sustained such industrial growth with its tenth year of increased grain output in 1971, though in 1972 a decline of 4 percent occurred.[16]

The seeming stability in the total number of persons employed in non-agricultural activities between 1961 and 1964, 45.2 and 45.8 million, respectively, is somewhat misleading, since the decline of the number employed in modern industry amounted to 9 million during the same period, a drop of about 40 percent. (At the same time industrial output fell off by almost 25 percent.) Employment in 1962 and 1963 most probably continued declining and then began a recovery during which reallocation of labor, started earlier, became a salient feature of the new heightened policy of supporting agriculture with huge infusions of laborpower from the urban areas as well as with growing inputs of fertilizers and a variety of machinery from expanding industry. From 1959 to 1963 about twenty million people were transferred from urban to rural areas.[17]

The reallocation of labor that was a significant characteristic of the aftermath of the GLF and its dislocations was also a principal determining factor in the changing structure of the labor force during the 1960s. The movement of tens of millions of Chinese (mainly industrial workers and their families) from the cities in the early part of the decade, the movement of millions of students and other activists during the GPCR, and the transferral down to the countryside of tens of millions of students, teachers, former peasants, unemployed, industrial workers, medical and paramedical personnel, etcetera (some only temporarily) attest to the deep commitment of the Maoists to make their model for economic development a reality. By 1972 the total number of persons employed in nonagricultural pursuits probably exceeded 55 million (up about 20 percent from 1964), with the mix undoubtedly quite different from that of 1957 and 1958 when the Soviet model was in sway.

Although we cannot analyze the structure of the labor force for the period 1961 through 1972 as we did for the earlier time span, we can construct a generalization based on estimates of what happened to the output of ten major industrial commodities. To that we can add, quite tentatively, our appraisals of what probably happened to other parts of the economy on which our information is principally qualitative.

The probability is quite high that for major industrial commodities employment grew solidly through 1972, with some setback during the GPCR. In 1964, we have seen, industrial employment numbered about fourteen million persons. There is some indication that employment growth in 1965 and 1966 occurred over 1964 at a 5 to 7 percent rate. In only one of the ten industrial areas being reviewed, petroleum or crude oil, is output growth continuous from before the GLF, "depressed" years being those in which output remains unchanged: from 1957 to 1968 output increased by over 600 percent. In this situation of practically continuous and solid growth the number of workers employed in petroleum activity undoubtedly increased, though probably by considerably less than the increase in output as new oil fields such as Ta-ch'ing were opened, and old ones were more efficiently exploited.[18]

In the nine other major industrial activities, output followed varying patterns, and employment changes likely were related to output changes, though probably not in the same proportions. Furthermore, the changes reflect the modified growth strategy in which industrial growth was to be related principally to the needs of an expanding agriculture. Output of steel declined sharply in 1961 to 8 million tons from a high of 13 million tons in 1960 (considerably higher if indigenous steel output is included). It recovered slowly up to 1966, ebbed in 1967, and rose to 12 million in 1968, 21 million in 1971, and 23 million in 1972. Slow recovery was deliberate and in line with the new strategy; the quality of output improved considerably in variety of product, better end products, and better organization of production. There was some increase of employment as production of steel went up, but that increase was undoubtedly slower than the growth of output given great unused capacities. The coal industry, on the other hand, never again attained the peak output of 290 million tons which it reached in 1959. In 1968, after rebounding from the drop in 1967, coal output reached 210 million tons. Coal output continued to rise in the years to 1972. Employment in coal mining very probably did not change much after the recovery of the sixties set in.[19]

In the seven other industrial areas output grew markedly from 1962 to 1966, and 1968 levels were comparable with the exception of electric power and chemical fertilizers. Sugar grew most, by 220 percent, as domestic output was pushed to provide for reduction in imports. The output of chemical fertilizers, a most valuable agricultural input, increased by over 160 percent. Cement, an important ingredient in industrial construction as well as in housing, expanded in output by 100 percent. The remaining industrial activities rose by lesser, yet appreciable, proportions: cotton loth by over 80 percent, paper by 80 percent, electric power by over 55 percent, and timber by over 30 percent. In all of these industrial activities employment undoubtedly rose with the expansion of output. For almost all of them capital use is intensive so that expansion of output was probably achieved with less than commensurate increase of workers.[20]

Another significant industry in the modern sector for which we have data extending into the sixties and which experienced sturdy growth after the setback of 1961 to 1962 is the machine-building industry, so important for industrialization and national defense. Starting in 1963 and continuing through 1966, the last year for which we have data, output for the industry increased in large annual jumps averaging 15 to 40 percent. Increase in employment must have followed this upsurge, though at a lower rate than that of production and probably with a time lag.[21]

For the rest of the labor force at work in modern and traditional components there are no systematic quantitative data to inform, even if tentatively, our sense of how the structure of work and workers has changed. This picture of work development is quite incomplete. We are left, therefore, with a sense of overall slow growth of the nonagricultural employment to over 55 million by 1972 with some idea of tempos of change in certain industrial activities.

There are some data on the growth of administrative and technical personnel from 1961 to 1971. The total of these workers increased from 9.3 to 12.0 million, an increase of almost 30 percent, with administrative personnel rising by almost 40 percent, from 3.4 to 4.7 million; and technical workers increasing almost 25 percent, from 5.9 to 7.4 million. Any of these increases, relatively, is more pronounced than the probable overall increase in the work force. The continuing strong commitment to this type of personnel is clear with the vigorous growth of industry calling for more administrative and technical workers.[22]

Unemployment

In economic terms unemployment is one measure of inefficient factor allocation; socially it epitomizes the failure to integrate large numbers of people in constructive work programs with attendant alienation. While workers employed in the Chinese economy have been growing in number and have been redeployed in the various ways sketched above, the regime has been confronted continually with the knotty problem of unemployment. In 1955, Li Fu-ch'un, chairman of the State Planning Committee realistically put unemployment in an extended time context: "The phenomenon of unemployment left over from the old China cannot be completely eliminated yet, and the surplus labor force still cannot be fully utilized. These problems will have to be solved by our continuous efforts in the second or even the third Five-Year Plan." [23]

Thus, inheriting an unemployment situation in the cities, the CCP has from the very start set up mechanisms to tide the problem over while its program for rehabilitation and industrialization has been pressed with the expectation that those without jobs would readily be absorbed in the upward motion of the economy. But only during the mass campaigns of the GLF in 1958 did this occur, if only for the moment, and thereafter the jobless in cities and in the countryside continued to vex the CCP leaders. The commune developed means for utilizing rural labor in its varied activities, but the unemployed in the cities were not as easily integrated into economic activity leaving alienated masses as a major sore spot. [24]

Though this problem (as well as underemployment) is one endemic to underdeveloped and emerging economies, it still poses a major economic and political challenge to the CCP. Countries in similar conditions of economic backwardness as China, such as Ceylon, British Guiana, East Pakistan, Egypt, Indonesia, Jamaica, and Trinidad, also experience high unemployment rates of from 7 to 20 percent. Unemployment reduces considerably the generation of capital from excess labor, contradicts the socialist claim for efficient planned work for all, and precipitates major social and political stress. From 1949 until the late sixties the troubling persistence of unemployment has resulted from a combination of factors of which an important one has been implementation of official policies such as wage increases which have unintentionally exacerbated the unemployment situation. [25]

The order of magnitude and range of fluctuation of male unemployment are indicated by the data in table 2.7. These data must be used with great caution, based as they are on population and labor force data with wide margins of error; the resulting unemployment residuals, therefore, ought to be used as suggestive only during a period of significant labor force change so that some notion of why this phenomenon persisted and who comprised this large group of workers can be fashioned.

For most of this period the labor force grew at a faster rate than the need of growing industrial and service activities for workers. The 1949 through 1950 levels of unemployment can be accepted as inherited, and apparently the regime's efforts to reduce unemployment made some headway in 1951

Table 2.7

Ranges of Male Unemployment, 1949–1960

Year	Total Unemployed (Millions)	As A Percentage of Labor Force
1949	6.6—13.8	18.2—31.7
1950	5.0—12.5	13.2—27.6
1951	2.7—10.3	6.8—21.8
1952	3.1—11.0	7.5—22.3
1953	3.0—10.9	6.9—21.3
1954	5.7—13.9	12.7—26.2
1955	7.7—16.1	16.8—29.6
1956	7.9—16.5	16.5—29.2
1957	9.6—18.3	19.5—31.6
1958	.2— 9.3	.3—14.9
1959	7.2—16.2	12.4—24.2
1960	10.7—20.2	17.3—28.3

Source: Chi-ming Hou, "Manpower, Employment, and Unemployment," in Alexander Eckstein et al., eds., *Economic Trends in Communist China* (Chicago: Aldine, 1968), p. 369.

as unemployment declined. But for the next three years, despite various official measures, unemployment persisted at about the same level. The regime claimed that from 1949 to 1955 over 32.6 million unemployed were put back to work. As the FFYP got underway unemployment, especially in the cities, started to mount again, and in 1957 it moved up more sharply to its highest level since 1949. A survey made in 1956 revealed that most of the urban unemployed were without skills and were relatively advanced in age with some of them being young people schooled to the higher primary level or somewhat above. There were two main causes for this swelling of the jobless: the growing income disparity between peasant and worker and the increasing unhappiness of some peasants with the extended co-operativization of agriculture. Both of these factors spurred peasants into the cities where incomes were higher and work tasks less onerous. During the FFYP about eight million rural people moved into the towns and cities. The marked rise in unemployment in 1957 probably was intensified by the increased income gap that resulted when workers received wage increases averaging about 14 percent in the 1956 wage reform. In 1958 joblessness seemed to have been dramatically reduced and on its way to being eliminated as the mass campaigns of the GLF were felt in industry and in agriculture through the newly formed communes.[26]

The phenomenon of substantial continuing unemployment from 1953 on was a consequence of the regime's implementation of the Soviet growth model whose effects carried over into the period of the GLF for urban workers. The regime's growth strategy of major emphasis on the development of industry while agriculture was being put through phases of cooperativization and squeezed of product for capital formation gave rise to subsidiary policies which were not easily reversed once the decision was made to revise the development strategy drastically. The new strategy placed the development of agriculture, so poorly suited to generate capital at all, at the top of the list with industrial growth to be encouraged but mainly to be put in the service of stimulating agriculture's technical progress. But this new program did not directly contribute to the containment of unemployment. The FFYP programs for the training of industrial and scientific personnel and the schooling of increasing numbers of youths were not readily curtailed or put to an end. The result was that large numbers of scientific and engineering personnel as well as greater numbers of students continued to flow from the programs at a rate still geared to the previously planned high levels of industrial production. This together with the influx of peasants into the cities swelled urban population while the FFYP developed, and when the gears were shifted during the GLF agricultural shortfalls aggravated the unemployment situation by reducing industrial output levels sharply rather than simply lowering their rates of growth as had been planned in the new strategy.

Though undoubtedly unhappy about the persisting unemployment question, the regime publicly acknowledged the difficulties and outlined the means for dealing with the situation: "For those unemployed who temporarily cannot find jobs and have difficulty maintaining a living, the People's Government has given them help in the form of relief grants, or by providing relief work, organizing them to make a living through temporary productive work, giving them training for new jobs, or sending them back to the villages to engage in agricultural production." [27]

At the beginning of the fifties various official directives and provisions were promulgated to tide the unemployed through the transitional period. But with the continuation of unemployment, more thought and action were demanded to deal with the problem, and relief measures called the "Four Ways" were developed. Budgetary provisions for relief as well as orderly arrangements for financing such relief were set forth. Table 2.8 sum-

Table 2.8

State Unemployment Relief Expenditures, 1951–1956

(In Millions of Yuan)

Year	Total	Cities	Rural Areas
1951	92.4	20.8	71.6
1952	181.4	37.1	144.3
1953	181.8	54.2	127.6
1954	410.7	36.8	374.0
1955	265.8	39.2	226.6
1956	186.5	71.0	115.5

Source: *T'ung-chi kung-tso* [Statistical work], no. 12 (1957), p. 32.

marizes state budgetary expenditures for unemployment relief through 1956, and undoubtedly such payments continued beyond that year.[28]

The totals in table 2.8 should not be considered as representative of all amounts paid to the unemployed, since other avenues outside the state budget were open. Relief payments to unemployed (often in kind) came from three sources early in the fifties: (1) contributions of 1 percent of the total payroll to an unemployment benefit reserve by all state and private plants, workshops, and commercial enterprises in cities covered by unemployment benefits; (2) central and local government relief appropriations; and (3) "charity" which covered a variety of possibilities including aid from trade-union sources and other mass organizations.[29]

Unquestionably the continuation of unemployment was a major factor in convincing the regime that the Soviet model was inappropriate for China. The unemployed could only be absorbed if industrial growth could be more greatly accelerated and spread throughout the countryside, an impossibility if agriculture did not provide an ever-growing amount of raw materials and other surpluses which could be used to acquire what industry needed. The realization that China's economic development could proceed smoothly and briskly only if agriculture flourished at once was at the heart of the GLF and the new design for growth.

But after the seeming success in reducing the jobless in 1958, their numbers swelled again in 1959 and 1960 as agricultural failures forced industrial cutbacks. In addition the withdrawal of Soviet technicians in 1960 caused shutdowns and reductions in industrial production. As industrial production began its contraction, the numbers of trained personnel flowing from the schools and institutes increased in greater proportions appropriate to the earlier strategy. Even though many industrial plants extended disguised unemployment through overstaffing, unemployment spread.[30]

In the trough of the economic contraction precipitated by the failures of the GLF in 1961 to 1962, the level of unemployment was quite high. To deal with this critical problem, aside from the newly designed development strategy which was aimed at absorbing workers over time, direct measures were executed. Starting in 1955, attempts at reducing urban unemployment took the main form of nonpunitive transferral of workers down to the countryside (*hsia fang*). The 1958 decline in unemployment may have resulted partially from this policy. *Hsia fang* continued on a large scale, and from 1959 to 1963 tens of millions of urban people were transferred. (Only a fraction of these millions were unemployed workers, since the total includes nonworking family members as well as unemployed.) Despite this mass movement to the rural areas there was still movement into the cities. In 1961 such movement into Shanghai was quite visible and, in response, rural labor recruitment for industry was prohibited for three years.[31]

The period of the sixties was one of constant transferral of workers as well as newly graduated students. Such movements were expected to succeed through the integration of most of the transferred personnel into communes; some transfers were temporary, but most were expected to be permanent. Difficulties undoubtedly arose in the period from 1962 to 1965, a time in which various kinds of private enterprise in agricultural as well as sideline activity developed. The likelihood is great that many transferred workers made their way back to the cities. With the beginning of the GPCR, movement between cities was stepped up as the Red Guards and workers took to the rails to carry on the ideological warfare that included work stoppages, in-plant conflicts, and sabotage. In this climate some workers who had been sent recently to the countryside probably returned to the cities to help swell again the ranks of the jobless.[32]

In the aftermath of the GPCR, as political organization was slowly stabilized, the economic policies of the Maoist model slowly began to take on clear-cut shape. The revival and intensification of the strategy of Walking on Two Legs included a strategy for maximum labor utilization: the integration of surplus industrial and service workers of the city into the communes to build a structure of indigenous industry, science, education, health services, and cultural activities. Additional millions of students, teachers, doctors, medical and paramedical personnel, unemployed industrial workers, former peasants, artists, and writers were transferred down to the communes. They as well as rural laborers were to contribute to the development of local and provincial industries and industrial services, community health services, and scientifically advanced agricultural techniques. The doctors and technicians as well as other former city dwellers were a major capital infusion of laborpower available to enrich the communes' and provinces' capacities to meet their own human and expanding production needs.[33]

Until the onset of the GPCR it was clear that the unemployment problem, though it might have been in the process of solution through the transferral of workers, was still not solved. During the later stages of the GPCR and afterward, tens of millions of people were transferred down to communes, provincial institutions, and other countryside operational units, the overwhelming proportion of them permanently. Though evidence of resistance to and discontentment with this movement can readily be gathered, it is clear that this mass movement was successful in greatly increasing the labor force in the countryside and in reducing the legions of the unemployed in the cities. There has been no unplanned return of large numbers of these assigned workers to the cities, and by 1971 the regime claimed that the goal of full employment had been reached. Whether this claim was literally true or not cannot be independently determined yet, but certainly at the least the proportions of the unemployment problem have been drastically reduced.[34]

Evidence on underemployment has not been uncovered. But its existence in parallel developmental situations in other socialist economies is a reasonable basis to expect that the Chinese face this problem too.

Labor Productivity

The extent to which labor or any factor of production is utilized effectively can be gauged in broad or macroeconomic terms, taking the measure of the global operations and effects of the economy; or, in narrower or microeconomic terms, the operations and effects of the smaller units of the economy, enterprise or industry or in both ways. (The two measures can be consistent with or contradict one another.) The widespread existence of unemployment in the fifties and sixties at quite high rates as well as unused industrial plant capacity in the trough of 1961 to 1962 reflect an inability to utilize factors of production efficiently in the macroeconomic sense. Whatever the mitigating circumstances such as the difficulties generated by rapid industrialization, the three years of bad weather (1959–1961), the disarray resulting from swift and poorly managed communization, the shifting of gears from the high speed of the Soviet model to the second speed of the evolving Maoist model, the continuous if fluctuating existence of millions of unemployed, all meant that the Chinese economy was operating significantly below its capacity. And yet the other (microeconomic) measure of efficient use of factors of production shows clearly, at least for the FFYP, that Chinese industrial workers were being used highly effectively along with materials and capital. Labor productivity rates which are measures of the output per labor input and therefore of the efficiency at the plant or in the industry show rises in industry generally and specifically.

The period of the FFYP is one which is relatively well covered by data on labor productivity, though the official statistics need refinement, so that we are able to see the general contour of factor utilization as well as variations among a number of industries. Tables 2.9 and 2.10 below give us the general and the specific picture. Data for the subsequent period have necessarily been put together in a less rigorous way, but they sketch broad development. Table 2.11 gives us these broad rates of labor productivity.

The rise in labor productivity for all industry during the FFYP was quite marked as the data in table 2.9 indicate. Annual positive growth rates in productivity, except for 1956 to 1957 when a slight decline developed, ranged from over 4 percent to almost 18 percent, the overall rise during the FFYP exceeding 42 percent before it dipped slightly in 1957. Certainly in a long-run context annual growth rates exceeding 3 percent are considered quite solid. The official index rate was even more buoyant: from 1952 to 1958 it rose by 64 percent. Even the refined data in table 2.9 document remarkable industrial growth during the FFYP.[35]

This swift and marked industrial growth followed from greater input and the more effective utilization of labor. In other words, output rose by more than the increase in employment of workers due to more effective coordination of the factors of production. About 45 percent of this industrial growth was due to increases in productivity, and 54 percent was due to increased numbers of workers. Over the course of the FFYP the average number of fixed assets used per worker rose by 49 percent, while the total capacity of power machines used per worker and the total amount of electricity used per worker soared by 79 and 80 percent, respectively. One student of these developments attributes the successful growth of productivity to the unused industrial capacities existing before the FFYP. If this

Table 2.9

Index of Labor Productivity,
1952–1957

Year		Annual Percentage Change
1952	100.0	—
1953	104.3	4.3
1954	111.5	6.9
1955	120.8	8.3
1956	142.2	17.7
1957	140.2	−1.4

Source: Robert Michael Field, "Labor Productivity in Industry," in Alexander Eckstein et al., eds., *Economic Trends in Communist China* (Chicago: Aldine, 1968), p. 647.

Table 2.10

Index of Labor Productivity
by Industry Branch, 1956
(1952 = 100)

All industry	142.2
Electric power	120.5
Coal	131.3
Ferrous metals	186.3
Metal processing	156.6
Chemical processing	162.1
Building materials	161.5
Paper	185.4
Textiles	134.5
Food	132.9
Other	133.8

Source: Field, "Labor Productivity in Industry," p. 650.

Table 2.11

Industrial Labor Productivity
Growth Rate Estimates, 1950–1966
(Annual Average Compounded Rates in Percent)

Period	Output per Man-Year All Industrial Employees
1950–1966	1.7— 2.0
1950–1965	1.4— 1.7
1950–1952	6.0— 8.0
1953–1966	1.1— 1.5
1953–1965	1.2— 1.4
1953–1957	6.0— 6.2
1958 to mid–1960	−33.0— −40.0
1960–1962	1.0— 2.0 [a]
1957–1965	− 2.0— − 2.5
1957–1966	− 1.5 to 0
1963–1965	4.7— 5.7
1963–1966	5.0— 6.0

Source: Barry Richman, *Industrial Society in Communist China* (New York: Random House, 1969), p. 598.
[a] For entire period.

were the principal cause for the rapid rise in productivity, then, being a self-limiting factor, it would foreshadow declining productivity once capacity were approached unless other factors came into play.[36]

As we look at the individual productivity performance of industries in table 2.10 we see that all of the nine branches upon which the productivity record is based improved in substantial degree from 1952 to 1956. Increase in productivity ranged from a low of 20 percent for electric power to a high of 86 percent for ferrous metals in the four-year span. The differential rates of increased productivity conform to the mandate of the FFYP under which heavy industry and supporting activities were given priority in greater investment, first choice for materials and laborpower, special administrative attention, and so forth. The heavy industries themselves: ferrous metals, metal processing, chemical processing, and building materials, fared best of the nine, save for the paper industry which was perhaps the darling of the bureaucrats. Coal and electric power, important sources of energy for heavy industry, did less well than any others, while textiles

*adres, workers, and technicians discussing a technical change, Shanhai-
_uan Bridge Girders Plant* (China Pictorial, *11, 1972, p. 34*)

Employing the Chinese Worker
59

and food, consumer industries, did only slightly better. The remarkable performance of all nine branches of industry, however, should not be overlooked. Scattered data on labor productivity in selected industries for 1957 reinforce the view that table 2.10 projects. From 1952 to 1957 in the coal, iron, steel, cement, and cotton textile industries, official statistics show respective increases in output per worker of 46, 138, 93, 74, and 8 percents (here the average daily output is used for coal and the average annual output is used for the others). The significantly lower rate of increase in productivity for cotton textiles is consistent with the priorities of the FFYP.[37]

The productivity rate changes described by table 2.11 project a wider time coverage beginning with almost the very start of the regime and carrying into the period of the GPCR. Though these data must be used with much greater caution than those in tables 2.9 and 2.10, they provide a reasonable basis upon which to generalize about trends. The data on productivity for the period from 1953 to 1957 are quite consistent with the rates in table 2.9. The picture that emerges is one of quite substantial improvement in industrial productivity over the entire period if the worst years of the GLF, 1958 to 1960, are omitted. Even if these years are included, and they were years we have already described as markedly depressed, the average annual rate of 1.7 to 2.0 percent for over fifteen years was just high enough to parallel population growth. That kind of performance in the long run would not make possible the realization of the CCP's development objectives. For China, however, the productivity growth pattern provides an optimistic basis for projecting attainment of long-run goals if agricultural growth of a modest and sustained kind such as in the period 1961 through 1971 persists.

The data on labor productivity attest further to the fact that the Chinese worker has been undergoing a pervasive transformation in organizational, managerial, technical, and human terms. As industry during the middle fifties was being rapidly socialized, the worker's environment was constantly being modified. Whether he worked in capitalist, joint state-private, handicraft, or state enterprise, the size and coordination of his work site were subject to the manifold demands of the FFYP transmitted through various mass organizations and supervised by plant managers. During the GLF the crescendo of demands, more insistent and more group oriented and inspired, pushed workers urgently toward physical as well as psychological limits as the numbers of workers, at least in the first year, swelled in plant after plant. Following the GLF when production was reduced sharply, many workers found themselves without jobs and under pressure to migrate to the countryside. Those who remained in the cities either with or without work were once again harnessed more tightly to the industrial engine that was being speeded up as recovery set in. By the time of the GPCR that engine was working again closer to capacity. It was slowed during part of the GPCR and then once again, after that trauma subsided, raced more determinedly to new peaks of output while agriculture sustained moderate growth which was essential to fuel the engine and its labor resources. In these critical and demanding circumstances the Chinese worker played an important, though short-lived for some, industrial role. Some workers continued to play that part; others were dispatched to the countryside to find that that role was only part of a more demanding function combining industrial know-how with the requirements of collective agricultural cultivation in a variety of communal farming, industrial, and service activities.

Three

Allocating Workers

As indicated in chapter 1, the generation of capital is crucial to solving the problem of China's economic backwardness by using surplus and poorly utilized labor to produce that scarce factor of production. This end result can occur when labor input is increased, its quality improved, or it is moved where it would be most needed; the achievement of all three contributes more fully to rapid increase in output and capital accumulation. Effective organization of such movement over time is essential for sustained growth.

In chapter 2 we saw that the Chinese work force had grown substantially and had moved into various occupations slated for development by the CCP leaders, though until recently unemployment had continued as a significant factor. To gauge more effectively the extent to which the regime has been successful in accomplishing its labor allocation and other economic objectives, even as its basic growth strategy has been modified, it is essential to achieve some sense of how mobile the work force is, how the CCP allocates workers among old and new jobs and locations, and how efficiently and within what framework of choice this is done. Toward that end we explore the area of labor mobility viewing the methods and results which have issued from party policy and practice.

The ready allocation of labor throughout the economy is an especially important objective within the framework of the Maoist model for economic modernization and development. Not only must capital be wrung from labor, but also, given the quite different training and allocation pattern of the FFYP, the effective execution of the radical Maoist model demands a different training orientation and deployment of tens of millions of workers and their families so that dualistic development can proceed. Such successful deployment must end unemployment, boost agricultural output, stimulate capital formation, and contribute to the development of the more sparsely populated hinterlands where nature's endowment in land and minerals invites exploitation.

Labor mobility, the ability of workers to be readily available with the necessary skills in the locations required, is, in the classical wisdom, considered a labor force characteristic essential to efficient overall production. In advanced countries labor mobility is associated with a healthy and progressive economy, and this ideal is held high in both the Soviet Union and the United States. In China, similarly, the regime considers labor allocation an instrument of importance but has approached the problem, especially after the FFYP, without any commitment to using the traditional labor market allocator to achieve desired results.

As one reflects on the meaning of economic mobility, two major aspects emerge. Vertical mobility, the upgrading of work skills beyond the level achieved by the individual worker in his particular job specification, stands out as absolutely essential if an economy is to sustain development. Horizontal mobility, the movement of workers into the geographic or plant locations, is distinct from the vertical type and yet in parallel fashion it can contribute to economic growth and development. Both types implicitly assume specialization and division of labor in the work force. Clearly, an economic system will have a high degree of labor mobility if there are few barriers to people getting job training and moving about the country to the various job sites. But there are combinations of training and job choices which do not meet the ideal of high mobility and yet allow relatively high efficiency in labor utilization. Institutional barriers may inhibit workers from moving from their plant; the longer they remain in the plant the greater the loss of wage, pension, and other privileges that they would have gained had they not moved to a new job in another plant. However, if newly arising sites and jobs could be filled by those entering the labor force for the first time, then the apparent immobility which some workers experience does not actually impair efficient labor utilization. Such a reality exists in Japan and apparently has not affected adversely the sustained rapid growth of the economy, presumably because horizontal mobility as regards new, young workers together with some vertical mobility within companies and plants is adequate for the rising work force needs of the economy.

Vertical mobility makes possible the widening of economic activity within plants and for the entire economy as more and more plants achieve this. As industrial plants develop, for example, they need a richer mix of technicians, engineers, and more highly skilled workers up to a point. This mainly is a qualitative requirement, since even if the plant work force were to remain numerically the same, more advanced production of, say, a wider variety of better steel products with the tonnage remaining the same would rule that more workers who could do so would perform more exacting tasks including better supervision, design, and management. To meet these needs workers and students need constant training to fit into the new slots.

Horizontal mobility is essential if new areas are to be exploited and if new plants are to be added to the existing stock of plants and equipment. As advantage is taken of newly discovered resources, new factories and mines are opened; and as modern industry is developed and indigenous industry retrenched, workers are both in short and abundant supply in different locations. If demands and supplies are to be balanced, workers must move from surplus to deficit locations, otherwise work force imbalance will upset production and development goals.

From the standpoint of economic objectives, therefore, allocating workers vertically and horizontally is an important determinant of the attainment of goals of economic modernization. The system of labor allocation also has an important bearing on the degree to which individuals have choices in shaping their own careers. The extent to which goals of the economy and of individuals are realized is a function of the mechanism handling labor allocation and training. In many contemporary cultures labor is allocated through a labor market in which supply and demand are kept in balance through fluctuations in price (wages). Where labor of varying skills is in short supply, wages rise to attract it; in areas where labor is in oversupply, wages decline to redirect workers to more remunerative jobs. In similar fashion, differential wage and salary arrangements for unskilled, semiskilled, and skilled workers, technicians, engineers, and supervisory personnel act as spurs to individuals by upgrading their skills so that they can be promoted to more demanding jobs. The opposite of the ideal or perfect labor market for labor allocation by central administrative assignment and social sanction. The central planners decide where labor is needed and in what quantities and then proceed through the administrative machinery to direct the movement of workers into the correct slots. The reality of labor allocation in all advanced economies falls somewhere along the continuum defined by the two extremes just described. The particular configuration usually has a combination of elements in which the role that wages play in allocation and the extent to which individual choice operates vary considerably. We seek in this chapter to define the system of allocation in operation in China and to see what the role of wages and choice is in that system.

The Socialization of Labor Allocation

The pattern of labor allocation in China has gone through several phases since 1949, some contradictory; others continuing a trend. The overall trend, as the Maoist model has evolved, has been clearly one of greater socialization and movement away from the market mechanism in directing labor into different sectors and different occupational slots. Over time, once the break with market and price allocation was made, individuals and groups have been channeled into required locations and occupations by administrative assignment, presumably in conformity with national, provincial or local programs and plans which were reinforced by developing social incentives.

Until the end of the FFYP, workers were directed primarily to jobs through the traditional market mechanism. In the rehabilitation period, 1949 through 1952, while the regime's efforts were geared mainly to the containment of inflation and the reconstruction of economic activity, and, while private enterprise still was a major part of total activity, workers moved from job to job or from unemployment to employment in response to the pull of the market, though employment administration was being set up. During the FFYP, as more enterprises became socialized, allocation of labor was more coordinated with crude labor and wage plans. By mid-1955 the inefficacy of a partly free labor market was recognized, and new labor allocation solutions were sought after. Reliance on wages to allocate labor, however, was still a principal means of achieving specific work force objectives: the wage reform of 1956 rationalized wage schedules and differentials in conformity with the specific aims of the FFYP and the new more heavily socialized nature of Chinese industry.[1]

At the same time as traditional allocative instruments were being utilized, party leaders were also developing administrative codes governing the movement of labor into and out of jobs and locations. The stubborn persistence of unemployment and the unwelcome flow of peasants into the cities (as well as out of them at intervals) throughout the FFYP became problems of serious political, economic, and social dimensions. The wage reform of 1956 exacerbated unemployment for workers in enterprises with fixed wage funds and swelled the ranks of the jobless with unemployed peasants attracted to the cities by the widening income gap between peasant and unskilled and other workers. Peasants also sought escape in the cities from the pressures of scattered agricultural depression and the stepped-up cooperativization in 1955.

Starting with the GLF in 1958, with variations only in emphases thereafter, the principal instrument for labor allocation became administrative assignment. The strategy of the GLF, calling as it did for mass mobilization and deployment of millions of city workers (and peasants) to launch huge capital construction projects in the countryside as well as on the periphery of many cities, rested heavily on allocation by fiat, though the execution of individual projects was decentralized. The nearly disastrous outcome of the GLF reinforced this pattern as increased unemployment among industrial workers (resulting from industrial contraction when crucial agricultural raw materials flows fell off) demanded moving these jobless back to the countryside to assist the weakened commune economy. Though the recovery strategy from 1961 to 1965 relied on heightened material incentive to resurrect worker and peasant motivation, the regime did not revert to the earlier dependence on wages and the market to allocate labor. The perennial work force imbalance was more urgent and had to be corrected, and throughout this period the transferring of personnel to the countryside was widely operative.

Once the eruptions and disarray of the GPCR had subsided and political and economic stability slowly returned, the continuing pattern of administrative labor allocation emerged more strongly. For now the organized resistance to this socialization process had been overcome. As general stability returned, the gradual implementation of the more clearly defined Maoist policies included a new, massive, and quite significant strategic reallocation of labor: the transferring down of tens of millions of youths, urban unemployed, and many professional workers whose services were needed in the countryside as part of the new capital-infusion policy. These included teachers, students, cultural workers, health service personnel, among others. The execution of this mass movement is reinforced continuously by campaigns in the mass media and among mass organizations emphasizing the importance of living and working in the countryside, "learning from the poor and lower-middle peasants," and "serving the masses." [2]

A duality is now at the heart of the labor allocation model: centralized horizontal (macroeconomic) mobility and decentralized vertical (microeconomic) mobility in *both* directions. The central regime is responsible for the broad movement of workers to different geographic and sectoral parts of the economy; at lower administrative levels the same is true: provincial and county administrators assign workers to the different areas of their jurisdiction. Within the framework of the enterprise (mine, factory, industrial complex, commune) workers are allowed and required to move up and down occupational and functional ladders with some opportunity for individual choice in response to available training programs. Thus horizontal mobility is more centrally and rigidly controlled in conformity with broad national plans, while vertical mobility is more subject to the flexible control of administrative units close to or at the operational level offering wider choice for individuals, within the usual constraints imposed by social and economic programs.

This mobility policy and structure is aimed at optimum labor utilization within the transeconomic framework of the Maoists. This framework includes such salient noneconomic objectives as the fusing of the city and the countryside (elimination of social and economic differences), the breaking down of narrow specialization and the fostering of more generalized occupational and job roles combined with specific skills, and the reinforcing of Communist work attitudes. Associated with these are significant economic goals: development of autarkic local and regional areas, saving of capital by keeping long-distance labor mobility to a minimum (once a suitable horizontal allocation is achieved), and generation of capital through dual utilization of labor (in capital projects involving work beyond the daily skilled work task: construction, land reclamation, etcetera).

Types of Employment

In factories, mines, schools, offices, railways, banks, and other work units of the Chinese economy, workers have been employed in clearly defined categories which determine their work responsibilities and rights, their pay scales, their labor insurance rights, and other similar obligations and perquisites. In the various industrial sectors of the economy three types of employment have operated. First, and foremost, is regular employment in which the obligations and rights of workers are most clearly defined. Next is temporary employment in which obligations and rights are less clear. And last is contract employment in which workers from other economic units are assigned as an organized group to a plant or mine or road project to work on specific work assignments after which they return to their parent group or are reassigned to another task.

Regular Employment

Typically workers have regular jobs with secure tenure and clearly defined responsibilities, rights, and benefits. These might be described as "permanent" in the sense that it is rare for a worker to be fired, though he or she may be reassigned if the manager or supervisors were so dissatisfied with his or her performance and his or her response to rectification efforts that no other alternative is available. Workers in regular jobs do move to other jobs either in individual reassignments or in group transfers—all administratively executed—so that the quality of "permanence" is a relative one.

Regular employment in enterprises, mines, institutes, schools, banks, or administrative bureaus covers the full range of nonagricultural occupations from apprenticeship to blue-collar workers to office workers to scientific and professional personnel. Presumably this type of employment was meant to be the only type with exceptions allowed for quite special situations, for the rules, regulations, and directives covering labor by implication apply to all workers. These standard labor operating codes provide for wage and salary scales with alternatives where appropriate. Bonuses and awards as well as special allowances (e.g., for cost of living or housing) have been open to regular workers. The entire array of labor insurance benefits (though trade-union members received higher benefits) from sickness and disability coverages to pensions and death benefits is available to workers in plants and enterprises with at least 100 workers. All regular workers are eligible for promotion according to specific standards. In addition, workers have certain rights such as housing and education which are usually variable according to the particular situation in the enterprise or other unit.[3]

The rights accruing to workers have varied according to the hierarchic level and function of workers though the variation has usually been in degree rather than kind. For example, pension rights are the same with the percentage paid being a function of longevity of service: the actual amount paid to two individuals with the same length of service varies only according to the difference in their base pay. Apprentices have been more circumscribed in their rights than other workers. Their term of apprenticeship is fixed to three years (though in some cases two years would acquit the commitment); they receive pay below the lowest grade worker and are not allowed, as are low-grade workers, to participate in piece-rate wage payments when they are used, nor are they permitted allowances accruing to workers, other than allowances for labor protection purposes (e.g., special shoes and other clothing). In other regards they enjoy rights similar to all regular workers, such as labor insurance benefits and the right not to be required to work on tasks not related to their technical or professional training. Upon completion of apprenticeship their level could be as high as grade 2 worker. In periods and locations of slack demand for skilled workers the apprenticeship term has been extended, and where new workers have been needed in smaller numbers than the available apprentices totaled, appointment of workers from among them has in the past been controlled through examinations. Though their status is unquestionably a cut below the lowest grade of unskilled worker, they have a clearly defined role and status and thus enjoy the advantages of regular employment.[4]

Temporary Employment

Strictly speaking the temporary worker as a major category is an anomaly in China; his existence and perpetuation fly in the face of ideological canons which proclaim homogeneity of all members of the working class. But in the same way as unemployment has persisted despite official concern and action, temporary workers continued to be employed widely throughout China until the GPCR, and they were a kind of buffer group enabling economic units to fulfill or come closer to fulfillment of output targets. Since in large numbers they are so clearly a contradiction to a variety of doctrinal values, and since very little information on their working conditions and rights has been forthcoming, their continued employment until the GPCR may have been another Maoist-Liuist bone of contention. After the GPCR and the transfers of many workers this group has been reduced considerably and operates in a different functional context.[5]

Workers were employed in this temporary classification because for various reasons they had not been able to obtain regular jobs due to certain social disabilities. Some were categorized as antisocial elements who were awaiting some procedural action including trial, or whose behavior did not warrant the taking of formal action. Delinquents, antisocialist elements, vagrants, petty criminals, and the like made up a small portion of this group. Another group included many workers who had completed criminal or informal reform terms. A third and quite large group involved large numbers of unskilled and semiskilled unemployed who had been assigned to work by cognizant labor bureaus. Peasants leaving the rigors of the countryside also provided a large supply of unskilled workers. Whatever their particular condition, the social aim of putting them into a temporary status was to provide an opportunity for them to reform themselves and enter the mainstream of workers.[6]

At the same time as the authorities envisioned temporary employment as a constructive means for reintegrating workers of this type, there was a patent economic advantage to the hiring of temporary workers: it usually cut down the total wages bill. Temporary workers did not receive, on average, wages as high as those of regular workers. In addition they were not accorded various fringe benefits (including compensation for sickness or disability, or vacation, pension, and death benefits) which regular workers enjoy, and which may amount to as much as 15 to 20 percent of the total wages bill. Temporary workers were not paid according to regular wage scales and did not enjoy piece rates when they were in use. Bonus and allowance arrangements which regular workers received were not generally available to the temporary worker.[7]

Assignment of workers to temporary jobs in particular plants or mines is the responsibility of the cognizant labor bureau in the operating unit's area. In the past some enterprise managers might have illegally taken advantage of the availability of temporary workers and hired them on their own to insure attainment of output targets while increasing the labor bill by considerably less than they would for an expansion of regular workers. From among the pool of temporaries there were probably some with special or advanced skills and others who were at least equal to the lower grade regular workers, some of whom might leave their jobs for a variety of reasons. For example, in Anhwei province late in 1957 it was recorded that over seventeen thousand temporary workers, mostly peasants, were employed "without the approval of higher authorities." In Hunan the year before, similar direct, unauthorized recruitment occurred. Though these practices have been subject to more rigorous control, over the years evidence of similar hirings has appeared so that the inference seems warranted that such practices were advantageous to enterprise managers. In any event, temporary employment achieved some flexible mobility of an unplanned nature.[8]

Contract Employment

The third category of employment, the contract labor system, developed extensively in the early 1960s (and still is in operation today) as an effective, low cost technique of labor deployment in which commune members could be utilized seasonally as workers in enterprises. Though contract labor had existed before the 1960s, it blossomed during the recovery from the GLF when labor was deployed on a large scale to implement recovery, and a variety of contract arrangements emerged. During the early sixties as commune members and workers were being spurred by renewed and heightened material incentives, various effective labor utilization schemes, later denounced in the GPCR as "bourgeois" and "revisionist," were put into effect to spur recovery in agriculture as well as in industry. The channeling of seasonally surplus commune labor to factories, mines, and construction projects which were mainly in need of large numbers of physical laborers periodically was one such scheme which offered obvious advantages to the commune and to the contracting enterprise and achieved a degree of labor mobility. The gains accruing to the contract workers from the system, denounced during the GPCR by Red guards as a "poisonous weed opposed to Mao Tse-tung's Thought," are less apparent.[9]

By 1964, contract labor was being used widely throughout China in various economic activities: mining; grain, oil, and cotton processing; cotton gins; textiles; building materials; aquatic products; lumbering; water conservation and power generation; building and road construction and maintenance; geological survey; post and telecommunications; and commerce. Though the details for contracting labor for such a wide variety of activities differ considerably, the basic characteristics of the system are simple and clear: (1) stipulation of specific labor tasks in the contracting enterprise; (2) specification of payments in money and kind to the commune as well as to the individual laborers; (3) establishment of work-point rights of contract laborers in commune annual payment distribution among members.[10]

An example of contract labor for maintaining roads in Hunan Province in South Central China during 1964 and 1965 reveals these general characteristics of the system. A fifteen-man contract labor specialized maintenance team was drawn from Ch'ao-shui Commune to carry out road maintenance responsibilities including upkeep of bridges, tree planting, and road administration for their 17.8 kilometers of highway. They worked as a team, in conjunction with other (noncontract) commune workers, and lived at their own commune homes. The team itself was divided into three subgroups under unified work squad administrative supervision. Contract workers had the same rights to time off over the year as other commune members: seven legal holidays and fifty-two rest days. The contract called for payment of ¥ 150 a kilometer each year with each contract worker earning ¥ 187.5 for the commune (since he is responsible for 1.25 kilometers of road). Of this total, ¥ 126 went to the worker's production team and ¥ 36 to the worker himself. The remaining ¥ 25.5 was allocated to the commune: ¥ 8 for tools, ¥ 6 for the worker's medical expenses, and ¥ 11.5 for small tool repair. Each contract worker on road maintenance also

got 2,400 work points in his production team's annual distribution of agr
cultural product (this came to 52 ¢ for each work day, which is the equiv
lent of ten work points) besides the ¥ 36 direct payment.[11]

Such contract labor arrangements had certain obvious advantages fro
the point of view of converting seasonally surplus rural labor into outp
or capital and was consistent with the idea of deploying labor into a varie
of economic activities from the same home base (the commune) at min
mum or no cost and keeping labor fully employed. The existence of th
system, also, raised some fundamental questions of propriety on ideolog
cal grounds of exploitation, perpetuation of the "bourgeois" and "rev
sionist" notion of "profits in command," and violation of revolutionar
working-class solidarity. We again use the road maintenance example t
look at the functional aspects of the system. The inferences are releva
for other kinds of activities. The claim was made that in the case of roa
maintenance on the Shao-hsin Highway in Hunan, state investment wa
reduced, and the quality of road upkeep was improved. To the extent tha
the contracted commune labor would have, in the absence of the systen
produced nothing or a lesser quantity in commune work, then substantia
savings could be realized. If the workers' road maintenance output wa
equivalent to what they would have produced on the commune, then th
possibilities of realizing much gain would be limited mainly to gains fro
organizational or administrative arrangements. Where the contract labc
was a pure gain over idleness on the commune, the state, the commun
and the individual could all share in the gains. On the evidence presentec
the gain to the individual was not significant and arose only if foregon
commune labor would have produced less in income than that obtaine
from the contract arrangements: 2,400 work points or 240 work day
which came to about ¥ 125 for the year. Organizational and quality gain
were also possible as were cost gains from the elimination of certain cos
of itinerant road workers such as moving, housing, and food. Under cond
tions of seasonal idleness or underemployment, therefore, gains fror
such a system could be substantial, but to the extent that the contract ir
volved work over the entire year some of the gain would be lost durin
peak agricultural activity periods when the foregone commune product c
the contract workers would be higher than the value of the road mainte
nance work.[12]

The spread of the contract labor system into the period of the GPC
must be seen as part of the post-GLF movement to revive economic activ
ity while millions of urban dwellers, members of the actual and disguise
unemployed, were being transferred to communes in the countryside t

e put to productive use. Once the GPCR moved into high gear and "bourgeois" practices were sharply attacked, the contract-labor system was sharply criticized. Contract labor was denounced as "a decadent system of capitalism" producing the "cheapest and most easily mobilized labor force." It was labeled part of the mechanism of "profit in command" which "regards workers as hirelings." Another complaint focused on the divisiveness of the system in shattering worker solidarity, creating "an artificial gulf within the working class" by putting contract workers "outside of the enterprises" where the regular workers "are the masters of the enterprise" which is "their home." Critics went further, assailing the system in economic terms by insisting that it "seriously impedes the development of productive capacity" by placing special burdens on workers because of the nature of hiring and the temporary context in which they work. The "mental" pressure which the system put on workers was seen as a major barrier to the "revolutionization" of the worker's thought, putting him "in a state of anarchy." The engendering of fear by the system was cited as an important impediment to workers' participating activity in political movements. As a matter of fact, contract and temporary workers were denied the right to be elected members of Cultural Revolution committees.[13]

The contract labor system in the past reflected continuing difficulties encountered in transforming surplus labor into capital. As the Maoist development strategy unfolds, labor utilization may be arranged in a neater, more unified package. The emerging more diversified activity of the commune, newly infused with a wider variety of technically and professionally trained people, may have regularized activities performed under the contract system through a more homogenized work force so far as rights and payments are concerned. Contracts between communes and other enterprises still do operate but in a generally changed context.

Horizontal Mobility

Horizontal, or site, labor mobility, the ability to move workers from one job site to another with the same or similar job functions, plays an important role in the development of new plants and new geographic areas. Such tunneling of labor power may take one of two routes: workers moving from one geographic area to another in the same or in a different industry, or workers moving in the same locality to a different plant in the same or another industry. These movements are lateral with the workers going from a job of a particular wage and skill grade to another position of similar wage and skill with variations of some degree necessarily occurring due to imperfect duplication of industrial and occupational conditions. In this kind of relocation the conditions of work and pay roughly correspond to similar jobs at other enterprises, necessary adjustments taking the form of cost-of-living differentials and payment of relocation costs.

Mechanisms

The allocation of individuals to new job sites separately or in groups is achieved by administrative assignment in conformity with requirements of labor plans. The individual, miner, lathe operator, teacher, or engineer is assigned to a specific position in a particular enterprise according to his skill and performance profile and the requirements of the job being filled. New plants usually start with nuclei of advanced workers from old plants. Attempts are made to impress upon the worker how important his moving to the new position is to the success of the collective effort. Where reluctance is exhibited subtle pressures rising in directness and intensity as resistance is encountered are applied, and for some even more coercive approaches may be employed. Party members are more likely to experience strong pressure if they resist, while ordinary workers are usually approached more carefully. The more advanced the worker, the more amenable he is to party pressure. In some instances if resistance persists the matter may be dropped. In one way or another, however, the labor requirement is met.[14]

Though the principle of administrative assignment sketched above has many obvious implications for labor allocation, it does not, per se, imply the mass transfer of groups of workers to meet urgent and far-reaching labor requirements. Such mass migrations have played an important part in dealing with problems such as developing a labor force in the hinterlands, unemployment, and labor shortages in the countryside. These massive movements of different configurations of workers occurred in the late fifties, in the post-GLF period preceding the GPCR, and in the period starting late in 1968 and continuing into the 1970s.

In these mass transfers the technique of *hsia fang* ("transferring down") is employed. This means that large numbers of individuals (with or without their families) of particularly identified groups in the labor force such as teachers, students, unemployed, medical and health personnel, industrial workers, and a wide variety of political, administrative, and party cadres are assigned to specific units in the countryside which are mostly communes but are also state farms, local, and provincial enterprises. The assignment of this sort may be temporary or permanent, for punitive and rectification reasons or not, for labor allocation or ideological purposes, for tactical or strategic economic objectives, varying in different periods and locations. The process of transferring down differs from the technique of individual assignment in several ways: the one is organized with ideological preparation and follow-up, the other is unobtrusive; the one involves the party in recruitment, resettlement, etcetera, the other is usually handled administratively in a routine fashion; the one relocates very large numbers of people, the other moves discrete individuals. Take as an example October through December 1968 when the GPCR campaign to repopulate the countryside with a variety of workers to provide large pools of labor for transformation into capital began. A quite incomplete survey of thirteen of the twenty-nine administrative-geographic units (provinces, major municipal units, and autonomous regions) shows that the widely publicized and prepared campaign to move large numbers of particular groups, such as cadres, students, teachers, and medical personnel, netted about a million people in the short period. Since that time it is clear that tens of millions of a variety of workers of all types have been funneled into the countryside in a series of *hsia fang* movements.[15]

This mass movement of tens of millions of workers is an integral element in the Maoist model for developing the commune as a multifaceted economic unit serving the needs, first, of agriculture and defense, and, next, of the entire configuration of economic activities from consumption of goods and services to the production, repair, and maintenance of an array of mechanical equipment necessary to the smooth functioning of the commune and beyond that of provincial and national industrial units. In this context, the unemployed, the students and teachers, the industrial workers, the various health personnel, artists, musicians, writers, and researchers, all are to contribute their special skills to the development of the commune or other economic unit as well as their general labor power, when not being used in their specialties, to varied agricultural tasks assigned by the commune managers. They are in the countryside to learn and to be remolded by the peasants as well as to provide the peasants with their know-how for optimum use in the commune's varied activities.

The technique of mass horizontal transfers of workers in China has been used over the years as a principal means of allocating labor whatever the particular strategic objective. Such mass movements are mounted under the command of the party and sometimes the People's Liberation Army

(PLA). The party has always conceived and engineered the recruitment, resettlement, and relocation of large groups of people by utilizing various techniques for initiating and sustaining mass movements of whatever nature (e.g., emulation or rectification movements). The PLA has often been involved in labor allocation projects. Demobilized troops have been resettled under its auspices. In a more salient way, the PLA has frequently provided the necessary laborpower, especially in remote, sparsely populated areas, to meet labor input requirements. This has been easily achieved, since the PLA has been throughout its history not only a military organization but also a shock work force with the skills, technical and managerial, to execute a variety of projects. For example, in 1954, the PLA Sinkiang Production and Construction Corps was set up to deal with land reclamation, water conservancy, cultivation (of one third of Sinkiang's arable land), industrial and mining development, and urban development. Also, in 1969 in a remote part of south China PLA units built and operated a chemical fertilizer plant. The existence of the PLA as a vertical economic and military organization has made possible the solution of certain labor allocation problems, but in the final analysis such support, although important in particular situations and as a model, can only contribute marginally to solving major laborpower problems.[16]

Vertical Mobility

All industrial societies provide the means for channeling members of their work force not only horizontally but also vertically into advanced positions of different technical requirements throughout the hierarchy of occupational rungs defining a specific industry or other economic activity. Such vertical mobility is especially urgent in an economy which not only is growing rapidly but also transforming many of its indigenous operations into modern formats. This movement of workers usually entails the upgrading or training in skills, functions, and responsibilities within a plant or enterprise, industry or administration, training or research activity, to provide for the evolving complexity of the function of economic units and configurations in a swiftly developing nation. Implicit in the idea of upgrading occupational dexterity is the furnishing of basic as well as graded training to enable placement of new workers and advancement of those already participating in production. Conventionally the upgrading of skills defines, in brief, vertical mobility; in China, however, such mobility is often a two-way street in which workers with particular skills may be transferred down to perform duties other than those related to their specific training as well as in their particular occupation, as described above.

Attempts in China to cope effectively with the problems of training adequate numbers of a wide skill arrangement of industrial, professional, and scientific workers have been somewhat complicated by ideological considerations. The ideal of expertness has always been coupled, at least rhetorically, with "redness," or demonstrating correct political and social attitudes and behavior. In different periods emphasis has varied though the ideal communist is to combine both. During the FFYP the emphasis clearly was on expertness, just as in the GLF "redness" was pushed to the fore. Similarly, when economic tasks were being dealt with mainly through the use of conventional material spurs, those who were technically expert were encouraged and advanced; while "redness" was placed on a high pedestal in periods of revolutionary exhortation and maneuver. The two qualities continue to be treated differentially; with the Maoist model strongly committed to "redness" the early post-GPCR period was one in which that quality was at the heart of a variety of policies: incentives, industrial and commune management, higher education, and vocational training. The primacy of correct political and social outlook was reflected not only in the role given to "redness" in payment schemes in agriculture and industry, but also in the vertical movement of a variety of workers. Major authority in industrial staffing was in the hands of party committees at different levels. This was of special importance in a period when so many workers of a variety of occupational talents were being sent down to the countryside. It is also clear that in moving up the management hierarchy, party membership assumed greater importance, and party membership was often a necessary requirement for appointment to and further advancement in top managerial positions. By 1973 evidence of a return in part to "expertness" became clearer as policy in general swung toward more moderate positions.[17]

Looking at the structure of training for occupational and professional placement reveals a situation in flux at this time. Since the GPCR the traditional education mechanism has been under tremendous pressure to change in revolutionary ways to "join theory with practice" and to "serve the people." But even while educational institutions, closed for several years during the GPCR, are being shaped and reshaped in molds more congruent with the Maoist model, a dual pattern of training for skill upgrading over time is still visible. Starting from the middle schools and up, students beginning their preparation for future work in China's varied nonagricultural activities as well as workers already in the economic structure have two avenues open for promotion in their career aspirations: the formal and less formal training routes.[18]

Formal Training Institutions

China has had a formal system of education which provided opportunities for students to prepare for industrial placement of varying degree of technical, professional, or scientific proficiency. Decisions on career plans were effected during the middle school period when certain general career choices were made and at the close of which many students ended their formal schooling and commenced work in factories, other enterprises, and offices. Those students interested in more advanced technical, professional, and scientific occupations entered specialty training schools after the middle school, the end of which signals twelve years of educational training after kindergarten. Beyond the usual five year higher educational training were postgraduate work and research.[19]

At the beginning of the middle school, the seventh year of formal education, some students proceeded on a general education track while others made early vocational choices. In the fifties, there were junior vocational schools starting in the seventh year, but since 1960 they have been discontinued; students planning to prepare for entry into specific industrial trades started their training in middle vocational schools beginning either in the ninth or tenth year and continued through the twelfth or thirteenth year after which placement in factories, plants, mines, offices, or unemployment occurred. Students anticipating a career as teachers in primary schools enrolled in either junior normal schools, in the seventh year, or senior normal schools in the tenth year. At the completion of middle school, therefore, almost all students from vocational schools went mainly into the different industrial jobs calling for minimal skills; those graduating from senior normal schools entered primary teaching; and those graduating from other middle schools went to institutions of higher education for teaching, engineering, and other professional training, as well as scientific disciplines. In higher education the general university, normal schools, and technical institutes and colleges prepared these middle school graduates for placement in the upper echelons of industry, administration, teaching, and scientific endeavor. Beyond the college, technical institute, or university level is postgraduate work and research. There is a sharp differentiation in China between university teaching activity and research, the latter being carried out in a series of specialized research institutes completely separate from the universities and under the general jurisdiction of the Academia Sinica.[20]

In this structure of formal education the choices open to students as they rose through the hierarchic levels narrowed. The different tracks followed provided options whose full exploitation depended upon the proficiency the student demonstrated in his formal educational performance as well as in special examinations for placement purposes in line with labor allocation needs. The correct social and political outlook (and class background) also bore on the determination of the student's next assignment in the preparatory training for future placement. Thus, the politically correct student who wished to enter a particular career track was supposed to have a higher probability of his choice being granted if his academic performance was quite high, the exact level required being a function of the demand for the profession he desired to pursue.

During the GPCR, dissatisfaction with elitism in education was trumpeted and became an important basis for "revolutionizing" the educational system. It was asserted that in the early 1960s students in higher education more and more came from privileged groups (party and other bureaucratic leaders, cadres, intellectuals,) and less and less from the working class and the peasantry. The educational system was denounced as "bourgeois" and the schools were closed down.[21]

In the aftermath of the GPCR when schools were finally gradually reopened, a new pattern of educational training for personnel at all levels emerged. The traditional schooling structure and institutions have been retained; but the link of educational activities to specific industrial and agricultural operating units has been made more direct, and other radical changes have been implemented. This "educational revolution" has been viewed by Lin Piao as a crucial element in the GPCR. Speaking at the party's Ninth National Congress for the Central Committee he maintained: "Whether the proletariat is able to take firm root in the positions of culture and education and transform them with Mao Tsetung Thought is the key question in carrying the Great Proletarian Cultural Revolution through to the end." [22]

The "proletarianization" of education runs the gamut from the middle schools to the university and involves "turning the schools into affiliated organizations of the rural people's communes, factories and the PLA." [23] In the cities this development has taken three forms: (1) factory schools run by individual or groups of factories with the school as a unit, or shop, of the factory; (2) neighborhood schools run by the administrative unit in the neighborhood; and (3) linkage schools, where the school is linked with factories, communes, and the neighborhood with the teachers and students participating regularly in labor. The first two forms existed before; the third is new. At the college and university level the relationship between the educational unit and the factory varies. University-run factories train workers directly; factory-run universities or colleges (July 21 Colleges, named for the date in 1966 of a report to Chairman Mao on proposed educational changes, have been extended in industry) furnish technicians for the factory. In carrying out the mandate that "education must serve proletarian politics and be integrated with productive labor," the regime has been extending the models of "socialist" institutions of higher learning. The programs developed at Tsinghua University in Peking and at the Shanghai Heavy Machine Tools Plant July 21 College have been publicized as the forms which all universities and factories should emulate.[24]

The main direction of this "educational revolution" was suggested by Mao.

> It is still necessary to have universities [and] colleges of science and engineering. However, it is essential to shorten the length of schooling, revolutionize education, put proletarian politics in command and take the road of the Shanghai Machine Tools Plant in training technicians from among the workers. Students should be selected from among workers and peasants with practical experience, and they should return to production after a few years' study.[25]

The full prescription for educational transformation was aimed at integrating the educational process with the production process. A "three-in-one" combination of workers-peasants-soldiers, "revolutionary" technicians, and members of the original teaching staffs is exhorted to tackle the chore of changing formats and curricula with teaching, scientific research, and production to be joined. Class struggle techniques, including having teachers take part in labor periodically, were to be continuously pursued.[26]

To insure that education becomes "proletarian" and serves the planned development of a decentralized, egalitarian economy, the admission of students has been radically reordered. Students are admitted to colleges, universities, and technical institutes only after having worked several years in communes, factories, or mines. They must be selected by their peers in these units as worthy of being educated. While at school they must continue to carry out productive labor as part of the linking of theory and practice. When their educations are completed formally they are expected to return to the commune, factory, mine, or other unit from whence they came to "serve the people." Advanced education and training are not to become escapes to rich urban living from the drudgery of agriculture and industry, but rather they are a vertical movement up the ladder of skills with return to horizontal *status quo ante*.[27]

As part of the revolutionization of education and of workers, Chairman Mao in a May 7, 1968 directive gave impetus to the establishment of May 7 Cadre Schools which were to become countryside schools for reeducating cadres or bureaucrats into revolutionary propagators of Mao's thought through continuous class struggle. Government officials of all kinds, including teachers, are required to attend such schools for regular periods, usually for six months but frequently for longer periods, to combine study of Mao's thought and other ideological material with physical labor at the school as well as in communes. These schools are not intended to be punitive but ideological-educational, and cadres receive their regular incomes while in attendance. The fundamental purpose of such schools is to forestall the bureaucracy's becoming elitist and detached from the realities of workers' and peasants' conditions of life. In some of their schooling cadres are taught and "reeducated by workers and peasants."[28]

Less Formal Training Routes

Committed as it is to the rapid expansion of its trained labor force, the CCP has promoted and reinforced the development and extension of several other avenues by which workers at all levels as well as citizens in general may upgrade their education and skills. Such programs have pragmatic as well as ideological foundations. Avoiding or at least minimizing expansion of formal, conventional educational facilities saves considerable quantities of capital as well as labor resources. Integrating work and study follows Maoist concepts on theory and practice. The widespread illiteracy among workers and citizens (before 1949 over 90 percent of the general population and 80 percent of the industrial staff were reportedly illiterate) has mandated not only the extension of formal educational opportunities but also the structuring of substantial and effective alternate routes for personal cultural improvement in general and specific training in skills. Before the GPCR such less formal means to knowledge and instruction had been organized mainly around and integrated with the factories, mines, farms, and other operating economic units.[29]

Interest in general or vocational advancement has been pursued either

A technical in-plant class for young workers, Fushun Excavator Plant
(China Pictorial, *1, 1973, p. 19*)

in programs which have been set up in places of employment or operating outside the work site. In the first type of program, education and training within the plant have covered areas comparable to middle school and higher educational levels in the formal school structure. These programs have been labeled *spare-time education,* and through them individuals have pursued general secondary level or higher educational curricula. For those interested in upgrading their skills or preparing for more advanced technical or scientific positions there has been an arrangement of suitable spare-time courses and programs. The spare-time curriculum has been offered at night and at other slack work periods. Those who improve their skills for advancement in work grades or occupational classification and pass examination requirements, which may or may not be formal, are advanced in their grade levels. Many workers do advance within their own plant, and workers have succeeded to such positions as workshop director, department head, vice-plant director, and director. By the end of 1959, according to official reports, 24 percent of the directors and 16 percent of the engineers in factories and mines under the Ministry of Metallurgical Industry had been promoted from the ranks of the workers.[30]

Paralleling spare-time education carried out in plants and other enterprises has been a widespread program of work-study or part work-part study, sometimes known as half-work and half-study. Though its format lends itself more readily to implementation in the countryside, it is employed also in factories. Such programs in a sense flow logically out of spare-time programs which usually were kept distinct from work routines and occurred at other times. In one precision grinding-machine plant in Shanghai a new type of worker-led college was set up combining study with productive labor. The college specializes in the design and manufacture of grinding machines, and its objective has been to train technicians from among the workers. Most teachers are workers and worker-technicians, and classroom teaching is combined with practice in workshops. Teachers as well as students are expected to learn through the process, and "graduation" occurs according to the individual's rate of progress. One week of each month is devoted to productive labor by the students; the remainder of the month involves classes and learning in workshop situations. This kind of training is very specific, and the students are very much goal oriented, anticipating specific position placement at the end of their training period.[31]

The average citizen or worker wishing to pursue general educational or vocational objectives that might not be covered in his own locale or at his job can participate in the spare-time offerings in plants (under trade-union auspices) or other public places. Specific spare-time schools offering broad programs or random courses are available. Regular agricultural and industrial spare-time curricula are offered from the lower-middle school level (the seventh year) through the fourteenth year of the higher educational level. In addition to such schools there are available a complete array of courses and curricula on a correspondence basis, rounding out the options which are open for general and technical training.[32]

Placement

Individuals trained either within the formal educational system or through the other programs which are offered are placed by the cognizant authority within a plant or locality according to criteria that include quality of performance, "redness" or proper social and political attitude, and the requirements of state plans for allocation and production. Students who finish formal education as specialists in professional or scientific categories are placed through administrative units covering their areas; workers and others advancing their training either through the formal programs or the other avenues which may be open are placed either within their own enterprises or through reassignment by the labor bureau supervising their enterprise and similar ones; where part-work–part-study programs operate, presumably the students are being trained for very specific billets.

One serious problem of administrative assignment is that individuals may be misassigned with resultant loss of production due to misallocation of labor resources. Imbalanced assignment with more workers than necessary at one location and too few at another is another kind of loss. Complications may also arise from the arbitrary allocation of individuals to locations and positions that they reject. Where a free labor market operates, such imbalances and misfits presumably are avoided through the wage mechanism, though other problems arise. In China the expectation is that planned allocation will work in the best way for production and development. But there is a realization that "many shortcomings" of a "serious" nature exist, and that they need to be "rapidly overcome." Chou En-lai, in 1956, addressed himself to these problems, admitting that among "five units under the Ministry of Light Industry, about 10 percent of our higher intellectuals are in posts for which they are unsuited. What a serious loss this is! We must take firm measures to correct this bureaucratism, sectarianism and departmentalism . . . so that specialists can be of service where they are most needed.'' Whether the misallocation comes from plain human error, hoarding of trained personnel, systemic malfunction, or corruption, its effects are negative and have been sharply attacked by the party.[33]

Control of Worker Mobility

Since the accession of the CCP to power in 1949, the regime has been beset by vexing problems arising from uncontrolled movement of people. Such movement, thrusting in several directions, has been mainly from the countryside into the cities arising from the varying impacts of land reform, land cooperativization, unemployment, and industrial wage increases. Movement within and between cities also was a principal characteristic of the fifties in which large numbers of urban unemployed became a continuing phenomenon swelling with the influx of peasants from the countryside and with the generation of workers newly idled from socialization of industry and social disaffection. By the late fifties the persistence of tens of millions of unemployed and of substantial migrations of peasants and workers while the CCP was concentrating its efforts on such priority programs as land reform, the FFYP, cooperativization, and socialization became an unavoidable major problem. This persistent problem was symptomatic of the Soviet model's inadequacy to meet China's fundamental needs. The GLF, which marked a change in the CCP's economic development strategy, was a comprehensive attempt to deal through a new, radical strategy with a wide range of questions which included unemployment and internal movement.

The CCP recognized early the dynamics of unemployment and set forth policy to deal with the problem, but it apparently expected the FFYP to channel labor, including the unemployed, effectively. As unemployment and other labor force imbalances persisted, the importance of exercising a greater degree of control was recognized and was reflected in the number of regulations on employment and movement which increased throughout the fifties. Temporary regulations, notices, decisions, and other such administrative controls on employment of workers from other areas, employment in general, firings, resignations, hiring procedures, and the like were issued as specific aspects of unchecked labor migrations were discovered. These edicts began to define policies on the handling not only of the specific day-to-day questions of labor administration but also the broad question of how workers were to be allocated.

Regulating Movement between Jobs

A review of administrative regulation of workers who are moving from job to job and are in search of jobs as well as of official responses to deviations from mandated procedures reveals a clear-cut and consistent broad policy on labor allocation over the years: labor is to be allocated by administrative decision of the cognizant labor bureaus in conformity with plans for industrial development, location, and socialization. To the extent that individual choice is officially honored, such choice must be consistent with the labor needs of the evolving collective economy. Where individual choice takes precedence, as it has in the movement of millions of peasants and workers, and misallocation ensues, the CCP leaders have reacted swiftly and strongly to attempt to contain such dysfunctional movement.

Early in the fifties the structure for controlling movement between jobs was shaped to assure that workers would be moved where they were needed by the plan for labor utilization. Aware of the temptation for factory and enterprise managers to lure workers to their units "without following correct procedures in order to fulfill their production quotas," the authorities set forth the ground rules for "unified labor utilization." For workers moving from jobs in one region to those in another, the Ministry of Labor would have to validate the move with a letter; while workers moving to jobs within the same region, though in different provinces or cities, required the formal approval of the region's labor department. At the same time as these regulations were promulgated to prevent undesired job turnover, to facilitate desired movement of workers the regulations insured that round-trip travel expenses were provided as well as an allowance for resettling in the contract defining the job.[34]

In 1957 the State Council added to the regulation of movement between jobs with guidelines to govern workers quitting or refusing jobs. Here, too, the aim was clearly to forestall undesirable and unnecessary labor turnover when mass migration had been quite high during the rapidly changing and upsetting period of farm collectivization and socialization of industry. Workers wishing to quit their jobs could be forestalled from moving by refusal of the particular unit to grant permission. The authori-

ies in the unit, however, were urged to use "persuasion and education pa-
tiently on those persons who are not happy in their work." When the plant
management found workers unsuited for their jobs they might reassign
such workers to more appropriate positions. When a worker turned down
such reassignment after persuasion and education had been carefully
applied, and he had not in any way violated work rules, he was free to re-
sign. These provisions apparently were aimed at reinforcing one another:
workers were not to leave their jobs at will; if they balked through disaffection at work and were not amenable to reassignment they faced unemployment.[35]

Despite the setting up of clearly defined procedures and rules for movement between jobs during the fifties, considerable movement occurred,
and quite large numbers of workers found themselves continuously unemployed (as chapter 2 revealed). This situation occurred during the FFYP
and abated somewhat while the GLF generated massive redeployment of
labor, agricultural and nonagricultural, in 1958. But as the GLF deterio-
rated, industrial production suffered, and retrenchment in plant work
forces rekindled the problem of unemployment with millions of workers
moving about to seek work. The CCP leaders responded tactically to this
and tried to ease and reverse the undesirable flows of population. Early in
the fifties while private and joint enterprises still operated, the tactic was
to keep as many workers in jobs as possible even though many of the jobs
became redundant as efficiency rose: "The managements or owners
should not try to solve their problem by dismissing workers and staff
members but should develop production and expand business, so that the
interests of the workers and staff will be protected, and an increase of
unemployment avoided." Unemployed intellectuals were to be made em-
ployable through retraining and political reform as were Kuomintang
officers and officials. The mass of unemployed in the cities were to be registered and individually dealt with. According to the profile of their skills
and talents, they were to be retrained in groups under the government
department covering their occupations and reemployed through that cognizant agency or provided "with proper relief." [36]

Despite these directives and arrangements the problem of unemployment not only persisted, but with the accelerated collectivization of agriculture in the middle fifties significant numbers of peasants drifted into
the cities, swelling the already unmanageable forces of unemployed, as
explained in chapter 2. In November of 1956 the State Council put a freeze
on increased employment among government units to cut off a major
source of demand for labor. In the next month the State Council issued a

directive on the prevention of the drift into the cities. Ideological educa
tion was carried out among peasants in famine areas to promote the
greater self-reliance to produce more and thus forestall their leaving fc
the city. For those "who drift to the cities blindly, merely because of admi
ing city life" the prescription was a heavy dose of education to acquain
them with the real situation in the city. Only those in serious famine area
who could line up jobs in the city through friends or relatives and get ap
proval of the appropriate administration, following resignation an
transfer procedures (which apparently were being violated widely), coul
move. Those already in the cities were dealt with according to their partic
ular circumstances. Those in jobs could stay; those without jobs, friend
or relatives were sent back to the countryside through local administra
tions which were responsible for their job placement. The directive re
iterated that economic enterprises were to follow established procedure
in recruitment and placement: "Private employment is not allowed." [37]

But the situation did not improve. Many enterprises persisted in direc
recruitment, ignoring labor control departments. Agricultural coopera
tives went along with such recruitment efforts as the cooperatives exper
enced difficulties of poor crops or labor utilization. Additional measure
were taken. In Canton, for example, as government agencies were re
trenched their released workers were distributed to various joint state
private enterprises. This followed the State Council's decision of No
vember 1956 to cut back on government employment. Now it issued a sup
plemental directive: the campaign to reverse the flow was to be steppe
up. Peasants in the cities were to be apprised of the very poor employmen
opportunities. Peasants contemplating moving to the cities were subjec
to similar entreaty and also were aided materially on the cooperatives t
forestall their leaving. At transportation hubs, special stations were to b
set up with representatives of local governments, transportation adminis
tration, and governments of areas from which peasants were flowing wh
would be responsible for persuading the peasants to return and for fur
nishing the means for such return. In similar fashion, the cities were to se
up special units to handle the return flow providing propaganda and f
nances for the peasants without jobs to return home.[38]

These measures had a short-lived success and then infiltration of unem
ployed peasants into cities and towns with limited employment opportu
nities resumed. The Ministry of Internal Affairs lamented in the spring c
1957 that in the preceding half-year over half a million peasants left famin
areas for city and town, and still the movement continued. It recom
mended several approaches, paralleling earlier suggestions. The more e

ective handling of famine relief and agricultural organization was one set of solutions; rigorous conformity of industrial and mining enterprises to regulations on employment was a big loophole which the ministry wanted closed.[39]

The continuing flow of peasants into populated centers and the ineffectiveness of the many measures which had been taken to stem the flow meant that unemployment kept growing in 1957, and that economic objectives and popular support were jeopardized. The critical labor utilization situation and the strategic veering away from the Soviet development model provide an impelling rationale for the radical approach which the GLF prescribed with its communization, decentralization, mass labor deployment, and launching of indigenous industrial activity in the communes (symbolized by but going beyond the backyard steel furnaces). The Central Committee of the Communist Party and the State Council, emphasizing the seriousness of the uncontrolled movement of peasants and workers and also acknowledging the ineffectiveness of earlier attempts to stem the tide, issued a joint directive in December 1957, on the eve of the GLF, to quell both the continuing peasant movement into the cities and worker misallocation. The same measures were repeated: ideological education among peasants in rural areas, stations in railroad hubs to hold peasants and persuade them to go home, return of peasants in the cities to their villages, reiteration of the prohibition against enterprises employing workers privately outside the prescribed channels, permission for newly arrived peasants in the cities to remain if they had jobs, expedition and coordination of the administration of returning peasants.[40]

Problems of Illegal Movement

The existence of laws and regulations outlawing any human behavior is not in itself evidence that the illegal activity does not occur. In assessing the incidence of any pattern of human action when reliable quantitative data are not available, knowledge of the legal or administrative framework is useful in gauging the degree to which violation of mandates is feasible or what the likely costs are to the individual who ignores the prohibition. In this context, whatever qualitative evidence is obtainable will be more useful. On the question of worker migration in China during the fifties and sixties, though the increasing restrictiveness of regulations is clear, and the costs of illegal movement appear to be readily identified, generalization on the degree of worker resettling is difficult because of the substantial un-

employment in the cities and discernible large-scale movements of peasants into urban areas until the mid-1960s. After that illegal movement subsided considerably.

The constraints against workers moving independently to new jobs
since the mid-1950s must be viewed against the societal realities within
which illegal migration might have been undertaken. Given the motivation
for a worker to quit his job to seek after another one in the same or a different geographic location, what obstacles existed, and how difficult was
it to circumvent them? For the worker attempting to move to a job on the
same or higher level in the same locale without official permission, the
move was possible if the management in the plant where he or she sought
employment, knowing the situation, wanted him or her, and neither the
management at his or her present job nor the cognizant labor bureau in
the area would invoke the law on administrative regulation. In that case, if
all parties were amenable, the move could be achieved by reassignment
in the regular fashion based on the principle that the reassignment was
for the good of all concerned, in particular for that of the plants involved.
It would appear, therefore, that an illegal move in the same locality
could occur if either all parties were amenable, erasing the illegality or
averting the unauthorized action, or the plant management in the worker's
present job location and the local labor bureau were indifferent to the
move.[41]

When a skilled worker attempts to move to a position on the same or
higher level in another geographic location, a set of regulatory difficulties
arise automatically, the first of which might be the forfeiture of severance
pay. Since each citizen is required to have a validated residence card, the
peripatetic job seeker whose residence card has been validated for his last
residence near the site of his former job is confronted with several problems. First, his illegal attempt to get a new job is revealed at once. The
manager of the plant, therefore, knows that placing the job seeker in a *regular* position conflicts at once with regulations which the local labor
bureau, as well as the plant management, is charged to uphold. Keeping
the worker on in a regular job capacity (regular and more highly skilled
positions receive more careful scrutiny due to the relative scarcity and
higher value of skilled workers and technicians) would entail considerable
conflict with the authorities once they were aware of the situation. To the
extent that management and the local authorities conspire to acquire an
attractive worker in violation of regulations, they are subject to denuncia-
tion from both local party cadres and higher authority, since such job pi-
racy undermines the administrative job assignment mechanism.[42]

Even if the worker does overcome this hurdle he would find other obstacles to surmount. Without a properly validated residence card he would not be able to secure the ration coupons he and his family would need to acquire certain staples such as grain, oil, cotton cloth, and any other goods being rationed. His right to a certain quality of housing might be forfeited. Most ration coupons are valid in only one location; special arrangements must be made for those on authorized travel. This impediment is not necessarily an absolute one: black market ration coupons have been available sometimes and certain consumer items can be obtained at higher prices. Relatives and friends are another possible source of food and other things. When the food supply is more plentiful, then the possibility of making out without ration coupons widens.[43]

The difficulties outlined for the worker who attempts to relocate in a new job without official authorization appear to be a function of his skill and income. Professional and scientific personnel would undoubtedly have the greatest difficulty: supervisors who might gain from hiring the worker would be most reluctant to take the risk involved and the worker himself would find the complications of reconstructing his living situation (food, housing, and other needs) quite onerous with a very high risk of failure. Skilled workers would also experience complications. On the other hand, unskilled workers and peasants seeking work in industry as semiskilled workers would be able to move about with less difficulty, not because the obstacles would disappear, but because lower grade workers and peasants, existing on lower levels of living, have less to lose and may find the difficulties of adjusting comparable to or better than their earlier situations. Peasants, for example, may find temporary positions in factories where the level of living provided by their wages would compare favorably with what many of them were used to on communes. Unemployed workers moving from one city to another and obtaining a temporary position would be much better off and workers with low-grade wages moving to temporary positions in another geographic site likewise might do relatively well. Individual workers with special situations, therefore, might move from one job to another aware of the risks and costs involved but determined for their own reasons to make the move. For large numbers of workers, however, the barriers to movement would loom high, appearing higher or lower depending upon the worker's and his family's stake in the present job and location. Statistically, therefore, illegal movement to new jobs is not likely to be a much traveled path for supervisory, professional, and scientific personnel or for most skilled workers in regular positions.

As the Maoist economic strategy has come into sharper focus after the

GPCR, the aims of labor allocation have fallen into place. The movement toward proportionate economic development is to receive its main propulsion from the rapid growth of the countryside through a fusion of city and countryside, worker and peasant, industry and agriculture. Toward that end the central authorities have moved tens of millions of workers horizontally from city to countryside, and the provincial and local authorities have deployed these people vertically within a variety of operating units.

> Every region, every province or city should . . . act in accordance with Chairman Mao's directive that local areas should devise means of setting up an independent industrial system and that first the cooperative zones and then the many provinces should, if possible, institute relatively independent though different industrial systems. We must devote attention to a rational geographical distribution of industry and an appropriate comprehensive development. Where possible . . . we should . . . enhance the capacity to assemble industrial products locally.[44]

The resettled workers and intellectuals have provided a mass labor pool for communes, county and provincial authorities, and regional administrators to utilize in the comprehensive Maoist scheme to raise China's countryside to the level of a new, revolutionary industrial society. Following labor-intensive techniques and deploying the new and old labor in extraspecialized ways as well as in traditional craft pursuits, the local leaders have developed small industrial and service activities; joined agricultural and industrial activities; reclaimed land; processed crude ores into usable forms for indigenous industrial work; converted a wide variety of industrial wastes into crude but usable raw materials; reshaped old equipment to meet current plant and equipment needs; organized comprehensive cooperative health services (making use of medical and paramedical personnel from the cities); extended part-work–part-study educational endeavors with the assistance of newly arrived urban teachers and students; put scientific and cultural staff to work; and generally moved labor around to meet the random, seasonal, developmental, and emergency needs of the area. These varied patterns of utilization of labor have, in conception, been aimed at maximum effective employment of labor power and have, at least inferentially, depended upon the widest horizontal and vertical mobility of that work force within the areal limitations of the operating unit. The mass assignment of people to the countryside has either put a major dent in the unemployment problem or reduced it to minor proportions.[45]

Four

Motivating Workers

In their reshaping of motivational mechanisms the Maoists have moved radically away from the models of the USSR and pushed headlong toward the more egalitarian ideals of communism. Material incentives and the socialist principle of remuneration have not been abandoned; their continued, if deemphasized, utilization merely reflects the transitional state of incentives in China today as the socialist consciousness of workers and peasants is being fashioned through continuous class struggle and reinforcement of ever-widening social or moral incentives. In the Maoist strategy for modernizing China the socialization of people to a state of greater socialist consciousness focuses in a major way on developing nonmaterial incentives which are based more and more on the group rather than on the individual. In this process, as the CCP leaders at all levels become aware that pressing these ideologically desirable mechanisms reaches limits, they usually ease the mechanisms and practice swings back toward earlier patterns. In this way zig zag movement toward the goal is achieved without generating cumulative opposition.[1]

Reviewing over twenty years of changes in the Chinese work incentive system reveals major functional and value transformations that reflect Maoist ideological goals in process of attainment. Three principal characteristics of these transformations can be discerned: (1) the system, which early in the period served as an allocator of labor among various sectors and occupations, now emphasizes more of an egalitarian payment arrangement with narrower hierarchic monetary differentials than before; (2) material compensation, the main element in the earlier mechanisms, has become a minimum base at each work level (narrow differentials above the base reflecting transitionally fair standards based on skill, experience and custom) with nonmaterial devices stressed more over time to exact increments of output; and (3) individual or personal motivating schemes have been replaced increasingly but slowly by group or socially defined mechanisms in which individual contributions are either submerged or filtered and evaluated. These characteristics are aimed at transforming individual "work" input into a broader "social contribution" concept in which the quality and quantity of work input is governed no longer by personal income considerations but by identification of self-interest with the interest of the group. To the extent that this transformation is achieved the individual's motivation becomes internal rather than external, "inner-directed" rather than "outer-directed." [2]

While the Maoists' emphasis has appeared to be on nonmaterial rather than material incentives, their more fundamental and far-reaching objective is to socialize incentives, to substitute the group as the basic motivational unit for the individual. Focusing on material versus nonmaterial incentives may obscure the fact that either type can be tied to the individual or the group as the motivated unit. Material incentives can be group oriented and, in fact, during the GLF and even after, such material incentives as piece rates were sometimes group linked. Likewise, nonmaterial incentives have often been tied to individuals (e.g., labor models). Since the GPCR, however, though material and individual-oriented incentives still operate widely, the main thrust is to develop nonmaterial, group oriented mechanisms; to socialize work incentives in the mold of the Communist ideal.

In all modern industrial societies wages and salaries play an important role in labor allocation, though in varying degrees. In China, for a considerable time after 1949, this continued to be so. But, as we have seen in chapter 3, the major unemployment problems persisting during the 1950s and continuing into the 1960s were dealt with, starting in 1958, mainly through administrative assignment and social motivation rather than through conventional labor market wage differentials or their manipulation. The egalitarian commitments of the Maoists have not only militated against setting up marked differential wage structures geared to labor allocation objectives but call for narrowing the wage and income disparities between peasants and industrial workers and technical and professional workers, setting up a compensation system consistent with the very modest standard of living projected for a "proletarian" China.

The material factor, too, is being transmuted to meet Maoist socialization objectives. Material incentives, traditionally more individual in their focus with single workers being paid wages on the basis of their individual performances, have been experimented with, the goal being to transform such schemes when possible into mechanisms where the individual's compensation is determined by the group within which he or she works and which pursues its work tasks as a unit. An individual's attitudes and cooperation take on major significance in the assessment of his or her work contribution and the determination of marginal payment he or she may receive above the standard wage.

These salient changes in the Chinese work incentive system came about while CCP policy underwent considerable modification, during which it sometimes shifted from one direction to another. Since 1949 incentive policy has undergone several shifts during five distinct periods: 1949 to 1952, 1953 to 1957, 1958 to 1960, 1961 to 1965, and from 1966 on.

From 1949 to 1952 the main concern over work incentives centered on questions of economic rehabilitation and regional, sectoral, and intra-industry wage disparities. Specifically, several difficulties arose. First, there were many wage scales with wide-ranging differences in maximums and minimums in the same kind of work and irrationalities and inconsistencies in payment. Second, the relation between performance and reward was often obscured. Pay differentials supposedly distinguishing gradation in skill commonly were minute; wage differences sometimes were based on sex or status distinctions; piecework mechanisms were not widely in use. Third, nonlabor income elements operated in the system in the form of bonuses for good attendance and traditional year's-end allowances in money and kind regardless of labor performance. Fourth, many interregional, interindustry, and interenterprise wage differentials stimulated the development of light industry in certain coastal areas in undesired ways. And fifth, a unified collective welfare program with benefits geared differentially to wage level was needed.[3] These important disruptive conditions issued naturally from diverse forms of ownership, different historical situations, the dualistic nature of Chinese industrial activity, different kinds of wage systems, and the large number of dissimilar industrial units. An effective uniform policy would not be possible until industrial conditions were more uniform. Socialization of industry, a process already begun, would provide a firmer basis for a national work incentive policy.

In the period of the FFYP, 1953 to 1957, a clear-cut, vigorous policy on work incentives in tune with the Soviet growth model was pursued. Material work incentives were rationalized throughout industry in conformity with the FFYP's goals to develop heavy industry rapidly. Wage mechanisms reflecting the differential importance the plan placed on certain industries and occupations were established and refined; they were often set up on a piece-rate basis. The array of differential wage scales was consistent with the labor allocation mandated by the FFYP. At the same time, some attention was given to the cultivation of nonmaterial, social incentives.

By the end of 1956 about two thirds of private industry had been transformed into state enterprises and the remaining one third took the joint state-private form. This more homogeneous grouping made possible more sweeping policy prescriptions on incentives, and in 1956 a major wage reform following the general line already sketched was carried out. Wages (following a "rational low wage policy" with increases limited to one half the productivity rise) [4] were placed on a more uniform and systematic basis with differentials, bonuses, promotions, and other payment features coordinated toward stimulating output and allowing for use of piece rates. Standard wage scales were set up for industrial, technical, professional, managerial, and scientific workers. Irrational and egalitarian features were eliminated. A general wage increase of about 14 percent was promulgated, and special adjustments were made to coordinate payment schedules. The reliance on a rational (market) material incentive policy à la Russe seemed unequivocal.[5]

During the GLF, 1958 to 1960, incentive policy, like general economic strategy, veered from the Soviet model to a seemingly opposite path in which the decentralized deployment of hundreds of millions of peasants in the newly created commune was based on a more revolutionary incentive strategy. Reliance was placed more on nonmaterial incentives with material mechanisms being reined in. Highly touted piece-rate systems were abandoned; bonus systems were cut back. Workers were exhorted to increase output in response to social goads with symbolic rewards replacing hard cash. Group oriented payment schemes were extended as material incentives generally were deemphasized.

The abandonment of the GLF in 1960 and urgent efforts to recover from its adverse effects and to give agriculture highest development priority resulted in a careful modification of incentive policy. The Maoist cast of incentive policy during the GLF seemed reversed as workers and peasants were more fully linked to material incentives. Rhetoric on nonmaterial incentives continued, but reality clearly showed that they played a less prominent role. Industrial workers were spurred on by reintroduced piece-rate mechanisms and bonuses. Late in 1963 about ten million workers had their wages raised one wage grade in the eight-wage grade scale through advancement. Throughout this period the anti-Maoist effort to recast Chinese development strategy grew strongly so that despite the varied pressures generated by the Maoist socialist education movement against "bourgeois" attitudes and mechanisms the extent and strength of material incentives deepened.

During the GPCR, incentive policy was abruptly reversed again once the

Maoist forces were in the ascendency. Until that time, the contending groups struggled vigorously over the appropriate policy: the Liuist group extended material incentives, raising workers' wages retroactively, and pushing further a variety of monetary emoluments in the disruption attending clashes in industrial plants; the Maoists denounced these practices as "economism" and "capitalistic" and stressed instead the urgent need to overcome "bourgeois" behavior and to transcend "self" in favor of group interest. When opposition to the Maoists had been surmounted, a program for development of nonmaterial and social aspects of incentives was put forth and the fundamental revolutionary emphasis on "Communist" spirit, first heralded during the GLF, was pressed vigorously.

For most of the period since 1968 incentive policy has been pushed further along the lines sketched late in the GPCR. Once the politically volatile situation was reasonably under control, more attention was devoted to programming Maoist economic policy, including a more revolutionary incentive policy with a material base, important nonmaterial (social) elements, and group focus for both kinds of incentives. In industry the national model for revolutionary emulation was the Tach'ing oil workers' incentive system which was the analog of the agricultural model (the Tachai production brigade) both cultivating group consciousness as part of the growing class struggle against "bourgeois" rewards and attitudes. In 1971 a modest wage increase similar to that of 1963 was implemented. In 1973 evidence, confirmed by the author's own observations in China, grew that material incentives were assuming more importance again.

Consciously modeling its system at the outset on that in the Soviet Union, CCP leaders did not depart from it in any important way until the GLF. Even today when the difference in the countries is substantial, the forms of material and nonmaterial mechanisms are often the same. In China the differentials in material reward have been generally narrowed, and the importance of material incentives in generating increments of work effort cumulatively has been reduced over time, though they will continue to be used for some time as fair remnants of a familiar reward system and will go through periods of resurgence. Instead nonmaterial consciousness-changing mechanisms of a group-oriented nature have been cultivated and expanded. Since 1953 material incentive systems in industry have become more uniform with the basic scales set up in the 1956 wage reform continuing in effect thereafter. The piece-rate systems which were developed in the 1950s and revived in the early 1960s are no longer in wide use.[6]

Material Incentives

Basic Wage Mechanisms

Today in Chinese industry workers are paid on a multiple wage-grade scale differentiated according to variations from unskilled to highly skilled categories. Whether the individual works on a time, time-plus-bonus, or piece-rate basis (when these latter mechanisms are in operation), there is a standard scale by branch of activity, except where special scales are used for workers in certain remote locations. In the late 1950s these scales were varied by branch in line with the regime's priorities for differential industrial development under the FFYP with ardousness of work an important consideration. Although the number of steps or grades in such wage schemes has varied, in most instances there are eight payment steps. This conforms generally to the situation in Soviet industry.

The following is a current medium monthly eight-grade pattern at the Peking No. 1 Machine Tools Plant which roughly corresponds to those widely in use throughout Chinese industry as to wage rates and ratio of highest to lowest grade:

Wage Grade	1	2	3	4	5	6	7	8
Coefficient	1.00	1.18	1.40	1.62	1.80	2.27	2.67	3.15
Monthly Wage (¥)	34.00	40.10	47.50	55.00	61.10	77.10	90.90	107.10

The roughly 3 to 1 ratio of pay of most skilled to least skilled categories is not a rigid one, but a rough middle-range ratio with ratios differing according to branch of industry and pressure on workers: in the past heavy industries with great strain on workers usually have had scales with ratios above 3 to 1, while light industries generally have had ratios below 3 to 1. Even with 3 to 1 ratios some industries may have a higher range such as 42 to 126. (Intergrade differentials are sometimes constant, but this is not always so such as in the above and two following scales.) In 1965 a scale for common heavy industries (roughly the 3 to 1 category) such as machine building, locomotive building, and electric engineering in Tsingtao was similar to the pattern above. Immediately below it is a scale above 3 to 1, also in Tsingtao in 1965, for heavy industries involving onerous duties for workers: [7]

Wage Grade	1	2	3	4	5	6	7	8
Coefficient	1	1.18	1.45	1.64	1.94	2.26	2.71	3.20

Monthly Wage (¥)	33	38.95	47.85	54.14	64.02	74.57	89.45	105.60
Coefficient	1	1.20	1.45	1.75	2.19	2.50	3.00	3.60
Monthly Wage (¥)	36	43.20	52.20	63.00	79.00	90.00	108.00	129.60

Distribution among grades varies somewhat. In industrial cities, the numbers of workers in grades is skewed toward the unskilled end of the continuum: about 40 percent fall in the first three (relatively unskilled) grades, the middle grades (4, 5, and 6) claim 45 percent, while the remaining 15 percent, the highly skilled, are in grades 7 and 8.[8]

Table 4.1 shows specifically how workers were distributed among a variety of industries. In this array, which is for the period before general wage reform and development of skills, the skewed nature of the distribution varies considerably. In older industries (coal mining and textiles) the proportions of skilled workers are greater, while in newer industries the pro-

Table 4.1
Distribution of Workers in China
by Wage Grade, 1955
(Percentage)

Industry	1	2	3	4	5	6	7	8	Average Grade
Power	6.7	14.7	24.5	21.3	15.2	11.2	5.2	1.2	3.8
Coal mining	1.1	4.4	13.1	28.3	29.6	18.7	4.5	0.3	4.6
Petroleum	3.4	10.9	31.2	30.8	14.2	6.2	2.5	0.8	3.7
Iron & steel	2.9	12.1	27.6	26.9	18.4	8.0	3.2	0.9	3.9
Nonferrous	2.2	12.1	31.7	32.3	14.8	5.3	1.4	0.2	3.7
Metal processing	5.0	19.0	26.7	20.9	14.5	8.9	4.0	1.0	3.7
Chemical	6.8	20.2	31.2	23.7	10.8	5.0	1.9	0.4	3.4
Building material	4.3	15.8	30.6	25.8	14.2	6.7	2.0	0.6	3.6
Textiles	2.1	10.5	21.7	29.0	19.5	12.0	4.4	0.8	4.1
Light industry and food	6.3	12.5	21.9	24.3	18.0	10.8	4.9	1.3	3.9

Source: *T'ung-Chi kung-tso t'ung-hsin* [Statistical work bulletin] no. 23, (1956), translated in SCMM, 4 February, 1957, pp. 29–30.

Motivating Workers

portion in the three lowest grades exceeds 40 percent, rising to its highest—over 58 percent—in the chemical industry.

Table 4.2 illustrates different kinds of eight-grade wage scales in operation in 1959 among a variety of industries. The first two represent industries requiring arduous work with a greater than 3 to 1 ratio between highest and lowest wage grades; the next five represent heavy industries requiring less demanding work with the eighth to first grade coefficient just about 3 to 1; and the last two represent industries having only seven wage grades with the coefficient less than 3 to 1 for the imputed seven grades and considerably less than 3-to-1 ratios. (The two industries are light if one considers the handicraft nature of much of the construction industry.)

While standard wage scales such as those illustrated above were being set up in 1956 for industrial workers, an array of wage scales for a wide variety of state employees (apprentice, clerical, general, technical, professional, engineering, managerial, administrative, and governmental) running up to the level of premier of the PRC was promulgated. Totaling, in some instances, up to thirty grades, these scales were much more complicated than the standard eight-grade scales in industry. They had eleven variants for different regions of the country (to reflect cost of living differences) with each region having its own scale, the wage variations for each grade extending up to as much as 40 percent among the regions. In addition to the regional wage differentials, provision was made in some instances to increase wage differentials further with living expense subsidies reaching as high as 93 and 97 percent above the standard wage in such outlying areas as the Tsaidam Basin and Tibet, regions in which the standard wage for each grade was the eleventh, or maximum, category. To take a specific example, under these scales the highest grade automobile driver (grade 1) in the Mang-ya area of the Tsaidam Basin would receive ¥ 196 a month, while his counterpart (also grade 1) in Shensi Province (the first regional scale) would earn only ¥ 78, or just under 40 percent of the Mang-ya driver's pay.[9]

Table 4.3 embodies some of the complications in the various monthly wage scales discussed above. Though it ranges only over ten wage levels, the wage differentials for each grade by the eleven wage regions are shown. The additional subsidies to which workers in certain regions are entitled are not indicated, but they range from 0 to 97 percent according to the varying cost-of-living differences and may be changed as such conditions vary.

The wage scales of more highly paid managerial and engineering per-

Table 4.2

*Basic Wages in China by Industries
and Wage Grades, 1959*
(In Yuan Per Month)

Industry and Enterprise	1	2	3	4	5	6	7	8
Coal, Fu-shun Mine	34.50	40.74	48.13	56.82	67.10	79.25	93.60	110.40
Steel, Anshan I & S Co.	34.50	40.74	48.11	56.82	67.10	79.25	93.59	110.40
Machinery, Mukden Wks	33.00	38.90	45.80	54.00	63.60	74.90	88.20	104.00
Electric Power, Hu-shun Station	34.00	40.05	47.19	55.59	65.48	77.15	90.88	107.10
Petroleum, Northeast Petroleum	34.00	39.88	46.78	54.88	64.36	75.48	88.54	103.70
Lumber, Forest Industries	33.00	38.61	45.17	52.85	61.83	72.34	84.64	99.00
Chemicals, Mukden Plant	33.00	38.61	45.18	52.87	61.84	72.37	84.68	99.00
Cereal, Mukden Flour Mill	29.00	34.00	39.90	46.80	54.90	64.40	75.40	—
Construction, Fu-shun	33.66	39.95	47.43	56.28	66.82	79.44	92.40	—

Source: Chugoku Kenkyu Sho, *Chugoku Nenkan 1959* [China yearbook 1959] (Tokyo: Iwazaki Shuten, 1960), p. 310.

Motivating Workers
101

Table 4.3

Wage Scales for the Workers of
State Organs (VI), July 1956

Levels	Wage Scales, Unit: Yuan/Month											Automobile Drivers	
	1	2	3	4	5	6	7	8	9	10	11		
1	78	80.5	82.5	85.0	87.5	89.5	92.0	94.5	76.5	99.0	101.5		
2	70	72.0	74.0	76.5	78.5	80.5	82.5	84.5	87.0	89.0	91.0		
3	62	64.0	65.5	67.5	69.5	71.5	73.0	75.0	77.0	78.5	80.5	Drivers	
4	55	56.5	58.5	60.0	61.5	63.5	65.0	66.5	68.0	70.0	71.5		
5	43	49.5	51.0	52.5	54.0	55.0	56.5	58.0	59.5	61.0	62.5		
6	42	43.5	44.5	46.0	47.0	48.5	49.5	51.0	52.0	53.5	54.5		Assist.
7	36	37.0	38.0	39.0	40.0	41.5	42.5	43.5	44.5	45.5	47.0		
8	31	32.0	33.0	34.0	34.5	35.5	36.5	37.5	38.5	39.5	40.5		
9	27	28.0	28.5	29.5	30.0	31.0	32.0	32.5	33.5	34.5	35.0		
10	24	24.5	25.5	26.0	27.0	27.5	28.5	29.0	30.0	30.5	31.0		

Source: State Council, "Notification on the Issuance of a Program of Wage Scales for Workers of State Organs," no. HSI-54, 1956, in *Compilation of the Laws and Regulations of nancial Administration of the Central Government* (Peking: 1956), pp. 226–47; U.S. Jc Publications Research Service, *Translations on Communist China's Management, Trade a Finance,* no. 79 (May 1966), pp. 1–55.

Notes: The wage scales listed above are of eleven kinds. In accordance with the commo prices and living standards in various localities, individual wage scales are provided for ecution in those localities. In localities where commodity prices are exceedingly high, s sidies for living expenses are added. Details of wage scales applicable to various locali and proportions of subsidies for living expenses are in the Wage Scales Applicable to Vario Localities and Subsidies for Living Expenses.

The wage scales of those technicians who are not listed above may be evaluated and de mined according to similar job titles and grades.

sonnel range up to ¥ 370 per month (without cost-of-living subsidies) according to the 1956 standard scales (see Appendix A for a few of these scales). Since the GPCR there have been no revised standard scales published, but there has been a general lowering of the actual wage scales of professional, engineering, and managerial personnel, as well as government officials, in conformity with the renewed stress on revolutionary and proletarian consciousness. Still, in 1973 in universities senior professors receive as much as ¥ 350 a month. It has been reported that the highest regular salary paid in China now (to top leaders in government, the party, and the PLA) is ¥ 400 a month and that the standard maximum salary for

Technical Workers					Cooking Personnel		Telephone Workers	
...ng ...ers	Electricians, Blacksmith, Boiler Repair Workers	Carpenters and Tilers	Gardeners and Elevator Drivers	Boiler Workers	Chefs	Other Cooking Personnel	Repair Workers	Operators

leading personnel in a sample of industrial enterprises was ¥ 210 a month which was about 30 percent below the standard maximum for the position. This represents a spread of about six to one from the top manager's pay to that of the least skilled workers (¥ 210 to ¥ 30–35). In most enterprises surveyed, however, the spread was even more narrow.[10]

The industrial wage payment pattern described above is used for time-rate workers in various industries as the basic pay mechanism. Each worker is classified by grade in terms of his or her skill and his or her function in the plan. Satisfactory performance of all duties entitles the worker to the standard wage rate for his or her category. Thus the least skilled worker in an enterprise employing the above scale would receive a standard monthly wage of ¥ 35. Other workers of varying skills would receive standard wages ranging up to ¥ 105 for the most advanced. When time-rate pay is supplemented by a bonus system or extra compensation for outstanding performance or, sometimes, reduced for inferior execution of required tasks, then actual wages depart from the standard for the grade.[11]

Piece-Rate Mechanisms

Piece-rate mechanisms in China have differed considerably, but almost all such means of payment have been based upon the multiple wage-grade system already discussed, and particular devices vary from that point on. Experimentation along many lines has yielded a great variety of specific techniques. Although the CCP once favored use of piece rates wherever feasible, there is no evidence of general use of *progressive* piece rates in which rates rise more rapidly than overquota output. This departs from practice in the Soviet Union where, in 1955, about 35 percent of industrial workers were paid on a progressive piece-rate basis. In China piece-rate and bonus payments above standard once totaled up to 20 percent of all wages but have usually been less.[12]

The basic element in piece rates up to the GPCR has been payment of wages above or below the standard for a particular grade, depending on the quantity and quality of the worker's output. For each grade there was a standard wage, higher by a few percent than the time-rate standard, which was paid if the worker approximated the quota. Output below the norm occasioned a payment less than the standard amount; output above resulted in wages exceeding the standard. The additional wage payments for extra production were not as great as the value of excess output but rose in step with such increased output.

Piece-rate systems were divided into limited and unlimited types. In the former type, premium pay for production above the quota was limited to a certain maximum amount, regardless of the degree of overfulfillment. Thus, the overquota part of the wage might be limited to 50 percent of the total wage. When the work group was capable of meeting its overall quota in a sustained way at or above a specified level, the unlimited piece-rate system was allowed to operate with piece-rate pay commensurate with output.[13]

Another classificatory distinction in piece rate was that between direct and indirect systems. The direct system based premium payments on the output of the individual or the small group. In the indirect type a large number of workers in a plant received wages above or below the standard grade rate depending upon the volume of output of basic production workers rather than on their own performance. In the Soviet Union, as well as in many other industrial nations, direct and indirect piece rates have also been used.[14]

An interesting piece-rate technique employed in a coal mine in 1959 included incentive awards, performance deductions, and subsidies. With the team of workers as the basic measurement unit, wages were a function of the degree of norm fulfillment. When the quota was exceeded, workers in the team were all paid the standard amount for their respective wage grades plus an additional amount equal to 80 percent of the scheduled piece-rate value of the extra production. If the team failed to meet the norm, workers were paid a wage proportionate to the amount of realized output. That is, if they produced an amount equal, to say, 75 percent of the quota, they received 75 percent of the standard amount for their wage grades. (In the Soviet Union a minimum wage exists within a similar context.) In addition, they were given a subsidy payment of 30 percent of the scheduled piece-rate value of the unfulfilled output portion to diminish the severity of the wage deduction. Thus, if the team produced only 90 percent of the norm, each worker got a wage of 90 percent of his standard wage grade pay *plus* a subsidy of 30 percent of production or 3 percent of the respective standard wage for a total of 93 percent of the standard pay for the respective grades.[15]

Another piece-work mechanism before the GPCR illustrates how quantity and quality of output were motivated. Three quality classes were set up for each of the usual eight grades. Those whose work quality satisfied all specifications were graded with an *A* and received the full standard pay for their wage grade if their output quota was fulfilled (additional output meant higher pay). For those whose quality of work did not quite meet *A* level, the grade *B* was given, yielding 92 to 94 percent of the standard pay for their grade. When *B* specifications were not met the grade was *C,* and the work was returned; no payment was received until minimum levels were satisfied.[16]

In textiles a complicated variation of piece rates also based on quantity and quality of production employed multiple grades as well as vertical classes within each grade. Each of the eight multiple wage steps had a regular standard rate; but in addition there were four other payment categories, two above and two below the standard rate, for a total of five different rates within each wage grade. A worker thus received one of the five rates in his grade depending upon the extent to which he met quantity and quality output reqirements.

To illustrate, if the wage grade's standard rate was ¥ 68, the other four rates (with differentials of ¥ 2) were ¥ 72, ¥ 70, ¥ 66, and ¥ 64. Thus, a worker satisfying quantity and quality norms received a wage of ¥ 68 for the month. If he met the quota for either quantity or quality and sufficiently exceeded it for the other one, his wage was ¥ 70, while overfulfillment in both by the required degree yielded the highest wage for that grade, ¥ 72. On the other hand, the worker who failed to satisfy either target by a set amount got a wage below the standard amount to ¥ 66. If norms for both quantity and quality were missed by a certain degree, the worker's wage was ¥ 64, the lowest for that grade. The rate of pay for workers in each of the eight grades was determined in the same manner.[17]

Another pre-cultural revolution variant of the piece-rate technique, based on Soviet experience, was developed at the Anshan Steel Works Refining Plant. Continuous production at the furnace was divided into several phases, each phase being given points representing a proportion of the total process. Total production determined the extent of piece-rate pay above standard wage grade payments.

The phases of production with their respective points were:

repair of furnaces	7 points
putting material in	29 points
melting	32 points
refining	32 points

The shift performing the first two phases was credited with 36 percent of the furnace's output, the other shift performing the next two phases with 64 percent. Each shift shared proportionately in any extra compensation arising from overnorm output.[18]

With many in the CCP viewing piece rates as too "bourgeois," there was considerable pressure, if such arrangements had to be used, to devise collective piece rates in which the individual's wage would depend on the quantity and quality of output of a work team or work shop. After the GPCR, however, piece rates were rejected and widely abandoned as a foremost example of "economism" and today they are only found in occasional industrial plants.[19]

Bonus Payments

When piece rates could not be employed due to difficulties of calculating individual and small group performance precisely, bonuses were often used to supplement time wages. The work goals were usually the same as for piece rates: production exceeding plans, economy in the use of materials, achievement of safety standards, and superior product quality. Extra pay came only if basic norms were achieved; then outstanding performance in any one of the specified areas warranted a bonus. In their nature such payments were based on evaluation of worker and group performance by supervisory personnel rather than on objective norms as in piece work. (The pattern in China also followed that in use in the USSR.) When production-cost reduction was the goal, 20 to 30 percent of the economized amount was frequently made available for bonuses. Such payments to individuals were in many instances restricted to a maximum of 15 percent of the monthly standard wage, a more severe limitation than usually applied to piece rates, with many enterprises keeping pay substantially below this level.[20]

During the 1950s several types of bonus techniques were used: (1) direct limited awards; (2) direct progressive awards; and (3) direct unlimited and contractual awards. The first involved bonuses paid up to a specified limit on the basis of an individual's or group's quota overfulfillment. The second technique, whose use has been quite limited, payed increasing amounts of bonus as norms were surpassed. These two types often led to rises in labor costs along with increase in output and to a wide disincentive effect on workers who felt discriminated against. The third type payed bonuses out of a planned total amount of wages. Since the amount for bonuses was fixed absolutely, added output stimulated by extra pay did not raise the wage bill. Today in China bonuses are not widely used.[21]

In many enterprises a negative bonus mechanism also operated in which the time wage for each grade was reduced below the standard if the worker failed to achieve his output quota. In these situations, higher wage-grade workers had their time wage reduced below the standard for their grade in proportion to the below-normal performance. In many units this rule was not rigidly applied to lower wage-grade workers who, in effect, enjoyed a minimum wage guarantee. A worker below the third wage-grade often got his full standard time wage so long as he fulfilled at least 90 percent of the quota. In some circumstances lower-grade workers were assured of 75 percent of the standard time wage even if output failed to reach the quota by more than 25 percent.[22]

Other Wage Payments

Other payments complete the range of regular monetary rewards. Wage supplements existed before the GPCR in the form of various allowances for overtime, night or holiday work, and difficult or hazardous working conditions. Pieceworkers who were temporarily assigned to jobs paying less than the average rate received extra pay in their permanent positions. Other pieceworkers who lost some earnings due to unfavorable working conditions (inadequate supplies, poor tools and equipment, and technical plant dislocation) were also given extra compensation.

Payments not directly related to work done on the job were also made to workers before the GPCR. Remuneration was often given to workers in training who were still assigned to an enterprise where they worked prior to training, a type of retainer payment. Those who instructed apprentices, foregoing perhaps high piece-rate pay, frequently received extra recompense. Some workers who wrote articles and gave lectures in addition to, but connected with, their regular jobs received supplementary income.[23]

Once the opposition had been overcome during the GPCR, the reaction against "economism" set in and wages in general were cut back: piece rates were almost abandoned; bonuses were reduced sharply; higher paid technical, professional, and engineering workers took substantial wage cuts in some instances; and scattered situations of workers taking reductions in wages were reported. This deemphasis of material reward as the principal stimulation of work input has only recently been halted.[24]

Payments for Invention and Innovation

In addition to the various forms of wage payment already described, schedules of monetary awards for inventions and innovations were first devised during the 1950s. Official regulations provided award classes and an administrative arrangement for evaluating and processing these creative endeavors. Such schedules paralleled early Soviet forms, though the Chinese never placed as much emphasis on such awards. In fact, the schedules listed below, promulgated in 1963 during the recovery from the GLF, reflect a considerable reduction in the level of earlier, preliminary payments set up in 1954. Since the GPCR, these permanent award schedules have been reduced or eliminated.[25]

The procedures for bestowing awards and administering inventions and technical improvements were the responsibility of the Scientific and Technological Commission of the People's Republic of China (also known as the State Scientific Commission) except for those relating to national defense, which were carried out by the Ministry of Defense. Recognition for inventions and technical improvements linked the honorary and pecuniary part of the award in five grades:

Grade	Honorary Award	Cash Payment
First	Certificate and first-grade medallion	¥ 10,000
Second	Certificate and second-grade medallion	¥ 5,000
Third	Certificate and third-grade medallion	¥ 2,000
Fourth	Certificate	¥ 1,000
Fifth	Certificate	¥ 500

Inventions were rewarded only once. Those of particular importance were honored separately as special awards after recommendation by the State Scientific Commission and approval by the State Council.[26]

Awards for technical improvements also fell into five grades:

Grade	Improvement Value *	Honorary Award	Cash Payment
First	Over ¥ 1,000,000	Commendation and Certificate	¥ 500–¥ 1,000
Second	Over ¥ 100,000	Commendation and Certificate	¥ 200
Third	Over ¥ 10,000	Commendation	¥ 100–¥ 200
Fourth	Over ¥ 1,000	Commendation	Under ¥ 100
Fifth	Less than ¥ 1,000	Commendation	No money

* Represents the actual value of higher production and economy in one year resulting from the improvement after the costs of implementation have been deducted.

By their very nature, technical improvements relating to industrial safety have to be rewarded without recourse to annual value of higher production and economy. Grades of awards were required to be set up according to the effectiveness and technical complexity of such improvements.

Social Insurance Benefits

The social insurance system in China provides benefits in money and kind to augment, when necessary, the wages of industrial workers. Under its provisions, laborers in industry as well as in other activities where 100 or more workers are employed are covered for sickness, injury and disability, death, maternity, retirement, and other benefits. Units not covered by the legislation were not precluded from establishing their own plans. The system is noncontributory with covered enterprises earmarking 3 percent of the total payroll for the various categories. Thirty percent of the amount collected each month has in the past been turned over to the ACFTU, which administered the system, for financing a variety of communal activities, such as sanatoriums, rest homes, and orphanages. (At the end of 1966 the trade-unions and their newspaper, *Kung-jen jih-pao,* or *Workers' Daily,* were suspended, as the GPCR gained momentum, and, the unions have only recently begun to function again. Presumably the social insurance functions of the ACFTU were carried out through enterprises and new committees.) The remainder is retained by the plant or factory for current costs of pensions, allowances, relief payments, and welfare units such as hospitals and clinics which were directly under its control. The government reported that in 1965, the last year for which such data were made available, 20 million workers and employees were qualified to receive benefits. For the most part the system parallels that in the Soviet Union.[27]

Although the system's main purpose is to provide minimal protection against certain hazards of living, there are also built-in incentive elements. Most benefits are graded according to wages. Another material encouragement is that special (additional) rights are bestowed on model workers and combat heroes (exservicemen) who work in covered units. Former nationalist officials and those convicted of certain crimes are excluded from coverage.[28] (See Appendix B for the official regulations governing benefits.)

Nonmaterial Incentives

Since the middle 1950s nonmaterial incentives, or mechanisms motivating individual and group labor input with psychic rather than material rewards, have assumed an increasingly prominent role in China. That role has fluctuated, becoming much more significant during the GLF and GPCR and after. During the aftermath of the GLF while material incentives were again emphasized, nonmaterial incentives were still in widespread use though they declined relatively in importance. For Maoist ideology nonmaterial or moral incentives are a vital means in the shaping of Communist man: all workers (and peasants) are expected to develop their socialist and Communist consciousness *while* they are industrializing and modernizing the economy, not *after* those goals have been realized. Nonmaterial incentives shaped into social or group forms are expected not only to exemplify an egalitarian reward system but to help unleash vast quantities of creative labor inputs which will hasten the realization of the regime's economic objectives.

CCP leaders maintain that, for the time, nonmaterial techniques must be joined with the material, a bourgeois remnant; but there is no question of the ultimate superiority of the former. Continued but reluctant reliance on material incentives also has necessitated constant use of indoctrination with nonmaterial incentives to forestall the undermining of socialism. Since the GPCR the deemphasis of material incentives has persisted until 1971: they have been denounced as a "hot-bed in which the concept of private ownership breeds" and "a poison which corrupts people's minds." [29]

The central role of the CCP in such campaigns is patent. Yet the effective execution of emulation drives and mass movements depends on the organization and operational efforts of various social, economic, and political agencies. Involved in such activities have been trade unions, youth organizations, women's groups, lower political organs, and non-Communist political bodies (e.g., Democratic Party). Even "capitalist" groups have been recruited. All potentially useful organizations become "transmission belts" for implementing drives that are part of the complex of nonmaterial incentives. [30]

The nonmaterial incentives used have involved individuals and groups vying with, as well as working closely with, one another. While many of these activities, especially when extended in extreme and onerous ways, have stifled incentive, good results have frequently ensued when the individual and the group have been positively committed to the venture. The success of most nonmaterial incentives depends on the participant's outlook. If the individual is negatively disposed toward society and the various groups he belongs to, most of these endeavors to elicit better performance would be likely to intensify his disaffection.

Thus, nonmaterial incentives by themselves may not work effectively unless they are accompanied by effective political indoctrination and education which are aimed at heightening personal awareness, putting a particular campaign or drive in proper perspective, and making its technical requisites clear. It is expected that such drives will not become meaningless rituals, producing little besides widely shared irritation. Through struggle-criticism-transformation campaigns, negatively disposed and indifferent individuals' resistances are weakened, and they may be more fully integrated into the group.[31]

We divide nonmaterial incentives into two types which are not strictly mutually exclusive but may reinforce or blend into one another and which continue in use today. They rest on the grounds that greater productivity or product derives mainly from (1) the desire to excel and surpass other individuals and groups: an individual and group competitive motive; and (2) the inclination to do better because of one's strong and close identification with the group: a social or cooperative drive. The first of these, the competitive urge, is built on the same foundation which underlies many material incentives. Actually, honorary awards are also distributive. Though what is distributed is not so costly as are the emoluments of material incentives, still excessive distribution debases the value of the unit. The second one, the social and cooperative drive, reflects more the individual's need to work as a social fulfillment, to be a successful member of a group. Over time this latter concept has been more intensely cultivated as Maoist ideology has emphasized a level of consciousness in which the individual worker's first consideration is to the manifold interests of the group or community.

Competitive Incentives

These incentives have usually been employed to achieve a clear-cut economic goal or set of goals. Contests involving individuals or groups have been fashioned for such interrelated ends as increasing output, improving the quality of production, raising labor productivity, reducing work accidents, and lowering costs. The exhortations in this kind of match have often focused on very specific means to these ends, as well as on the ends themselves. Veteran workers are invited to help tyros to adjust quickly and effectively to work situations; agile workers are encouraged to transform the slow into likenesses of themselves; all workers are urged to contribute to technical improvements and inventions and to assist in the improvement of management and administration.[32]

Competitive emulation campaigns are many in number. Such drives may be organized on any one of several levels according to the specific purpose in view: production group, shift, department, factory, or industry. Whatever the unit involved, the contest may be on a local, provincial, regional, or national basis. Since the advent of the GPCR, competitive emulations have been deemphasized.

Individual Competition

Individual workers are spurred on by a variety of formal and informal rewards all of which serve to raise the self-esteem of the honored and perhaps to inspire, by example, numerous unknown admirers to improve their work performance. The contests and campaigns in themselves motivate workers through their desire to win, but in addition this type of competition distributes a large number of nonmaterial rewards (sometimes tied to a token material award) to commend outstanding performance. These include titular honors, opportunities for occupational advancement, attendance as representatives at conferences of outstanding peasants and workers, meetings with Chairman Mao (in the past) and other celebrities, chances to join the CCP and to be elected to various political and governmental bodies, and special vacation and travel privileges.

The bestowal of honorific titles on outstanding workers is one simple and possibly quite effective manner of encouraging not inconsequential numbers on to greater effort. Labeled Model, Labor Hero, Advanced or Outstanding, the honored worker enjoys a status of esteem and qualifies for certain perquisites in proportion to his accomplishments. Advanced or Outstanding producers are those who surpass a certain standard of performance. Models are higher on the scale; they excel over time and are named from among the most advanced workers. Labor Heroes are at the pinnacle of performance and have been honored in the past for unusual activity not frequently duplicated.[33]

Individuals honored with these various titles have also often been given tangible evidence attesting to their elite status, such as medals, banners, and money, the latter in addition to cash bonuses. Gold star and regular gold medals as well as certificates of merit have been awarded publicly to those with outstanding achievements. Public presentation of title winners without emblems is practiced too. Banners signaling great accomplishments are also bestowed upon those qualifying; such emblems may be red flags or other symbolic badges such as dragons of an hierarchic order.[34]

Individuals in emulation contests have also been spurred on by honorary awards. One such example reveals the technique employed. An emulation contest in a steel company's coke factory set up honorary award classes based on six aspects of work, hence Six-Good Workers, to speed up output and spur on laggard workers. Each day whoever met the standards in all six regards had a small red flag placed on the wall poster. At the end of the month, awards were made according to the number of flags posted: Category A, 25 or more flags, designates "Standard-Bearing Six-Good Work Soldiers"; Category B, 20 to 24 flags, designates "Red Standard Bearers"; Category C, 15 to 19 flags, designates "Reserve Red Standard Bearers."[35]

In the 1950s model and advanced workers realized gains in other ways. Extra paid vacation periods at well-known attractive locations gave further meaning to honorary awards. Sometimes elite workers, individually or in groups, were sent on special trips to foreign countries on vacation or in political or technical exchanges. They also helped as hosts and guides for visiting foreign workers.[36]

A crowning achievement for some model and advanced workers during the 1950s was to be sent as representative to the periodic regional and national conferences held to extol elite workers and to glorify their image in the public eye. There they were greeted, lionized, and propagandized by the highest officials of the party and in their particular field. Their mission was defined, and they were given high praise. They lived in relatively luxurious surroundings, ate well, saw the sights, tasted of various cultural activities, and generally got a feel of life at the higher levels of society in Peking or in a provincial capital. A few were even presented with token gifts by Mao Tse-tung. Such conferences are not as widely and frequently held now.[37]

Group Competition

Group emulative mechanisms utilized to stimulate production and improve its quality have paralleled individual competitive mechanisms: challenging another unit to a production contest, attempting to surpass the unit's previous record, trying to exceed a quota, and working with a backward unit to raise its levels of performance. The success of the unit involved is rewarded, as with individuals, through a variety of honorary awards, reaching up in the same way to the national conferences described. Such challenges and contests have also been a feature of socialist emulation in the USSR, though in China they have played a more important and long-term role.[38]

The keen rivalry between units is often harnessed to generate large increments in output. Many of these rivalries have all of the earmarks of a league sports contest in which the standings constantly change as all units vie to win or be close to the top. The flavor of this type of competition is suggested by "emulation battles" among locomotive units in the Tsinan locomotion division in 1959. After each series of contests, the norms for distance, speed, and load were changed at five hierarchic levels, with each locomotive crew attempting to meet the highest standards and thus gain the best dragon name: Great Dragon (*chu lung*).[39]

The engineer and crew of each train that met or surpassed the norm were entitled to the appropriate dragon name. The category of dragon names and criteria in descending order were:

1. Great Dragon (*chu lung*) where the team completed scheduled run on all five days, attained a specific speed index, maintained a clear safety and economy record, and reached all intermediate stations one minute ahead of schedule
2. Large Dragon (*ta lung*) where the team made one safe and economical round trip and reached all intermediate stations one minute ahead of schedule
3. Medium Dragon (*chung lung*) where the team made one safe and economical one-way trip and reached all intermediate stations one minute ahead of schedule
4. Red Dragon (*hung lung,* applies to shunting engines, booster engines and those on short runs) where the team attained safe, economical, and high-speed performance marked by good cooperation.
5. Wind Dragon (*feng lung,* applies to passenger locomotives) where the team made safe, punctual, economical runs, smooth in starting and stopping

Another competitive form which exerted heavy psychological pressure on group members was the family emulation drive which was pushed early in the 1960s. In one such publicized contest a father, son, and two daughters working on closely related operations in the Tientsin No. 1 Dyeing and Weaving Mill undertook the family competition in a plantwide emulation drive for reduced waste and increased output. The standards set in the plant campaign provided the index for each family member's performance so that comparisons among the four could be made readily to show who was ahead and who was lagging. Discussion at home dealt with not only relative progress and individual improvement, but with the technical problems which each met and their solutions. The elder daughter became the lagging member of the family team and was subject at home to criticism of her shortcomings. As a result, it was claimed, she stepped up her work and became a top quality performer. The family's overall performance eventually received public praise.[40]

Another important form emulation has taken is the interplant competition. In such campaigns the number of plants involved may vary widely. The contest revolves around any one or a combination of objectives such as output or economy. One such contest was held among four sewing machine manufacturing plants in Shanghai to raise their technical level. There were over four hundred sewing machine quality norms that were made explicit. On this basis, a grading system with a maximum grade of 100 was set up, and each plant was evaluated quarterly. The lead among the four factories varied quarterly, and each one was under pressure to improve so that it could take or maintain first place. In many such campaigns a rotating red flag was given temporarily to the leader in the contests and, periodically, reevaluation could bring about a change in its custody.[41]

Since the GPCR, emulation drives have been modified in important regards to reflect more faithfully the Maoist goal to revolutionize workers' consciousness. The types of emulation drives discussed above have been denounced as "so-called emulation" developed by "Liu Shao-Ch'i and his agents" to undermine the development of genuine socialist consciousness with "production campaigns" that depend on competition rather than on social interest.[42]

Essentially the difference between the old type of emulation and "revolutionary" emulation is that in the former, success in meeting production targets was the main consideration; while in the latter, ideally the advancement of proletarian attitudes and work styles takes precedence *even if production suffers.* The ideological assumption is that even though production may suffer while proletarian consciousness and cooperation are being nurtured; production will be enhanced in the long run, because the revolutionary socialist work style is more creative and more inclined to stimulate fruitful work effort. In other words, the very condition for a better life for all individuals is collective work.[43]

Here, then, the old competitive incentive mechanisms are being transformed into cooperative devices as part of Maoist "revolutionization." In the same way as material incentives are expected to be socially oriented, so too nonmaterial incentives, which in ways similar to traditional material incentives start out oriented to the individual, are counted upon to lose their individual ("bourgeois") orientation.

Cooperative Incentives

Cooperative incentives have also been used widely in China and will be more widely and intensely employed as Maoist ideology is more extensively promulgated. Most of them contain competitive elements, but for ideological and pragmatic reasons the main emphasis is on cooperation, and after the GPCR the competitive elements were attacked and sometimes eliminated. They are considered an important means for developing a Communist society in which material incentives are no longer to be of great motivational significance. Cooperative incentives are used widely in industry to increase output, to elevate the technical production levels of new and old industrial workers, to stimulate technical innovation, to reinforce "proletarian" attitudes, and to combat "bourgeois" states of mind and practice (self-interest).

These incentives have usually involved mass participation techniques dealing with various production problems. Mass meetings have been held to discuss and review production experiences and concrete programs for improvement of performance; to deal specifically with ways of raising labor productivity; to "exploit the masses' wisdom" on how to increase output; to devise means for stimulating innovations and rationalization proposals; to raise the level of "backward" units through disseminating the experiences of "advanced" units; to rectify individual work attitudes and habits through criticism and self-criticism; in sum, to develop various aspects of decision-making. Paralleling emulation drives, and often intertwined with them, mass participation or mass movements have been used on both large-scale projects in the public's eye, such as the gigantic dam construction schemes during the GLF, as well as on less dramatic pursuits. While most of these forms were used in the USSR, the Chinese have used them in more varied ways and with greater intensity and continuity.[44]

The successful organization and utilization of China's masses for sustained economic growth rests on the regime's ability to motivate large and small groups to exert themselves in sustained fashion with relatively little material reward. Success in the conception and execution of cooperative incentives is one means of achieving this end. A social psychological breakthrough here would unleash millions of extra workdays with minimal economic cost and reinforce the proletarian qualities the Maoists hold in high esteem. The doctrinal rationale for cooperative incentives is not inconsistent with certain advanced social psychological theories and practice that see behavior modification in terms of token rewards and interactions which increase group solidarity.[45]

Cooperative incentives often have operated in ways paralleling what contemporary social psychological theory prescribes for increasing psychic productivity. The effective operation of certain types of group decision making, criticism, and goal-oriented mass movements is predicated on fundamental psychological needs being met. The individual's needs for affection, for a sense of being included in important affairs, and for feeling some control or influence over events which shape his life may be positively carried out through some or all of these cooperative incentives.[46]

Even if the heavy reliance of the CCP on incentives (particularly the nonmaterial type in recent years) has reasonable expectations in psychological terms, the question of micro- and macroeconomic efficacy remains. Much of the conventional wisdom would place weighty emphasis on allocative efficiency and customary heavy capital formation and downgrade the growth effects of incentives. But a growing body of economic literature questions this and focuses on the much greater potential for growth through organizational and motivational changes and investment in human capital. It is just this configuration—stress on human factors: the "role of man"—which is at the core of the Maoist strategy for economic development and transformation of human consciousness.[47]

Communist reliance on the fervor of the worker has been a salient means of increasing output. For example, a mass campaign to increase coal output sharply was based on the "revolutionary zeal" of the miners. The campaign was carefully organized to control the production efforts of the miners through education and psychological pressure. The blueprint for executing the campaign plans was set forth: first, about one hundred fifty cadres were convened in a conference held by a party committee to undergo orientation on the existing conditions, the desired output goals, likely problems, and the necessary approach to the workers. The cadres were then sent to organize about two hundred fifty mass meetings among their respective working groups in which the tasks ahead were projected, and heavy doses of indoctrination were also dispensed. The miners were made aware of all key points in the production process. The meetings also made explicit individual and group production guarantees. The aim was to give every miner the sense that the success of the campaign was inextricably linked with and dependent upon his efforts being linked to those of the others. These activities resemble production conferences in the Soviet Union.[48]

Another technique aimed at increasing labor input through heightened cooperation involved public evaluation of workers, an aspect of the "evaluate-rectify work-style" movement (*Chen-tun tso-feng*). In the 1950s, the emphasis was on criticism and self-criticism; in the 1960s the meetings stressed praise rather than criticism; since the GPCR the two are combined in mass struggle-criticism-transformation sessions. The first method was supposed to lead to improved individual performance positively through intensifying identification with the group or negatively through fear of lowered status. The second method aimed at better individual work habits through closer group integration.[49]

Another method employed to arouse worker ardor has been mass decision making, developed during the GLF as an aspect of political emphasis and control in industrial plants. In industry, decision-making authority was moved from the manager to the party committee and today is in the hands of the revolutionary committees which were set up after the GPCR.

Mass decision making does not mean that the workers make managerial decisions, but rather that they discuss basic management alternatives, under party guidance, and come to conclusions as to what the "correct" decision is and why it is so. Perhaps they contribute to the ultimate decision through occasional insightful suggestions, but the main consideration from the viewpoint of cooperative incentives is the psychological impact of such decision-making meetings on the individual and group. If the individual feels that he is contributing to the group "decision," that he has some "control" over it, his interest in and involvement with the group aim will probably be greater than if he feels only that he is one of many workers going through onerous motions to make a meager living. Workers with a deep sense of solidarity can more effectively carry out work chores than a set of alienated individuals.[50]

Another type of mass participation technique is the exchange of technical experiences between "advanced" and "backward" individuals and groups. In its earlier form the emphasis was on individuals and small groups and was mainly competitive. In the 1960s the stress was on larger groups in which "comparing, learning from, over-taking, and helping" became the means by which large masses were to raise significantly their contributions to production. After the GPCR such emulation practices were developed further with leading groups used to stimulate and teach those who were less advanced.[51]

This campaign has been developed to put large numbers of workers in direct contact with one another. For example, over a period of a year numerous factory directors, technical and managerial staff employees, and rank-and-file workers in industry traveled to Shanghai, Tientsin, and

Workers exchange experiences in water recharging at Shanghai No. 17 State Cotton Mill (China Pictorial, 7, 1972, p. 4)

Shenyang to exchange their work experiences and learn skills, techniques, and procedures from their opposite numbers; and advanced units have returned these visits to teach them. This mass movement's aim was to make comparison of work experience an effective means of transferring knowledge, arousing interest, and raising production.[52]

These various cooperative nonmaterial incentives have been modified and integrated as a result of the upheaval of the GPCR. Many individualistic features of earlier mechanisms have been discarded as workers have been exhorted to transform their pursuit of "self-interest" into a zealous concern for the interest of the work group, the plant, and society.

The national model for workers in industry to follow in meeting the various demands of production is the worker group of the Tach'ing oil fields. The great success of these exemplary workers was in constructing in three years, through practicing "self-reliance, hard work [and] diligence and thrift," a modern petroleum base on the desolate plains of Heilungkiang Province which has made China self-sufficient in the manufacture of this important fuel. In 1964, Mao called upon industry "to learn from Tach'ing," and ever since that time this work group has been projected throughout China as one to be emulated.[53]

The Tach'ing model for cooperatively motivated labor input operates *in addition* to the standard wage scale which each worker of a particular skill level receives for his work. The generation of greater worker output depends upon the effective implementation of several features of a nonmaterial incentive mechanism set forth in the Anshan Iron and Steel Company Constitution. The mechanism's five components are: (1) "politics are firmly in command": all plant activity including production is subordinate to considerations of plant, regional, and national policy considerations as defined by Mao's thought; (2) party leadership is strengthened and constantly defined for the workers; (3) vigorous mass movements are to be launched as problems dictate: workers are to be involved in mass campaigns requiring elaborate educational and technical preparation and continuous feedback once the campaign (say, converting waste material into usable raw materials) is under way; (4) institute cadre participation in labor, worker participation in management, reform of irrational and outdated rules and regulations, and effect close cooperation among cadres, workers, and technicians: flexible and innovative production practices are to be encouraged through cooperative interaction of various tiers of personnel; and (5) accelerate technical revolution: shape modern technological knowledge to the special needs and constraints of Chinese industrial reality. This configuration of a team of workers of all levels dealing with an array of routine as well as particular work problems without regard to the usual considerations (rules, regulations, job definitions, etcetera) is the model which the Maoists expect will unleash great quantities of enthusiastic labor input and will increase social solidarity and through that sustain rising levels of output—without increasing wage outlays.[54]

In the unceasing pressure on workers to raise the quality and quantity of their labor, the dynamic ideological model of "struggle-criticism-transformation" is invoked to resolve conflicts (contradictions). The first phase, struggle, calls for definition of the problem, discussion of its many aspects, and analysis of the experience of other units by all those confronted with the problem. Then there ensues an expression of opinion on the best solution to the problem. Since these opinions will vary and contradict one another, the second phase, criticism, is set in motion. The profered solutions are subject to the mandate of "politics in command" and therefore must meet the interests of the larger community and society. Critics in sessions also inflict censure upon individuals expressing "bourgeois" ideas and force rectification of erroneous views of individuals and groups. The resolution of the problem, intellectually, is the final phase, transformation, in which the correct model for action is agreed upon with criticisms of ideas, attitudes, and approaches having been assimilated, and a new, more advanced awareness of the problem and how to meet it emerging.[55]

Five

Organizing and Managing Workers

Implementing labor policies effectively, including the incentive system already reviewed, demands more than the mere proclamation of party policy to workers. Some organizational structure, either separate from or a special part of the internal plant or enterprise administrative machinery, is required if the canons of industrial discipline are to be operationally effective. Various possible mechanisms exist, but, as in other Communist countries, the CCP has, until the GPCR and now in 1973 again, relied heavily on trade-unions to carry the responsibility for maintaining the morale and discipline of the work force.

The trade-unions in China have carried out several functions: acting as a "transmission belt" in communicating and executing CCP directives, agitating to maximize output, carrying out a wide range of political education to heighten the activism and consciousness of workers, and administering an array of programs affecting workers' welfare (social insurance, safety regulations, wage mechanisms, etcetera). Trade-unions have been a nonparty, mass organization implementing important party policies in which "the party committee [in the plant] exercises over-all leadership over the trade unions all the time." [1] The extent to which emphasis has been placed on two of these functions has varied in line with policy changes in other areas. The "transmission belt" and administrative functions have been relatively constant, but maximization of plant output and propagation of ideological education have been pushed differentially as the CCP's major strategic policies have been modified.

Trade-union accent on production or political education usually entailed a group of related policies revolving around each of these. When political education was the main thrust of trade-union activity, organizational decentralization was also pushed with a larger role being given to the regional (horizontal) trade-union apparatus. Reliance was placed on young, rising union leaders who were not so professional and bureaucratized (more "red" than "expert"). When ideology and decentralization were stressed, so were nonmaterial more socially oriented incentives. In the opposite policy model, there was emphasis on production; centralized vertical (industrial) union organizational activity in which older, more "expert" leaders held rein; one-man management operated in factories; and material incentives with economism (increasing material emoluments as means to greater production) holding sway. The Maoist view has given highest priority to ideological education as a primary moving power for industrialization through first socializing workers and industry with deemphasis on economism and compulsion and more reliance on participatory forms of political education, struggle, and mass movements. Proper ideological control by the party over the trade-unions would reduce bureaucratic tendencies.

Reviewing trade-union policy since 1949 reveals periods in which either one of the two policy models or a mixture of both, neither predominant, obtained. Trade-union emphasis on production emerged most clearly in the beginning period of the FFYP, 1953 to 1955. The political education policy model was approximated during the GLF, 1958 to 1960, and during parts of the GPCR. In the period from 1961 to 1965, after the disarray of the GLF, policy turned sharply in the direction of production emphasis though the Maoist preference for political education was reflected in the widespread socialist education movement and other trade-union-sponsored mass movements. In the two periods, 1949 through 1952 and 1955 through 1957, trade-union policy clearly involved a mixture of both production emphasis and political education.[2]

Overall the Chinese trade-unions have not been utilized so widely, continuously, and vigorously as have the Soviet trade-unions in direct stimulation of production through conventional economic incentives. This characteristic of the Chinese trade-union scene arises from ideological and pragmatic motives. It is clear in the Maoist framework that political consideration about revolutionary consciousness, struggle against "bourgeois" ideas, and egalitarian ideals has prevailed over economic factors. Deviations from this set, especially in the period from 1953 to 1955 and, to lesser degrees, in the time spans of 1955 to 1957 and 1961 to 1965, occurred because of either the temporary ascendancy of non-Maoist leaders or the exigencies of the post-GLF economic contraction. The overwhelming predominance of China's peasants in the work force confronts CCP leaders with the need to minimize the gap between worker and peasant income. To allow that gap to widen, therefore, would be to court labor misallocation and peasant discontent. Implementation of an array of material production goads in industry might raise industrial production at the expense of peasant labor disaffection with a deleterious effect on capital formation projects in the countryside. The injunction of Lai Jo-yu, then head of the ACFTU, in December 1957 that "the living standards of the workers should not be too high compared with that of the peasants," reflects, even while the outstanding industrial success of the FFYP was being enjoyed, the extent to which the peasant was a prime factor in policy prescription.[3]

The Ideological Basis of Chinese Trade Unions

The different roles that Marxist ideology dictates for trade-unions to play under capitalism and under communism are quite clear. Under capitalism trade-unions are important instruments in the revolutionary struggle: they are targets for Communist penetration and domination, and they may serve as actual instruments in the struggle leading to the seizure of power. In either situation they become proving grounds for shaping groups of workers into effective cadres for realizing Communist goals. Through active participation in trade-union work, communists expect to demonstrate that they consistently and devotedly pursue the interests of the working class.[4]

The responsibilities that trade-unions are to carry out once the revolution has triumphed are also clear. In the Soviet Union's early history the assumption that since the trade unions were leading units of the industrial working class, they would naturally fulfill requirements of the revolution was dramatically shattered by opposition of trade-union leaders to certain party policies. The early notion that the trade-unions were to be autonomous and not part of the governmental and state apparatus yielded to the now more universally accepted idea that the trade-unions are subordinate to the state and the party and are to coordinate their activities as outlined in party and governmental pronouncements.[5]

As Marxist ideology has evolved in the USSR, the trade-union has become an important vehicle for advancing the program of the party and the government. For the Soviet party, the interests of the proletariat and the socialist state have been considered as one, the main avenues for trade-union activities being clearly marked: increasing production, political education extending welfare and cultural activities of workers, and protecting workers against various defects in working conditions. Contradictions between workers and the state or party were assumed away. Since the interest of the proletariat and the state is safeguarded by the Communist party, its control over trade-union policy is decisive. To insure this control party members occupy the most important trade-union posts, especially at the highest levels of the trade-union movement, in both the USSR and China.

In China, however, Mao has introduced an important ideological qualification to this view that has affected labor policy significantly: contradictions continue after the revolution both *between* the people and the "enemy" and *among* the people. This means that conflicts between workers and the trade-unions, the party, the government, etcetera are not only to be expected but may be aggravated because of "bureaucratic practices of certain state functionaries" and are not to be resolved by "coercive, high-handed methods." As a result, labor policy in China has been more flexible and less authoritarian than in the USSR.[6]

The legal basis of trade-union activity in China is found in the Constitution of the People's Republic of China and in a variety of labor laws and regulations enacted since 1950. The Constitution broadly defines workers' rights and obligations. Various labor laws and regulations spell out in greater detail the structure through which rights and obligations are carried out.

Without actually mentioning the words *trade-union,* the Constitution defines generally what workers are expected to do and what they can expect in return from government and society. Article 1 places workers in the forefront of the society: "The People's Republic of China is a people's democratic state led by the working class and based on the alliance of workers and peasants." In Article 16 the state's role in encouraging "the working enthusiasm and creativeness of citizens" is set forth after work has been labeled a matter of honor. Articles 91, 92, 93, and 100 complete the broad delineation of workers' rights in China. Article 91 asserts the right to work and requires that the state "gradually [provide] more employment, [improve] working conditions and [increase] wages, amenities and benefits." Article 92 puts forward the workers' right to rest and leisure and requires prescribed working hours and systems of vacation. Article 93 establishes the basis for social insurance: "Working people in the People's Republic of China have the right to material assistance in old age, and in case of illness or disability. To ensure that working people can enjoy this right, the state provides social insurance, social assistance and public health services and gradually expands these facilities." And Article 100 enjoins citizens to "observe labour discipline." [7]

The Constitution's failure to mention trade-unions in any way resulted from the fact that it was adopted the year after the adoption of a constitution of the trade-unions which deals extensively with their membership, organizational structure, and financing. Its preamble sets forth clearly the way trade-unions are to contribute to the early realization of the regime's economic goals. Since "the interests of the state and the common interest of the entire people constitute the fundamental interests of the working class," trade-unions are called upon to "strive for the development of production, for the constant increase of labour productivity, for the fulfillment and over-fulfillment of the production plans of the state, for the speedy industrialization of the country and for the steady advance towards socialism." Although trade-unions are also counted upon to be concerned with improving living and working conditions, since they are expected to act as "firm social pillars of the people's democratic state," and since the duty of trade-unions "to raise production" is reiterated several times as conforming to the fundamental interests of workers, it is clear in the context of the early 1950s that the priorities of economic growth strategy placed the raising of production and the increase in labor productivity at the top of the scale of functions for trade-unions. In the view of CCP leaders, the trade-unions are "transmission belts between the Party and the masses" and the interests of the workers were viewed as encompassing those of all the people and the state.[8]

Trade-unions have a well-defined relation to management: they are expected to "strengthen their unity and cooperation with the management of the enterprises concerned. This is an important question that has a direct bearing on whether fulfillment of the tasks assigned by the party and state can be insured and whether the trade unions can play their full role as a pillar of the proletarian dictatorship." In this context, trade-unions are expected to "support the management in every sphere of its work, organize the workers successfully to fulfill the state plan as well as tasks assigned by the management and observe the rules and regulations of the enterprise."[9]

The Structure of Trade Unions

Union structure has had a dualistic nature, both vertical and horizontal. Operating unions are organized on an industrial basis, drawing membership from blue- and white-collar workers, and on a local and regional basis. The national industrial unions are vertically integrated while local, provincial, and regional units, organized horizontally to represent the variety of industrial unions in the geographic area, parallel structurally the government and party organization. The peak of the organizational pyramid is the All-China Federation of Trade-Unions, the national trade-union center, representing in 1965 about twenty-one million workers. The ACFTU derives its mandate from the All-China Congress of Trade-Unions (ACCTU), to be convened every five years. The dualistic character of the union structure has allowed for flexible emphasis: when policy has stressed production and one-man management, the more centralized, vertical structure has lent itself to effective policy implementation; when policy has stressed politics, struggle, and local initiative, the more decentralized, horizontal apparatus has been more useful.[10]

The basic unit in the factory, mine, or other enterprise is the primary trade-union committee comprised of at least ten members. Where fewer than ten are employed in an enterprise, they may join the nearest basic trade-union unit or establish a basic unit with others. Each primary trade-union organization is shaped according to guidelines prescribed in the constitution of the trade-unions. The membership elects a chairman and several vice-chairmen and establishes the permanent or temporary working committees required by the nature of the basic unit. The general membership is supposed to meet at least once a year to receive and approve reports on the activities of the basic unit and its auditing commission, to receive reports on the enterprise's administration, to define the aims and programs of the basic unit, and to elect the various leaders and committees of the unit.[11]

Depending on enterprise structure, other trade-union organizational sub-units may be established. The primary trade-union committee may set up department committees to carry out trade-union activity in specific enterprise departments. Each department committee elects a chairman and, if it is large enough, several vice-chairmen as well as the necessary working committees to carry out its functions adequately. Below the department level, trade-union units may be formed according to the production or office operating organization. Each of these units elects a group leader and, if required, a deputy leader, as well as a labor protection inspector, a labor insurance steward, and cultural and educational assistants for the group leader. In these ways the local trade-union unit is organized down to the actual operating unit.[12]

Where the basic trade-union unit is large enough, full-time trade-union functionaries are provided to carry out the work of the trade-union on a continuing basis. The number of workers employed in the productive or administrative unit (factory, mine, business establishment, farm, institution, or school) determines how many full-time trade-union officials are required. The following table gives the numerical basis for full-time trade-union officials:

Number of Workers and Staff	Number of Full-Time Trade-Union Officials
200– 500	1
501–1000	2
1001–1500	3
1501–2500	4
2501–4000	5

Where over 4000 workers are employed, another full-time official may be added for every additional 2000 workers. In enterprises with fewer than 200 workers the primary trade-union unit may employ a full-time trade-union official. With the permission of a higher trade-union committee, the full-time trade-union officials are paid by the trade-union at a level at least equal to that of their previous income. Such paid officials are guaranteed their original jobs or jobs at the same rate of pay after they complete their term of office.[13]

Space, equipment, and facilities for the use of trade-union committees must be provided by management. When 100 or more workers are employed, separate offices, furniture, and utility facilities are to be made available gratis. If fewer than 100 employees are in an enterprise, and separate offices cannot be provided, then special desks are to be set aside for trade-union use. In either event, space for general membership meetings or representative conferences is to be set aside.[14]

Trade-unions' funds derive from membership admission fees, membership dues, proceeds from trade-union events, and management contributions. The admission fee for new members is 1 percent of the total wage in the month preceding admission. Membership dues are also 1 percent of the member's monthly wage. Income is also received from cultural and sport activities carried on under trade-union auspices. The management of each enterprise is required each month to pay 2 percent of the total wages of all workers, including payments in kind, to the trade-unions. Three fourths of this amount is set aside for the promotion of cultural and educational activities for workers. All trade-union funds are to be expended in conformity with budgets which have been approved by their higher trade-union organization and must be in accord with regulations of the ACFTU. Reports on a regular basis both to membership and to the higher trade-union units are required. Such reports on financial accounts are examined and validated by the chairman of the auditing commission.[15]

In 1965 there were 160,000 primary trade-union units organized into national industrial unions. Although each primary trade-union sets up its own leadership group, it is also subject to direction by the higher level national industrial union officials who in turn transmit policy prescriptions from the national union federation and the Communist party. In similar fashion, trade-union federation congresses and regional, municipal, and county trade-union councils provide doctrinal leadership to all the trade-union units in their various areas. In 1965 there were twenty-one provincial, two municipal, and five autonomous regional trade-union councils.[16]

Each of the sixteen national trade-unions has the same organizational structure. (The sixteen national unions include memberships composed of heavy industry workers, light industry workers, coal miners, petroleum workers, water conservancy and electrical workers, machinery workers, textile workers, building workers, geological workers, railway workers, road transport workers, seamen, post and telecommunications workers, agricultural and forestry workers, financial and commercial workers, and educational workers. Perhaps there is a seventeenth national union for the defense industry.) The national union is organized by its national congress (as the ACFTU is by the ACCTU) which is to convene every three or four years and is comprised of representatives from the various trade-union bodies whose members are in the industrial activity defined by the national union throughout the country. The national congress elects the national committee which runs the national union in the periods between congresses, carrying out the congress's directives as well as those of the ACFTU and electing a presidium to direct the national union's continuing activity. The congress receives and approves reports made by the national committee. Likewise reports of authorities of the government are received and policies enunciated before the membership. In this context, the congress defines and shapes the policies and goals of its national union, retaining the power to amend and approve regulations of the national union. The main function of the national union is like that of all hierarchic trade-union groups: to act as a "transmission belt" in the continuous campaign to mobilize China's workers for the purposes of the party.[17]

The hierarchic organization of trade-unions cutting across industrial lines proceeds from the locality up through the other geographic subdivisions leading eventually to the national level. It parallels the organizational relationships from the primary trade-union group to the national industrial union with the ACFTU at the peak. At each geographic level there is an organized unit which brings together all trade-union organizations within that jurisdiction regardless of the industrial function at the primary level. (This is analogous to the city trade-union councils and state federations of labor organizational structure of trade-unions in the United States.)

Starting with the basic industrial trade-unions at the enterprise level and leading up through a geographic hierarchy to the ACFTU, trade-union representatives from the operating primary trade-unions in each administrative unit (that is, town, county, province and so forth) are organized into units cutting horizontally across the industrial trade-union structure. This parallels the organization within each industrial trade-union from the local operating unit up to the national industrial unit organization. In the administrative pyramid that reaches to the ACFTU from the many local trade unions, an effective structure is realized for the purposes of implementing those trade-union and related functions which transcend narrower industrial union concerns. The industrial union hierarchic organization from the actual operating units to city, provincial, and national industrial union organizations is directed toward solving those trade-union problems which relate specifically to output and productivity in the actual industries covered by the industrial organizational units. Functions such as ideological and political education and mass production campaigns and emulation drives can be carried out more effectively by units that cut across industrial lines as the horizontal geographic organization does.

For each geographic area, congresses with representatives of the various industrial unions are to be convened every two years. These congresses receive reports on trade-union activities and the auditing commissions of their respective levels, define broad trade-union tasks, and elect auditing commissions and the trade-union committees for the respective levels. Congresses of trade-union councils of cities under provincial jurisdiction and of industrial unions in cities and mining areas are to be convened every year by their respective committees. In the periods between congresses, committees of provincial and city trade-union councils and industrial unions implement the last congress's decisions. These committees carry on the everyday work that has to be done through elected chairmen and vice-chairmen and members who make up a standing committee.[18]

Members of trade-union committees elected by the workers are required to be protected against sudden transfer or discharge by management. The trade-union law states that such management action requires prior trade-union committee approval. The trade-union committee on which the member to be transferred or discharged sits must not only give its consent but must report to the next higher trade-union committee for its approval; then, according to the trade-union law, transfer or discharge is permitted.[19]

The ACCTU, which had met every four years up to 1957, when the interval between meetings was extended to five years, is the representative body of all trade-union groups from which it derives its mandate and powers. This national congress broadly sets forth major trade-union tasks and selects those who will direct the activities of the national trade-union federation on a day-to-day basis. A complex of continuing functions is carried out from day to day by the ACFTU and its various departments for the units represented in the congress.

The ACCTU, which gives legitimacy and structure to the ACFTU, focuses on the means to help fulfill the economic goals of the party and the government and relates the Chinese labor movement to fraternal labor movements throughout the non-Communist and Communist world. In carrying out the first function it elects its executive committee (140 members and 69 alternates in 1957) and receives and approves their reports; it also amends when necessary the constitution of the trade unions. In defining the tasks and policies of Chinese trade unions, the congress receives economic planning reports of different units of the central government. Its deliberations reflect the major concern of trade unions in taking all necessary measures to guarantee that workers make a maximum contribution to production and take all steps necessary to insure that economic plans are fulfilled or overfulfilled. The ACFTU reached the rank and file daily through its newspaper, *Kung-jen jih-pao,* or *Workers' Daily,* until its suspension at the end of 1966. The Chinese labor movement's relationship to the international working-class movement has been defined by the congress whose representatives visit other countries as delegates to their national trade-union meetings and also have participated in the activities of the World Federation of Trade-Unions. Foreign delegations from Communist and non-Communist countries, in turn, have visited China and attended sessions of the congress. During 1966 while the GPCR was under way the ACFTU ceased paying dues to the WFTU which the CCP considered was dominated by the USSR.[20]

The executive committee of the ACFTU, which is elected by the congress, is charged with implementation of the congress's decisions and direction of trade-union activity throughout the nation. Its plenary session elects a presidium, a secretariat, a chairman, and several vice-chairmen. In effect it is the presidium of the executive committee which carries on the activities of the ACFTU, holding four meetings a year. The secretariat carries on routine bureaucratic activities while the presidium is responsible mainly for execution of policies of the national congress and the plenary session of the executive committee.[21] (See Appendix D for income and expenditures of the ACFTU.)

During the GPCR the trade-unions, allied to Liu Shao-Ch'i's faction, were under attack by the Red Guards, and by the end of 1966 the ACFTU and the entire trade-union apparatus were suspended. The trade-unions and in particular the leaders of the ACFTU were closely related to the CCP hierarchy, and thus the assault on the CCP perforce required an attack on organizational allies which opposed the Maoist line. The trade-unions were also assailed for their "economism," their emphasis on production and development of professional skill, and their being a "trade-union of all the people," accepting for membership exlandlords, excapitalists, etcetera instead of being instruments of "class struggle." The suspension of the trade-unions posed, therefore, the structural problem of temporary or permanent replacement of the old trade-union hierarchy if the policy and administrative functions of the ACFTU were to be carried out.[22]

For some time trade-union functions apparently were carried on in an ad hoc manner, and then a substitute structure was set up beginning in late 1967 with the establishment of numerous workers' congresses under the initiative of the revolutionary committees the GPCR spawned to replace the regular CCP organization with Maoist organs. The new congresses were expected to carry out vigorously the political education, propaganda, and "struggle" functions of the old trade-unions, while combatting "self-interest" and repudiating "revisionism, unionism, syndicalism and economism." These novel labor groups were shaped to the struggle-criticism-transformation (political and psychological) mechanism which the Maoists increasingly employ in their efforts to transmute the worker's and peasant's consciousness.[23]

This ad hoc execution of trade-union functions is apparently coming to an end, and trade-unions are now in different stages of reactivation over much of China. The process has been in effect since early 1971 when reference was made to ACFTU activities, and it appears to be following the pattern of post-GPCR reorganization of the party first and then nonparty mass organizations. The 1973 New Year's joint party-PLA editorial (in *Jenmin jih-pao, Hung-ch'i,* and *Liberation Daily*) called for the rebuilding of the trade-unions and other mass organizations. Since then, in the spring of 1973, trade-union congresses have been held or are in preparation in major industrial centers of China: Shanghai, Peking, Harbin, Shenyang,

Taiyuan, Sian, Hofei, Hangchow, Chengtu, and Huhehot. New leading groups have been elected from these congresses and similar congresses have been held or are in preparation in provinces, municipalities, autonomous regions, and other cities.[24]

The movement to reorganize and reactivate the trade-unions is now clearly under way. Apparently CCP leaders feel that the Liuist elements among workers have been eliminated or transformed, and that trade-unions can now carry out more effectively their political and ideological role without fear of revisionist errors. *Jen-min jih-pao,* or *People's Daily,* in Peking finds that "the ranks of the Chinese working class have become purer . . . and are now more united and militant. China's working class . . . is worthy to be the leading class. . . ." The trade-unions are now expected to carry out the fundamental task—"to grasp class struggle firmly and persist in the socialist revolution. Perhaps the next step will be the resurrection of *Kung-jen jih-pao* or *Workers' Daily.*" [25]

Trade-Union Functions

In all Communist countries trade-unions carry out the same functions. They transmit the party line to workers, encourage production through a variety of techniques, engage in political education, and execute a range of welfare chores (social insurance, spare-time education, safety regulations, recreation, etcetera). In China, as has already been suggested, the emphasis on production and political education has varied, reflecting an important ideological and existential difference of view among party groups. With the end of the GPCR and the success of the Maoist group, their fundamental stress on political education and class struggle has emerged more clearly and strongly. The higher utility value that they place on political education reflects a basic conflict with older party views. Starting with the notion that if workers are effectively indoctrinated and organized ideologically they can increase production prodigiously, the Maoists see revolutionary order and commitment as ideologically and pragmatically superior to the Soviet mix of economism and compulsion.

The trade-union's role as "transmission belt" has been unequivocally set forth time and again by party ideologues: "trade unions must be completely subject to the unified leadership of the party and give full play to their organizational role under this leadership. This is a basic principle for carrying out well trade union work." This leads inevitably to party programs taking precedence over other considerations typifying the Leninist doctrine of "politics in command" which the Maoists have extended further so that class struggle comes before production. The party requires the trade-union, therefore, to coordinate its activities in line with the attainment of political goals.

In its work, the trade union must also strengthen its unity in cooperation with the management of the enterprise. This . . . insures fulfillment of the tasks of the party and the state [in which] the trade union, like the management of an enterprise, works under the unified leadership of the party. [Its] basic task is the same—to run socialist enterprises successfully by relying on the masses for fulfilling the tasks assigned by the party and the state. . . .[26]

The encouragement of production has usually been a principal role played by trade-unions in Communist countries. This has also been so in China where the Trade-Union Law calls upon trade-unions to "educate and organize the workers and staff members to adopt a new attitude towards labour, to observe labour discipline; organize labour emulation drives and other production campaigns in order to ensure the fulfillment of the production plans." [27] In this context, the goal of maximum output has been the paramount one with all trade-union efforts being coordinated toward that aim. Over time and with the increasing pervasiveness of Maoist doctrine, however, the goal has become Communist consciousness or revolutionary commitment to the group. Not that production is anathema, but rather that proper Communist consciousness leads to maximum output in the long run and it, rather than production, requires the continuous attention of the trade-union as well as of other cadres.

Before the GPCR the trade-unions emphasized, with varying degrees of intensity, the importance of generating more and better labor input to fuel expanding output. The particular tactics and techniques employed differed according to the period, following the pattern defined at the outset of this chapter. When the Soviet model was being closely followed, from 1953 to 1955, the trade-unions cooperated with the individual managers to stimulate workers with economic goads and to discipline them to the output mandates of the FFYP. At other times production was encouraged through nonmaterial ways: during the GLF the focus shifted markedly as political indoctrination with revolutionary exhortation became the central labor focus for the time.

In directly aiding production, trade-unions have not followed the methods familiar in Western industrial countries. Wages were established by the central administration once the economy was coordinated in the mid-1950s. Unions played a role in handling grievances, but that role was often shared and was not usually decisive. When production schedules were set or speeded up, the union's main obligation was to reinforce them and to determine the norms for work discipline to be followed by all workers. When violations occurred the trade-union cadres were expected to put pressure on the offending workers. The unions kept workers aware of the importance of production goals in the interests of society and themselves.[28]

When the focus was still on production, but the means were mainly nonmaterial, the trade-unions carried a major responsibility. They were called upon to elicit greater amounts of work and to interest workers in new jobs often at remote locations. This demanded not only effective implementation of the various incentive mechanisms but also careful day-by-day oversight of workers to insure that norms were being met and, where problems arose, to make certain that they were resolved correctly at once.

Following the leadership of the CCP, the trade-unions relied on their officers and *activists* to execute their responsibilities to maximize labor input. Conceived as "bridges between the trade unions and the masses," activists are trade-union members who commit themselves to carry on specific trade-union chores (e.g., chairman of a workshop trade-union group) in addition to their full-time production duties. They are the eyes and the ears of the union in the basic work units, and the successful implementation of trade-union production policy depends on their competence and ideological commitment. The number and effectiveness of these trade-union sergeants and corporals have varied considerably among the over one hundred fifty thousand primary trade-unions in China. Ideally trade-union leaders aim at recruiting as many activists as possible, since production plans can best be realized if every worker is fully committed and exercises himself in every way to bring about their realization. In one engineering processing plant in 1962, activists totaled 31 percent of all workers, a quite substantial group, rising from fewer than 1 percent in 1959.[29]

To evoke the worker response essential to greater and better quality labor input in the positions and places where needed, the trade-unions pursue various tactics. They see that material incentive mechanisms operate smoothly, uncovering problems which may arise; and they also attempt to eliminate bugs in the wage schedules. At the same time they carry out special programs tailored to particular aspects of work performance. Mass or selective emulation drives may aim at more output, less waste, or better products. Group campaigns are organized in which model or "advanced" workers tutor the "backward" to imitate their more efficient and diligent performance. Or the groups are oriented to improve their work habits by exposure to technical demonstrations. Unworthy workers whose absenteeism, tardiness, or laggard execution of work tasks threatens labor discipline and attainment of production quotas are fair game for reform. Campaigns to stimulate worker innovation or rationalization proposals are coordinated with plans to implement product restyling.

In the effort to mount these programs successfully, trade-unions have used various techniques. Mass decision making, criticism, self-criticism, study groups, and the like, treated at greater length in chapter 4, are all employed to achieve the same ends that properly structured material incentives aim at but do not always reach under the best of conditions. In all of these methods, however, the trade-union's officers and activists have had a major role to play, and their successful performance has sometimes had a great bearing on the extent to which greater and better labor input result.

Political education suffuses all trade-union functions and has always been given an important role as an ideological "school for communism" even when production has been greatly stressed. In its usual operation, political education has exhibited dual aspects: to indoctrinate workers in the party's modernization and industrialization goals and to socialize and raise workers' consciousness toward the end of shaping Communist man. The former role has tied in neatly with efforts to maximize production; the latter has often been in tension with immediate production objectives and has been zealously pursued in periods of great revolutionary agitation such as the GLF and the GPCR.

Harnessing political education in the service of maximizing production was developed as a technique during the 1950s when a variety of emulation campaigns, such as those illustrated in chapter 4, were mounted. These campaigns were focused principally on increasing the production of an individual, a work team, a plant, or an industry in which the goal was unequivocally to raise production.

In the GLF, during certain aspects of the socialist education movement from 1962 to 1965, and in the GPCR, emulation campaigns were mounted in which the purpose was clearly to advance "class struggle," raise "revolutionary fervor," or combat "self-interest and economism." The coordination of trade-union work with these more purely psychological goals of political education, following party dictates, has become the recent hallmark of Maoist policy: "if people concentrate on production without putting

Worker meeting, Shanghai Boiler Plant (China Pictorial, *5, 1973, p. 2*)

proletarian politics in command, they will be led astray and serve the restoration of capitalism." [30] Transformation in the consciousness of man takes priority over production with the doctrinal notions that unless man change, any success in production will lead to "revisionism"; and the successful transmutation of man must in the long run generate robust output: "so long as we are imbued with the revolutionary spirit of self-reliance and hard struggle, we can create what we lack materially." [31]

In pursuit of direct ideological rather than production objectives, trade-union as well as party cadres have been charged with responsibility for effective political education of workers. Toward that end class struggle goals have been stressed: mass ideological movements, group study of Mao's thought, struggle-criticism-transformation sessions, development of joint worker-party-army groups in factories, revolutionary emulation, and the like have been carried on unceasingly. Negative attitudes such as "trade-unions for welfare," "production first," "technique first," "self-interest," "economism," have been denounced constantly. Positive traits of selflessness, political awareness, cooperation, and class consciousness have been stressed and reinforced in all such political education techniques. [32]

In socialist revolutionary emulation, one of the pure forms of political education, distinction is made between it and earlier emulation forms in which production was stimulated by competitive contests among individuals and work units. Such a revolutionary emulation was started in 1969 by the Peking Capital Iron and Steel Company, never considered a model of productive efficiency in earlier years, which exhorted workers to "grasp revolution." The enterprise's goals were broadly psychological and organizational with no reliance on any material or individual rewards such as more wages or bonuses or money prizes. Five main points were set forth for the campaign: (1) the use of Mao's thought and mass criticism to develop revolutionary consciousness; (2) revolutionization of cadres' thinking through their regular participation in labor; (3) aim at higher and economical output for the building of socialism and defense; (4) elimination of unreasonable rules and regulations; and (5) stimulation of mass involvement in technical innovations. Though some of these goals might have been found in earlier nonrevolutionary emulation, the essential quality of revolutionary emulation is clearly different. Achieving correct socialist awareness and behavior takes precedence over greater production. Better to have production suffer and proper attitudes developed than the opposite. And ideally, the development of proper attitudes will lead to greater output. [33]

The trade-union's concern with "the material and cultural life" of workers extends into several areas: factory safety; administration of the various social insurance programs; and the provision of social, cultural, recreational, and other facilities. To the extent that these trade-union responsibilities are carried out effectively the workers' levels of living and quality of life are improved.[34]

The commitment of the CCP and the Chinese government to insuring safe working conditions has been set forth unequivocally and emphasized in many documents. In the Common Programme adopted in 1949, in the Constitution, in the Trade-Union Law, in the Trade-Union Constitution, in decisions and regulations of the State Council, in instructions on safety given by Mao Tse-tung, and in many other pronouncements and works, the fundamental importance of safety in industrial plants and other working situations has been reiterated. To carry out this commitment a structure of regulations and inspections supervised by the trade-unions and aimed at making working conditions as safe as possible has been erected. To the extent that safety requirements conflict with production fulfillment plans, the primacy of the latter may weaken safety controls. Mao himself sensed the problem: "if attention is paid only to [increasing production and practicing economy] while [safety and health are] forgotten or neglected even to a small extent, this is a mistake." [35]

The importance of securing workers against safety and health hazards in factories and mines is self-evident, especially in an industrializing economy with poor quality and rapidly expanding work force, extensive old machinery, and much new machinery being introduced rapidly. Practical considerations of worker morale and productivity make labor protection a realm of great importance for any economy aspiring to rapid industrialization, a situation which is acknowledged explicitly by party leaders.

The primary trade-union is responsible for checking factories and mines to insure adherence to safety and sanitation regulations. The ACFTU and the Ministry of Labor have jointly carried out these regulations in the past. The maintenance of safety and sanitation standards is assigned to plant management, and labor protection departments have been established in large and medium-sized firms. In smaller units special personnel are selected to supervise the implementation of standards determining working conditions. Such personnel, recruited from among rank-and-file workers, are sent through special training programs and over time exposed to further education. From 1953 to 1958 hundreds of thousands of such workers enrolled in various training programs which included courses, forums, broadcasts, exhibitions, demonstrations, and periodical and poster propaganda. Periodic national conferences on labor protection have also been held to focus on safety and sanitation problems, the role to be played by "labor protection activists" and trade-unions, and development of official regulations dealing with the problem. The local trade-union is required to coordinate these labor protection activities, to see that the regulations are carried out in each operating unit, and to conclude agreements with management stipulating how general labor protection standards are to be implemented in the enterprise.[36]

While mass programs to encourage better safety and health conditions were developed, research institutes to deal with various scientific aspects of the problem were established in governmental units, enterprises, and technical schools and colleges: the Institute of Scientific Research on Labor Protection and the Division of Research on Labor Sanitation function in the Ministry of Labor and the Chinese Medical Science Research Institute, respectively. In the Ministries of Metallurgy, Coal, Chemical Industry, Railway, and Construction, similar research institutes and other agencies study ventilation, heating, and noise elimination. Research institutes and other units are also to be found in provinces and cities. Large enterprises such as the Anshan Iron and Steel Company support institutes studying industrial sanitation and safety techniques. Departments and special courses in technical schools and colleges deal with industrial safety and health, and industrial design institutes often study these problems.[37]

The technical and legal basis for implementing safety and health safeguards is found in the voluminous regulations on working conditions promulgated since the early 1950s. These regulations cover general requirements for maintenance of factory safety and sanitation as well as specific provisions on particular industries and occupations. Temperature and ventilation control, fire prevention and sanitation measures, controls on silica dust and coal tar in mining and manufacturing, restrictions on heavy physical work, provision for special garments and shoes to be used as protection against acids, alkalies, and petroleum are some major areas of safety and sanitation tackled by the trade-unions.[38]

Careful scrutiny of the available evidence on labor protection indicates certain clear-cut patterns. Concern with the problems of safety and sanitation has been consistently expressed by trade-union, governmental, and party leaders; and considerable resources have been put into training programs, development of extensive regulations, national publicity and conferences, trade-union activity, and the like since early in the 1950s. At the same time, evidence of difficulty in getting well planned, effective safety and sanitation programs into operation is widespread. Some of this difficulty is a function of the stage of China's development and the level of technology and education. And yet the pressure of increasing industrial capacity at a rapid rate has undoubtedly contributed to a slower realization of labor protection standards. Excessive overtime work suggests concessions to output goals. The FFYP detailed the ways in which China was to surge ahead industrially. The absence of any discussion of the role of labor protection in this gigantic effort suggests for that period the competitive force working against better standards reminiscent of the experiences of earlier industrializing economies. A recent visitor to China reported less than adequate (in terms of advanced industrial societies standards) safety precautions in an array of different enterprises.[39]

The trade-union organizations at all levels participate financially and operationally in the administration of various aspects of the social insurance program for industrial workers. They receive revenue from the noncontributory labor insurance part of total wages; they provide certain facilities to meet health, old age, and disability needs of workers; and they oversee the administration of all aspects of social insurance at the enterprise and various regional levels. Membership in unions is officially encouraged, since union members receive higher social insurance benefits than nonmembers. Yet all workers do not belong to unions.[40]

The money necessary for trade-union operation of such collective welfare activities as sanitoriums, rest homes, orphanages, houses for the aged and disabled, vacation centers, and other types of centers comes from the premium of 3 percent of total wages set aside by each enterprise as the labor-insurance fund. Thirty percent of the premium is paid to the ACFTU for financing the various centers for the sick, aged, and vacationing workers. The remaining 70 percent of the premium is the fund from which enterprises, under plant trade-union management, pay the scheduled benefits covering sickness, injury, retirement, death, and childbirth.[41]

The communal activities set up by trade-unions to service workers' social insurance needs are found throughout China, some in choice locations and climes. Hundreds of thousands of workers enjoy these facilities each year. The numbers of such establishments have increased over the years, starting from very modest beginnings and growing absolutely and relatively. Late in 1952 there were 51 sanitoriums with room for over five thousand people, 374 overnight sanitoriums with fourteen thousand beds, 35 rest homes accommodating over three thousand, and numerous establishments for housing aged and disabled workers. In 1965 these numbers had changed greatly. There were over twenty-eight hundred sanitoriums and rest homes with about ninety thousand beds run by trade-unions and enterprises. In addition, trade-unions and enterprises carry on other welfare activities: housing developments, medical and health centers, nurseries, kindergartens, public baths, and canteens.[42]

The actual administration of social insurance benefits is carried on from the level of the ACFTU down to the local union. The ACFTU has "full responsibility for overall planning of labour insurance work throughout the country." But the Ministry of Labor is the final authority in labor insurance affairs. The primary trade-union committees in the individual enterprises throughout industry are required to supervise labor insurance fund collection, to supervise various other direct payments required of management by labor insurance regulations, to effect improvements in enterprise clinics and hospitals, and to handle the benefit details. Specific labor insurance committees are established by the primary unions to execute the unions' responsibilities in labor insurance matters. These committees are charged with educating workers about labor insurance rights, processing and approving benefit applications, and supervising payments and accounting of the system. The union auditing committees are required to audit and publicize the labor insurance accounts monthly. A labor insurance secretary is elected by the primary union to propagandize, visit the sick and disabled, and organize any mutual assistance necessary for individual workers and their families.[43]

Trade-unions also encourage and organize cultural, social, recreational, and other similar programs at the national, regional, provincial, local, and enterprise level. Deriving financial support for such activities from the trade-union working fund, the primary union develops specific programs. The working fund is filled by 2 percent of the total wages made available by enterprises. Forty percent of the amount goes to the ACFTU for national communal cultural and educational projects; 10 percent is for provincial, municipal, and industrial trade-union use; 25 percent is for enterprise part-time schools; and the remaining 25 percent is available to the primary union for various cultural and other activities for workers in the plant.[44]

In-plant educational programs are organized and developed in cooperation with plant management by unions starting at the primary trade-union level. Such "spare-time" education provides both general education curricula as well as technical programs aimed at raising workers' technical levels. General education often ranges from literacy courses to the university level. After the GPCR the link between universities, colleges, and technical schools and plants and enterprises was widened.[45]

Labor Disputes

Although labor disputes have been considered ideological anomalies by leaders in Communist countries, their existence has been admitted and on occasion even reported openly. In the USSR such disputes were explained in terms of human aberration. Lenin attributed such conflicts which arose early in Soviet industrial relations to "bureaucratic distortions of the proletarian state and the remains of the capitalist past and its institutions, on the one hand, and the political and cultural backwardness of the laboring masses, on the other." [46] Basically, the early Soviet view was that the abolition of the private ownership of the means of production eliminated the basis for class conflict and thus labor disputes were nonfunctional: there was no capitalist owner-exploiter against whom to strike, ergo strikes would not occur.

Given the functions of trade-unions in China, the question of conflict between the trade-union as arm of the party and the trade-union as representative of the workers when they have grievances poses itself. This kind of tension has been apparent to workers and trade-union officials. Lai Jo-yu, chairman of the ACFTU in the 1950s, gave public recognition to such "contradictions" and asserted that the trade-unions should support the "correct views" of the workers. Many trade-union cadres were keenly aware of the problems they faced, some felt great anguish at the conflict between workers and management because "proper demands may arbitrarily be rejected by the managing directors, department heads, party committee secretaries, branch secretaries, workshop heads and work section heads." [47] When grievances were not satisfactorily resolved but festered and eventually erupted into a labor disturbance of one form or another, the party usually entered the scene to attempt a satisfactory solution.

Such labor disturbances have occurred at various times in China, and some have been officially reported and commented upon. Table 5.1 lists some labor disputes occurring during the 1950s. It was during the Hundred Flowers period in 1956 and 1957 that such disputes occasioned extended ideological comment on the nature of a variety of "contradictions" in a socialist society and on the appropriate way to deal with them. Mao Tse-tung acknowledged that "in 1956, small numbers of workers and students in certain places went on strike [and] members of a small number of agricultural cooperatives also created disturbances. . . ." He cited as main causes for such conflict "bureaucracy on the part of the leadership and lack of educational work among the masses." This official response also appeared in *Jen-min jih-pao* or *People's Daily* which held that labor troubles came about "where bureaucracy assumes serious proportions and workers [are] compelled to follow the trouble-making path when their problems cannot be solved in the normal way of 'unity-criticism-unity.' " [48]

Mao's view of labor and other disputes was more than mere repetition of Lenin. He developed not only an ideological distinction between "antagonistic contradictions" and "nonantagonistic" ones but also indicated how nonantagonistic contradictions should be dealt with to yield positive results for society:

> Our people's government is a government that truly represents the interests of the people, yet certain contradictions arise between the interests of the state, collective interests and individual interests; between democracy and centralism; between those in positions of leadership and the led, and contradictions arising from the bureaucratic practices of certain state functionaries in their relations with the masses. All these are contradictions among the people. Generally speaking, underlying the contradictions among the people is the basic identity of the interests of the people.[49]

This principle represented a modification of some moment in the earlier, rigid view held by Marxists that contradictions could not exist between the people and the government in a socialist society except as rare aberrations. Mao's understanding of such conflicts accepted the common reality of contradictions continuing in the socialist development of society and called for struggle to resolve such conflicts correctly, dialectically. The right to strike under certain conditions was even asserted by officials.[50]

A longshoremen's strike in Canton starting in November 1956 and continuing until April 1957 was reported in the official press and provides an interesting case study of conflict in trade-union functions. Discontented generally with bureaucratic indifference to their living conditions and reacting specifically to the imposition of new work norms and lower piece rates at the beginning of the year, the workers gradually absented themselves from their jobs. By March and April attendance on the day shift was at its low point, only 60 percent of normal; almost half the workers were out. On the night shift, little more than a third of the work force showed up. Those who appeared for work performed in dilatory fashion with a result-

Table 5.1

Reported Labor Disputes in China, 1956–1957

Unit	Period	Nature of Disturbance	Number of Workers Involved	Cause	Outcome
1. Capital Construction Bureau, Ta T'ung Coal Mine, Shansi	Mid-April to Early June 1956	Workers confronted director with grievance demands	over 200	Poor medical treatment and living conditions for apprentices	Apprentices put off with implied threat of punishment
2. Chungking Machine Tool Factory	October 1956	Workers confronted director with demands and strike threat	over 50	Inferior work assignments for apprentice graduates	Probably some concessions
3. Canton Marine Transportation Bureau	January 1957	Workers ended unloading work promptly; refused to work overtime	over 25	New strict, punitive attendance system	Status quo maintained
4. Preparatory Administration Office, Electrolytic Chemical Factory, Canton	March 1957	Planned protest; slogans written in toilets	50–70 (?)	Temporary workers claimed reneging on permanent status	CCP committee reviewed situation and grievance resolved favorably for workers
5. Canton Marine Transportation Bureau	March–April 1957	Strike: absenteeism and slow down	over 200	New shift system, higher norms, lower pay	Negotiated settlement
6. Public Baths, Shanghai	Early March to Early April 1957	Workers demanded to be rehired	over 200	Transfer to countryside with sharply lower pay	Persuasion of workers to return to countryside
7. Peking City Paint Factory	Mid-March	Protest of election of union leader	over 20	Welfare fund and wage grievances	Status quo maintained; threat of punishment

	April 1957				
9. Lien I Machine Factory, Shanghai	Early May 1957	Quarrel with director; property damaged	over 20	Incomplete wage increase	Status quo maintained. Workers persuaded by visiting cadres
10. Fêng Fêng Mine District, Han Tan City, Hopei	Early May 1957	Grievance petition presented	40	Disparities in rent payments	Status quo maintained; workers persuaded
11. Wood Work Coop, Ching Te Chen, Kiangsi	Most of May 1957	Work slowdown and threatened strike	15	Work reassignment	Status quo maintained; self-criticism for five workers; newspaper criticism of coop authorities
12. T'ung Yung Machine Factory, Hangchow	Early June 1957	Promotion and fringe benefit demands	50 ?	Worker discontentment	Status quo maintained; workers persuaded
13. Kweilin Building Company	Late June to Early July 1957	Strike and beating of cadres	over 600	Discontentment with cadres' handling of worker grievances	Some worker proposals accepted; two leaders executed; others sentenced to several years in jail
14. Chungking Machine Tool Factory	July 1957	Demonstration at director's office	over 30	Arbitrary reassignment from school to work	Arrest of three leaders as counter-revolutionaries
15. Canton Trucking Company	June 1957	Petition demanding return of welfare and repair funds	over 200	¥ deducted from wages	Status quo maintained; workers persuaded; worker-capitalists subject to self-criticism

Sources: *Chung-Kuo Ch'ing-Nien Pao*, 2 June 1956; *Chung-King Jih-Pao*, 27 September 1957; *Ch'ung-Kung Shih-Nien* (Hong Kong: Union Research Institute, 1960), p. 301; *Jen-Min Jih-Pao*, 9 May 1957 in SCMP 1551, 17 June 1957, pp. 12–13; *Nan-Fang Jih-Pao*, 10 May 1957; *Kwang-Chou Jih-Pao*, 12 May 1957 in SCMP 1569, 15 July 1957, pp. 28–30; *Sin-Wen Jih Pao*, 27 April 1957; *Peking Ta-Kung Pao*, 9 May 1957; *Kwang-Chou Jih-Pao*, 10 May 1957; *Sin-Wen Jih-Pao*, 16 May 1957; *Jen-Min Jih-Pao*, 9 May 1957; *Peking Ta Kung Pao*, 22 May 1957; *Hang-Chou Jih-Pao*, 26 June 1957; *Kwangsi Jih-Pao*, 16 October 1957; and *Kwang-Chou Jih-Pao*, 20 August 1957.

Organizing and Managing Workers
147

ing sharp drop in productivity. Ships were slowed down considerably in their turn around and cargoes flowed to their inland destinations long behind schedule, pushing costs of such delays quite high.[51]

The longshoremen of Canton, according to the official account, began in 1955 to feel alienated from their trade-union and party leaders. Early that year the longshoremen had worked on the construction of dormitories sponsored by the Canton Harbor Marine Transportation Bureau, their employer. The longshoremen expected to enjoy the benefits of the new housing, but upon the project's completion staff members of the bureau occupied the housing. The longshoremen's complaints were discounted, and their expectations were labeled "egalitarianism" by union and party cadres.[52]

Another demoralizing development was the cumulation of grievances arising out of callous administration of the bureau's clinic. Complaints against inconvenient hours and inability to get credit for medical bills below ￥ 1 reflected workers' dissatisfaction. An incident in which refusal of the clinic to provide a longshoremen's sick son with prescribed medication because the boy's mother was short nineteen cents and closing the clinic while she was borrowing the money became the symbolic confirmation of many workers' complaints. Some responded; "Yes, we have become the masters, but our life is not worth nineteen cents."

The discontentment of the longshoremen grew in intensity as time brought no improvement in their treatment. Starting in November 1956 they began to strike informally, absenting themselves from work in growing numbers. The resulting decline in output and productivity was met by management's implementation of severe penalties for absenteeism, tardiness, poor performance, stalling tactics, and disobedience with suspension from work the ultimate punishment. In addition new, higher output norms, lower piece rates, and changed work shifts were established. When the new system was first imposed starting 1 January 1957, tardy workers were locked out from work. The workers retaliated by stopping work promptly at the end of their shift, which required that cargo vessels which were almost unloaded remain in port until after the next work shift began unloading.

The change in working conditions and pay precipitated the longshoremen into more intense strike action leading to a high rate of absenteeism for March and April 1957. The daily work-shift pattern was modified: a three-shift pattern was set up with a rotation system whereby each longshoreman worked three shifts in two days to effect the rotation. The workers maintained that the shift rotation gave them inadequate rest time, impairing health and increasing accidents. While shifts were modified, work norms were raised, and pay for specific tasks was reduced. General norms were raised by over 7 percent and for nine main cargo categories and thirty-two major working processes the increase was over 18 percent. Most of the work performed was heavy manual labor, and the workers felt that the higher norms were unreasonable, and that some of the piece rates for certain cargo tasks were irrational and ridiculously low resulting in more and more longshoremen refusing such work.[53]

The official party line then on strikes was that "in most cases, troubles [i.e., strikes] occur where bureaucracy assumes serious proportions and workers are compelled to follow the trouble-making path when their problems cannot be solved in the normal way of 'unity-criticism-unity.' " When such "trouble" arises it should be dealt with in line with Mao's guidelines on the correct handling of contradictions among the people. Ideally, such "trouble" should not arise, but when it does either the workers do not understand and reject the situation and thus have to be properly educated, or the workers' interests have not been correctly represented by party, union, and management and such "bureaucratism" has to be counteracted.[54] This follows Mao's position:

> In 1956, small numbers of workers . . . went on strike. The immediate cause . . . was the failure to satisfy certain of their demands for material benefits. . . . But a more important cause was bureaucracy . . . of leadership. . . . Another cause . . . was that the ideological and political education work done among the workers . . . was inadequate. . . .

> We do not approve of disturbances, because contradictions among the people can be resolved with the formula "unity-criticism-unity," while disturbances inevitably cause losses and are detrimental to the advance of socialism. . . . But this does not mean . . . there is no possibility of the masses creating disturbances. . . .

> In handling any disturbances, we should work painstakingly. . . . The guiding spirits in disturbances should not be removed from their jobs or expelled without good reason, except for those who have committed criminal offenses or active revolutionaries who should be dealt with according to law . . . it is nothing to get alarmed about if small numbers of people should create disturbances; rather we should turn such things to advantage to help us get rid of bureaucracy.[55]

The Canton longshoremen's strike was treated officially as a "disturbance" justified because of bureaucratic error. The local CCP committee organized an inspection team to determine the facts and announced that the ideologies of the bureaucratic cadres were rectified and the contradiction between the workers and the cadres was properly handled. The clinic's routines and policies were corrected, accommodations in the dormitories were made available to workers, and the shift rotation system was modified. The output norms imposed in January 1957 were replaced by the 1956 set until other more appropriate ones were devised. Mao's directive to "turn such things to advantage" seems to have been carefully followed. The overriding role played by party officials puts in clear perspective the restricted part the trade-union had in dealing with the crucial interests of workers.[56]

Six

Workers' Welfare

Any appraisal of how workers' welfare has changed since 1949 must be seen against the major Maoist egalitarian thrust that has occupied, more recently, a central position in the CCP's development strategy. The commitment to eliminate, or at least reduce considerably, fundamental differences between industry and agriculture, town and country, and mental and manual labor is a principal element of Maoist policy. For workers, this policy imposes definite limitations on the extent to which their welfare can improve so long as that of the peasants remains low. Among workers themselves these limitations demand narrower rather than wider income spread. A "low wage policy" is followed.[1] The economic wherewithal available to raise welfare levels is now definitely allocated in massive quantities toward improving peasant life with relatively lesser amounts channeled toward workers.

This more recent development in income and welfare policy is a reversal of an earlier course of action affecting workers' livelihood. Until the eve of the GPCR, except for the period of the GLF, workers were slated for improved levels of living as part of, first, the Soviet model development strategy, and, later, the modified Chinese growth design. Real gains in their levels of living did occur. But such improvement, even at a modest rate, while peasants were remaining at their considerably lower levels, only widened the income gap between workers and peasants and complicated, both politically and allocatively, the problems of CCP leaders intent on executing their new development strategy of the early 1960s.

Taking the measure of workers' welfare under the best of circumstances is a difficult task. In advanced industrial societies, where such projects supposedly have been perfected, recent queries about the quality of life have placed under a shadow presumably definitive sophisticated quantitative gauges of welfare. Output per capita, detailed income distribution data, disaggregated consumer expenditures, and similar multidimensional indexes of the material well-being of large numbers of people have been called into question, not as to accuracy, but as to completeness. Concern has spread to incompletely measured and unmeasured dimensions of goods and services and, now, an array of free goods and services heretofore taken for granted, such as water, air, lakes, rivers, oceans, beaches, and wooded areas.

The problem of quantifying the principal dimensions of Chinese workers' welfare includes the above quality aspect as well as other considerations stemming from statistical deficiencies in undeveloped countries and the particular data blackout in the PRC since 1960, which is now easing somewhat. This means that from only 1953 to 1960 is it possible to determine a reasonable if limited picture of workers' livelihood in a narrow, quantitative sense. After 1960 the paucity of data demands a piecing together of bits here and there to come up with a meaningful approximation of the reality of workers' welfare. Starting in 1971, official release of some economic data has helped to refine this approximation somewhat.[2]

Two aspects of the Chinese situation make these approximate generalizations of the 1960s more probably accurate as reflections of well-being. The first is the egalitarian distribution pattern. Since dispersion of income from the average is limited, an approximate average reflects, more or less, the condition of a very large proportion of workers. Secondly, since wage data on workers come mainly from large state industrial enterprises, their quality is relatively good. Recent visits of scholars, correspondents, businessmen, and government officials to China have yielded confirmatory evidence of these important indexes of workers' livelihood.[3]

To the different available indicators of workers' living levels must be added a variety of information, quantitative and qualitative, on the quality of the worker's life: various aspects of health, education, culture, recreation, and the like. Death rates, incidence of disease and epidemics, numbers of persons actively pursuing an array of educational programs, numbers of both theaters and people in attendance, sports arenas and their capacities, and similar measures of the many dimensions of living can help inform our search for the welfare. Ideally, welfare should also include some measure or sense of freedom and social solidarity once the intercultural value question is solved. But even if adequate psychometric techniques were available for such purposes, we have no means of putting them to use in China today.

Workers' Wages and Real Earnings

Since 1949 the wages and real earnings of blue-and white collar workers as well as engineering, professional, supervisory, and managerial personnel as a group have risen substantially. This overall improvement has fluctuated in shorter periods as the contractionary impacts of the GLF and the GPCR have been felt. The more highly paid professional and technical personnel experienced the same general movement in earnings for only part of the twenty-odd year span, for during the GLF and since the GPCR their earnings have been telescoped somewhat in the egalitarian thrust of Maoist policy. By 1970 the spread between the average workers' wages and those of most of the highest paid personnel had been narrowed considerably.

Table 6.1 provides a useful framework for analysis of these changes and a beginning for our rough measure of workers' living levels. Its details on wages and cost of living have been pieced together from several sources and must be taken as approximations of reality rather than refined indexes of wages and prices. They sketch the annual rise and fall in workers' earnings, monetary and real, from the regime's accession to power through 1959. The gaps thereafter, informed only by the 1965 figures, need explanation for which we have some pieces of hard information and general knowledge which make possible some meaningful inference. The relative stability in prices starting in 1953 (with prices rising less than 2 percent by 1965) is a factor which simplifies our analysis. More important, though, it is a reflection of stability in controlled markets, simplifying income policy.

The rise in workers' average earnings from 1949 to 1957 followed in the wake of general economic expansion heightened by the FFYP, the spurt of the last two years resulting mainly from the 1956 wage reform. The increase in real wages of over 60 percent in the eight-year span from ¥ 362 to ¥ 584 ($145.00 to $234.00 in pre-1973 U.S. dollars), with the rise in the last two years alone reaching 17 percent, marked a substantial achievement for workers. More highly skilled personnel, such as technicians, supervisors, engineers, and directors whose pay scales were raised sharply in 1956, fared quite well, and their higher incomes lifted the average markedly for all workers.[4] The spread between blue-collar workers and staff employees widened to a maximum by 1957 as higher salary schedules and fattened bonuses swelled employees' pay envelopes. Top plant personnel received about four to five times the average plant worker's income.[5]

Table 6.1
Money and Real Earnings of Chinese Workers and Employees, 1949–1965
(Yuan Per Year)

Year	Average Money Wages	Cost of Living Index (1952 = 100)	Wages in 1952 Prices	Index of Real Wages (1952 = 100)
1949	262	—	—	—
1950	322	89	362	81
1951	379	99	383	86
1952	446	100	446	100
1953	496	106	468	105
1954	519	107	485	109
1955	534	107	499	112
1956	610	107	570	128
1957	637	109	584	131
1958	551	108	510	114
1959	531	108	492	110
1965	583	108	540	121

Source: N. R. Chen and W. Galenson, *The Chinese Economy Under Communism* (Chicago: Aldine, 1969) p. 172.
Note: The official exchange rate for the Chinese Yuan was approximately $.40 in the above period.

The data for 1958 and 1959 must be interpreted carefully: the apparent decline in real earnings is misleading even though they began a downward trend into the 1960s. The declines of average money wages and real earnings, the latter by 13 percent in 1958 and 3.5 percent in 1959, were the result of the huge influx of unskilled and semiskilled workers into industry at low wage grades which brought the average down. (Table 2.1 in chapter 2 reveals that employment in the modern sector jumped from almost 23 million in 1957 to over 44 million in 1958.) Such a general decline in average earnings, therefore, did not represent any real decline in income for most workers since the new, low-paid workers undoubtedly made as much or more than in their former pursuits and the old, more highly paid workers made as much if not more than before the influx.

This decline in average money and real earnings for 1958 and 1959 became a real decline starting in 1960 when the disruptive effects of the

GLF began to be felt widely in industry following the disarray in rural communes. The drop probably reached bottom in the period from 1961 to 1963. The rise again in workers' incomes started at the end of 1963 when a general wage increase was implemented. This increment benefitted a large range of workers, though staff personnel did better than blue-collar workers. The highest paid plant personnel received three to three and a half times the average wage, with wages not yet reattaining their 1957 spread due to the egalitarian effects of the GLF.[6] The low point in workers' real earnings in the 1961 through 1963 period probably reached the 1952 level, a drop of as much as 15 percent when the distorted 1958 and 1959 real wage situation is taken into account.

Starting at the end of 1963 and continuing into 1966 money and real earnings rose each year with the worker-professional income gap widening. The increase in 1965 to levels surpassed only in 1956 and 1957 was likely to have been outstripped by the 1966 level when the 1956 and 1957 conditions were probably more closely approximated. In 1967, average earnings most probably declined though the picture is quite murky. That GPCR year was the one of greatest conflict and disarray. Industrial production is estimated to have declined from 1966 to 1967 by 6 to about 23 percent with the likely rate of decline around 15 percent.[7] With output down due to disruption and strikes in industrial enterprises, workers' pay inevitably declined. But part of the disruption involved raising workers' wages (some of this even retroactively), giving bonuses, and instituting a variety of welfare benefits—all of this denounced by the Maoists as "economism" and "capitalism"—resulting in some rise in money earnings. On balance, however, the downward pressures were greater than the upward ones, and the result might have been a decline in real earnings of as much as 10 percent.

From 1968 to the present, workers' wages have risen, though not greatly. Prices have remained fairly stable, though certain specific prices, that is, those of medicines and transistor radios, have been lowered. It is reasonable, therefore, to assume that the cost of living today is roughly at the 1968 level or somewhat lower. As to the actual level of wages today, reports from correspondents and other visitors traveling in China during the spring and early summer of 1971 provide a rough estimate of average blue-collar wages. In August 1971 many workers in the three lowest wage grades were moved up one grade retroactive to 1 July 1971. Lowest grade workers who began work before 1966 received an increase of about ¥ 6 a month as they moved to the second wage grade; second grade workers who began work before 1960 likewise rose in grade, earning about ¥ 7 a

Workers' Welfare
155

month more; and workers of the third grade who held jobs since before 1957 were raised to the fourth grade with about ¥ 8 more a month. Thirty percent of the workers in a Peking knitwear factory enjoyed these increases. These reports of average wages in industrial plants in several cities yield a range of ¥ 600 to ¥ 750 a year ($240.00 to $288.00). This writer's observations and information while in China fit into this pattern. Since it is quite likely that the plants visited had wages above the national average, this writer assumes that average to be toward the lower end of the range—¥ 630. In terms of 1952 prices this would deflate to ¥ 583, a real wage level 31 percent above that in 1952 and a little over 8 percent above the 1965 level.[8]

A recent official Chinese account of the level of living reports average wages for workers (other than those recently joining the labor force) for 1970 were ¥ 650, over 50 percent above the 1952 level. Using our cost of living index, the ¥ 650 would deflate to ¥ 602 which exceeds the 1952 level by over 35 percent. This discrepancy between our estimate of the increase in real earnings and the official claim rests entirely on the cost of living index, since the figure used for 1952 average money earnings, ¥ 446, is the official Chinese estimate. The index which I have used is a refinement of official data. Chinese leaders, by implication, claim that the cost of living today is almost 5 percent below that of 1952, while certain United States economists who have refined official Chinese data suggest that by 1965 prices were 8 percent above the 1952 level. Even though the 15 percent difference in real wage increase is significant, it is quite clear that wages—a principal component of workers' welfare—have improved steadily since 1949 with the noted exceptions during the GLF and GPCR.[9]

Since the GPCR the situation for higher level engineering, professional, and supervisory personnel has not followed exactly the same course as that of blue- and white-collar workers. These staff workers have been under constant pressure to accept lesser material emoluments, and many of their salaries have been reduced considerably below the maximums for their salary scales. One visitor during the GPCR reported the ratio of maximum pay to average workers' wages in tens of industrial enterprises at less than 2.5 to 1. The maximum pay found among over thirty-five enterprises was ¥ 210 a month (a quite unusual rate these days and higher than this writer discovered in the enterprises he visited in 1973), or seven times the minimum pay to the least skilled worker. Today this telescoping of upper echelon industrial salaries is much more widely in practice and the spread between average pay for all workers and more highly paid employees is narrower. Top salaries ranging between ¥ 150 and ¥ 200 a month are less in evidence so that these maximums are about five times what the least skilled worker receives.[10]

Egalitarian pressures against high salaried staff personnel have led to reductions in their earnings. Bonuses have been eliminated in the main. Certain differentially advantageous benefits have also been retracted. For example, in earlier years managers, engineers, and other professional staff enjoyed superior housing accommodations. Today many of these employees are housed together with workers in the same types of apartments with no special advantages. In fact, since their pay is higher, their rent—2 to 5 percent of their wages—is, too.[11] Thus the main losers over the years among workers have been those who in the earliest years of the regime up to 1957 reaped the principal benefits, the highly trained, technical staff upon whose shoulders the FFYP and the Soviet growth model placed so much responsibility.

The above analysis of earnings for all types of workers has to be qualified by an important factor already discussed in chapter 2, unemployment. Unemployment means that the actual overall earnings of *all* workers are considerably less than the average indicated for employed workers. In earlier years when unemployment was widespread, workers' average earnings reflected too high an average income for all workers. By 1968, as the GPCR ended its tumultuous phase, the numbers of urban unemployed began to subside as tens of millions of city dwellers were reassigned to communes and other nonurban areas. By 1972 as many as 30 million people had been resettled; and unemployment in cities was undoubtedly at its lowest level since 1949, reducing the negative income impact on workers' earnings, the average of which more closely reflected the income reality for all workers.

Consumption Patterns

Our analysis of workers' earnings gave us a general idea of what level of goods and services workers in China could command with their income, but it did not give the measure of consumption. In addition to reviewing how workers spent the money they earned, we must also take into account nonincome sources of consumption, such as goods and services provided through public agencies, which add to the level of living made possible by wage earnings.

The general ability of the economy to provide consumer goods and ser-

Table 6.2

China's Net Domestic Product, Total and Per Capita,
1952–1965

Year	Net Domestic Product (Billion/952 ¥)	Population (Millions)	Net Domestic Product per Capita (1952 ¥)	Index of Net Domestic Product per Capita (1952 = 100)
1952	71.4	582	123	100
1953	75.3	590	128	104
1954	79.3	599	132	107
1955	82.3	608	135	110
1956	92.1	619	149	121
1957	95.3	630	151	123
1958	108.0	640	169	137
1959	104.4	650	161	131
1960	95.9	658	146	119
1961	92.2	667	138	112
1962	94.0	676	139	113
1963	98.1	686	143	116
1964	104.2	695	150	122
1965	108.1	705	153	124

Source: Joint Economic Committee, U.S. Congress, *An Economic Profile of Mainland China* (Washington: Government Printing Office, 1967), p. 50; and Leo Orleans, "Propheteering: The Population of Communist China," *Current Scene,* 15 December 1969, p. 17.

vices is reflected in the data in table 6.2 which shows increases and decreases in total and per capita domestic output from 1952 to 1965. Though the experience of the USSR reminds us that robust growth in total output need not necessarily include great strides in raising the consumption level, the strategic situation in China changed after the FFYP. That change included greater concern for basic consumption levels especially of peasants.

The data in table 6.2 on total and per capita output fluctuate in the already familiar pattern. Up through 1958, output both total and per capita expanded annually, the greatest accretions coming late in the FFYP and in 1958, the first year of the GLF. The marked decline to a low point in 1961 to

1962 measures the severe contraction wrought by the disarray of the GLF. The recovery from 1963 to 1965, the eve of the GPCR, raised total and per capita output above their 1958 and 1957 levels, respectively.

After 1965 we know that total and per capita output declined during the GPCR to a low in 1967 and then recovered again. For 1970, based on data which Chou En-lai reported to Edgar Snow, we infer (assuming a population of 757 million) that total output surpassed 1958 and 1965 levels, while per capita output rose but did not yet reach the 1958 to 1959 high. Any increase in consumption levels for workers in 1970 therefore must have been achieved either through a modified output mix, since per capita output in 1970 was still below the 1958 to 1959 figures and little if any greater than the 1965 level, or through a reduction in the numbers of workers, or both. In 1971, 1972, and 1973, output continued its rise to new peaks.[12]

Table 6.3 illustrates changes in workers' expenditure patterns in Shanghai from 1929 through 1930 to 1956. Although we cannot assume that these patterns were representative of all workers in China, the data suggest what might have happened for many workers.

The most important question on the quality of consumption, once basic needs are met, is the extent to which workers can engage in discretionary expenditure. If such expenditure is quite narrow, the quality of consumption is considered poorer than if expenditure for a wider variety of goods and services is possible. Table 6.3 reveals that discretionary expenditure seemed to widen between 1929 through 1930 and 1956 in Shanghai.

The decline in total food expenditure by 6 percent and the quite sharp drop in expenditure on food staples are two salient factors in the probable improved quality of consumption in 1956. With less spent on food, more could be spent on nonfood products; with less spent on food staples, a wider choice among other foods was possible. The drop in food expenditure in 1956 was more than offset by the rise in expenditure on nonfood products. More was spent on clothing and other products in 1956. Among foods more was spent on meat, fowl, and eggs than in 1929 through 1930.

Among services the changed pattern in 1956 was striking. Though expenditures on services were a higher proportion of total expenditure in 1929 through 1930 than in 1956, in that year workers spent a higher proportion of total expenditure on all services, save rent, than in 1929 through 1930. The sharp drop in expenditure on rent from 8.5 percent to 1.9 percent made this possible. With rent payments nominal in 1956, expenditures on other services rose. Expenditure on recreation tripled over that of 1929 through 1930; that on transportation doubled over 1929 through 1930. How much of the latter increase represented improved or increased

Table 6.3

*Family Expenditure Structure of
Workers and Employees in Shanghai,
1929–1930 and 1956
(Percentage of Total)*

	1929–30	1956
Food	58.5	52.5
staples	28.9	15.6
other	29.6	36.9
Nonfood products	17.4	24.4
clothing	7.1	11.9
other	10.3	12.5
Services	24.2	23.0
rent	8.5	1.9
other	15.7	21.1
Total	100	100

Source: N. R. Chen, ed., *Chinese Economic Statistics* (Chicago: Aldine, 1967), pp. 435–36.

consumption is not clear. The expenditures on medical care fell from 1.4 to .5 percent of total expenditure between the two periods; this reflected the lower prices for medicine and medical services rather than a decline in quantity of service. A major part of medical care had become a free service.

Unfortunately there are no comparable data on family expenditure patterns in China during the 1960s or since. Bits and pieces of information suggest patterns. Cotton textiles, cooking oil, and grain are still rationed but in sufficient quantities to meet basic needs. The proportion of total income spent on food seems to have declined further. The wide array of basic goods available in ample supply in shops at low prices in 1971, 1972, and 1973 attests to generally improved consumption conditions. Food expenditures for some families are about 35 to 50 percent of total expenditure. If this is representative of large numbers of workers' families, it means a greater degree of discretionary expenditure than that of the 1956 Shanghai pattern. Savings, stressed greatly by party media, play a role too in expenditure patterns, though not one of great moment given the relatively low level of income. Usually it is a residual after all expenditure and may amount to a few yuan a month. In 1970 savings accounts totals were reported to be 28 percent higher than in 1965.[13]

The actual level of food consumption has varied considerably since 1949 following the vicissitudes of grain production, a bellwether of general economic activity. Workers' fundamental well-being, therefore, has rested heavily on food production and on grain in particular. Table 6.4 gives us a rough idea of how workers' food consumption probably fluctuated. The refined grain production data are reasonably good, though the population series and therefore the per capita output figures are less certain. The pattern, if not the degree of fluctuation in per capita output, is a fairly good reflection of reality.

The total and per capita output of grain has made a slow but steady advance except for the near-disaster years of 1959 through 1962 when output sank to 1952 levels with the population almost one hundred million greater. As a result workers suffered serious cutbacks in food consumption. It is fair to infer that up to 1959 workers enjoyed adequate basic food supplies. From 1959 to 1962 we know this situation was reversed, and, despite millions of tons of grain imports and makeshift crop cultivation on every available piece of free land, city dwellers fared poorly, because their grain and nongrain food intake had been reduced considerably. More equal distribution of food than occurred in pre-Communist days mitigated somewhat the negative effects of the sharp decline in grain output. By 1963 the situation began to ease, and by 1965 earlier adequacy levels for grains and nongrain foods were being approximated. Steady expansion of grain, nongrain crops, and vegetables each year has certainly led to attainment of new high levels of food output by 1971 with 1952 per capita levels being surpassed in 1966. In 1972 grain output declined to the 1970 level as unfavorable weather took its toll. Today workers enjoy the best food consumption levels since the advent of the regime in 1949.[14]

Unfortunately, there are only limited quantitative data available on the output, variety, and distribution of nonfood consumer goods since 1949. For the period from 1949 to 1959 there are statistics on the physical output of industrial commodities including consumer products. For the 1960s there are only rough estimates of industrial production which have already been employed. The inferences drawn for the 1960s and the early 1970s are based on: (1) the general estimates of industrial production; (2) pieces of information gathered by correspondents and other visitors who had recently been to China; (3) my sense of the situation, derived from reading a variety of material originating on the mainland and my own personal im-

Table 6.4

Estimated Grain Output in China, 1949–1973

(In Million Metric Tons)

Year	Output	Index of Output (1952 = 100)	Population (Millions)	Output per Capita (Tons)	Index of Output per Capita (1952 = 100)
1949	134	81	561	.239	84
1950	144	87	567	.254	89
1951	155	93	574	.270	95
1952	166	100	582	.285	100
1953	170	102	590	.288	101
1954	176	106	599	.294	103
1955	182	110	608	.299	105
1956	188	113	619	.304	107
1957	187	113	630	.297	104
1958	205	123	640	.320	113
1959	170	102	650	.262	92
1960	150	90	658	.228	80
1961	160	96	667	.240	84
1962	170	102	676	.251	88
1963	182	110	686	.265	93
1964	195	117	695	.280	98
1965	200	120	705	.284	100
1970	240 [a]	145	757	.317	111
1971	250 [b]	151	768	.326	114
1972	240 [c]	145	779	.308	108
1973	255 [d]	154	790	.323	113

Source: Kang Chao, *Agricultural Production in Communist China* (Madison: University of Wisconsin Press, 1970), pp. 227, 246; Leo Orleans, "Propheteering: The Population of Communist China," *Current Scene*, 15 December 1969, p. 17.

[a] Chou En-lai's figure.

[b] *Jen-min jih-pao* [People's daily], 1 January 1972.

[c] *China News Summary*, no. 455 (February 1973).

[d] Author's Estimate.

pressions as a visitor; and (4) the basic strategy of the CCP since the end of the GLF for the economy to grow proportionately, giving consumers a greater share of total output than under the FFYP.

During the 1950s workers' consumption probably rose steadily as industrial production on consumer goods industries grew continuously, though less robustly than producer goods. The output of textiles, paper, and commodities in daily use swelled from 1949 to 1957, the end of the FFYP, from almost threefold for textiles to just over threefold for commodities in daily use to about sevenfold for paper over the 1949 levels. These increases from 1952 to 1957 were: textiles, 37 percent; paper, 120 percent; commodities in daily use, 75 percent. All increases clearly were adequate to compensate for population growth and still allow for substantial real increases for workers.[15]

Figures indicating actual physical output of a variety of consumer goods during the 1950s are shown in table 6.5. They document some of the actual advance in workers' living levels that our earnings data implied. Clearly, Chinese workers enjoyed an appreciable improvement in the consumer goods they demanded as a consequence of the FFYP's industrial successes. The soaring percentage increases in growth of certain consumer goods such as bicycles, radios, clocks, penicillin, Chinaware, violins, and accordions, attest to the very low levels of consumer output that Chinese economic activity had generated in 1952. The general levels of consumer output reflected in table 6.5 demonstrate dramatically, despite the robust advance during the FFYP, the vast challenge confronting the Chinese economy before fundamental nonfood consumption needs (in China's terms) can begin to be met.

The progress made by Chinese workers by the end of the 1950s was abruptly reversed by the economic contraction following the GLF. The general decline in industrial output from 1959 to 1962, the year of lowest output, by almost 35 percent undoubtedly saw a similar if less sharp decline in nonfood consumer goods production. This severe setback probably put workers' consumption in the category back to the 1957 through 1958 level for those not forced into the ranks of the unemployed.[16]

China's economic recovery started late in 1962 and proceeded at a fairly strong rate; industrial production rose by 10 to 15 percent each year through 1966, the first year of the GPCR. Workers' nonfood consumption shared in this revival of output.[17] The array of consumer goods available to workers in 1966 at their labor input costs is shown in table 6.6. Though we do not have information on the degree to which such products were generally at hand, some idea of supply is suggested by the relative labor input

Table 6.5

Output of Consumer Products in China, 1952 and 1959

Commodity and Unit	1952	1959	Percentage Increase
Bicycles (1000)	80	1,498	1,773.
Sewing machines (1000)	84	563	570.
Radios (1000)	17	295 [b]	1,635.
Clocks (1000)	152	5,700	3,650.
Penicillin (Kg.)	46	72,607 [c]	15,684.
Antibiotics (tons)	0	198	—
Colored, printed cloth (million meters)	1,924	3,460 [c]	80.
Woolen fabrics (thousand meters)	4,233	31,100	635.
Woolen yarn (ton)	1,980	9,540 [c]	382.
Woolen blankets (1000)	717	920 [a]	28.
Domesticated silk (ton)	3,548	7,250 [c]	104.
Silk fabrics (million meters)	65	264	306.
Cotton undervests (1000 dozens)	2,875	9,566 [b]	233.
Socks (1000 dozens)	29,930	36,463 [b]	22.
Coats and pants (1000 dozens)	800	1,926 [b]	141.
Cotton underwear (1000 dozens)	1,898	4,091 [b]	116.
Towels (1000 dozens)	18,640	23,375 [b]	25.
Paper (1000 tons)	539	2,137	297.
Newsprint (1000 tons)	61	122 [b]	100.
Cigarette paper (tons)	5,028	8,803 [b]	75.
Cigarettes (1000 crates)	2,650	5,505	108.
Alcoholic beverages (1000 tons)	682	1,091 [c]	60.
Soap (1000 tons)	117	272 [c]	132.
Rubber footwear (1000 pairs)	61,690	182,360 [c]	196.
Matches (1000 baskets)	9,110	11,070 [c]	22.
Chinaware (1000 pieces)	16,238	1,621,560 [b]	9,886.
Pencils (1000)	148,262	484,760 [b]	227.

Commodity and Unit	1952	1959	Percentage Increase
Fountain pens (1000)	39,498	130,000	229.
Thermos bottles (1000)	5,536	37,000	568.
Violins	5,778	70,025[b]	1,112.
Accordions	734	22,679[b]	2,990.
Organs (sets)	4,781	21,365[b]	347.
Aquatic products (1000 tons)	1,666	5,020	201.

Source: Kang Chao, *The Rate and Pattern of Industrial Growth in Communist China* (Ann Arbor: University of Michigan Press, 1965), pp. 120–32.

[a] 1956.

[b] 1957.

[c] 1958.

of different items. For example, basic items such as shoes must have been in relatively good supply given the low price they commanded and the absence of rationing of shoes.

In 1967 output declined again directly as a result of the GPCR's disruption. Workers' consumption also suffered a brief setback. With the 1959 output level regained by 1968, workers began to realize several years of increasing quantities of consumer goods at new peak levels. Price reductions for selected items such as medicine enhanced consumption. The quantity of consumer goods has risen and the variety has widened each year to the present.[18]

The consumption of services by workers includes those paid for directly by individuals and families out of income as well as those received gratis. Services more than commodities include substantial quantities of free consumption in housing, transportation, health care, recreation, education, and the like. These are areas, also, in which quality is quite important but extremely difficult to gauge.

The housing situation did not improve considerably for workers as a whole over most of the period under review. In the last few years, however, more marked housing gains have been registered. Rents, of course, are nominal, with some reaching a maximum of 4 to 5 percent of the worker's basic monthly income. In most instances the actual cost of housing is more than the rent so that free or mainly free services are in effect given to workers' families. Those who enjoy new housing constructed under the

Table 6.6

Cost of Products in Terms of One Day's Pay
(Chinese Worker Earning ¥ 60 Per Month)

Product	Approximate Number of Days' Pay
Man's cap	$1^1/_2$ — 2
Child's cotton suit or dress	1 — $2^1/_2$
Cotton socks	$^3/_8$ — $^5/_8$
Wool socks	5 — $2^3/_4$
Man's or woman's conventional two-piece cotton suit	5 — 7
Man's two-piece wool suit, military cut	30 — 50
Man's or woman's wool (cashmere) sweater	7 — 15
Man's Western-style suit, cheaper material	35 — 50
Man's Western-style suit, good material	60 — 90
Man's light overcoat	70 — 80
Woman's cloth overcoat	90 — 120
Man's or woman's shirt or pajamas, Western-style	4 — 6
Meal at a fairly good restaurant	2 — 7
Chocolate bar	$^8/_8$ — $^1/_4$
Pack of cigarettes	$^1/_5$ — $^2/_5$
Large bar of soap	$^1/_2$ — 1
Bottle of wine or alcoholic beverage (gin, vodka, brandy, whisky)	3 — 15
Sunglasses (without case)	$^1/_3$ — $^1/_4$
Flashlight	$1^1/_2$ — $^1/_3$
2 standard flashlight batteries	$^1/_4$ — $^1/_3$
Box of matches	negligible
Cheap clock	5 — 6
Watch	30 — 60
Radio (including transistor radios)	25 — 50
T.V. set (14" to 17" screen)	165 — 425
Camera	25 — 50
Film (roll of black and white)	$^1/_2$ — $1^1/_2$
Child's cloth shoes	$^1/_3$
Child's leather shoes	1 — $1^1/_2$

Product	Approximate Number of Days' Pay	
Men's or women's cloth shoes	2	— 3
Men's or women's leather shoes	5	— 10
Adult's leather sandals	3	— 6
Lady's simple leather handbag	2½	— 4
Suitcase (leather or similar material)	15	— 25
Sewing machine	75	—100
Bicycle	60	— 90
12-piece set of home furniture (cheap wood)	at least 350	
Single bureau with mirror	40	— 50
Car (if allowed to purchase)	more than 12,000	

Source: Barry M. Richman, *Industrial Society in Communist China* (New York: Random House, 1969), pp. 808–09.

factory's auspices may receive more housing than the average family. Such factory apartments usually include one or two bedrooms, possibly a sitting room, den, or balcony, a small kitchen, and a lavatory and/or toilet which may be shared depending on its make up. As urban population swelled to peaks in 1958 and 1965 through 1967, the quantity and quality of housing per family probably fell off. After the GPCR as millions of people in the cities were relocated in the countryside, housing accommodations probably improved. The population of many cities has remained stationary or declined somewhat.[19]

Though effective evaluation of changes in transportation service is not possible given the lack of information, the fact of subsidy is clear. A worker today may spend as little as ¥ 3 a month on bus fares to and from work, six days a week. This is 10 percent of the worker's minimum pay or 5 to 6 percent of the average worker's pay and is clearly a modest sum, less than the cost of transportation.[20]

So far as recreation and education go, here too any evaluation of quality, for education particularly, would be at best very tentative, even if we had basic information. Broad quantitative data indicate that more recreational facilities for more workers have been provided through various agencies such as factories, unions, and local administrations. The recent imposition of responsibility on schools and universities to set up regular links with factories in addition to in-plant programs already in existence means that more and more workers have opportunities to get a variety of formal course and program training.

Besides being an important source of workers' well-being, health care also provides substantial amounts of free goods and services in the form of medicines, glasses, and medical, dental, nursing, and other services. Workers do pay for some of these: in 1956 in Shanghai they spent 5 percent of their income directly on medical care. In fact, though, the cost of the array of health service provided to workers is much greater, reflecting subsidy.

From 1949 until the GPCR, health services for workers were expanded more or less continuously as output grew. In periods of economic reversal it is unlikely that such services were contracted significantly. As we saw in chapter 2, the number of trained doctors rose greatly. By 1968 there were 115,000 Western-style doctors and approximately 500,000 who were practicing traditional Chinese medicine. In urban areas, about 10,000 hospitals supplied 500,000 beds. In the period from 1960 to 1963—one of economic contraction—urban health facilities were expanded: clinics almost doubled in number from 43,000 to 84,000.[21]

The year 1968 marked a significant turn in health services for workers in cities. Mao Tse-tung had issued a directive on public health in June 1965 demanding equalization of health care provisions for people in the countryside as part of his strategy to reduce differences between town and country and worker and peasant. He charged the Ministry of Health with neglect of rural over urban areas and was reported to have said:

> You may tell this to the Health Ministry. That Ministry renders service to only 15 percent of the nation's population, and among this 15 percent mainly people of some position or rank. The broad masses do not get medical treatment; they have neither the doctors nor the medicine they need. The Health Ministry does not belong to the people. It would be better renamed Urban Health Ministry, or Urban "Lords" Health Ministry instead.[22]

Mao called for up to one half of all health workers to be transferred from cities to rural areas to set up health bases and programs. On-the-job training and short courses were to be used to develop "barefoot" doctors. By late 1968, at the end of the GPCR, Mao's line was being implemented and large numbers of health personnel were relocated in the countryside. In the succeeding years this relocation continued and rural health services spread. The workers remaining in the cities had fewer doctors, dentists, nurses, and facilities for their health care starting in 1968. To reduce the likelihood that health care would deteriorate in cities, training programs for urban counterparts to "barefoot" doctors have been undertaken.[23]

The Quality of the Worker's Life

Some aspects of the quality of the worker's life have been provisionally reflected in the consumption data noted above, but our analysis of patterns and levels of consumption is inadequate for gaining a real sense of the quality of life that workers enjoy in China today. The inadequacy stems only partly from the fact that our quantitative information is incomplete. More significantly, the fullest quantitative data on what and how much workers can command in a market would fail to answer the question of quality of life, because some of its major components fall outside conventional economic welfare measurement.

Today even in an economic context we are more sensitive to important existential realities which indicators such as GNP fail to account for: air pollution, quality of products, noise levels, all of which are part of the process which generates output. In addition, observers of the social scene are much more aware of a variety of social indicators, such as life expectancy, infant mortality, quality of public health, crime rates, and the like, as well as simple concerns such as how dirty are the streets, how secure one feels while walking at night, or how free one feels, which embody the concept termed quality of life.[24]

We make no pretense of drawing a complete picture of the quality of life of the Chinese worker, let alone his state of freedom. In terms of our culture the Chinese worker is subject to many constraints which we would consider unbearable, but it is also clear that certain basic needs are cared for. Our objective here is merely to add somewhat to our sketch of the quantitative components of the worker's life with some limited comments on the situation of his total welfare.

One obvious and important aspect of the worker's life are the conditions of work: the hours of work, the degree of arduousness, the perils on the job, the congeniality of the work situation. The standard work week in industry is an eight-hour day with a six-day work week. It is a common practice to work in shifts: regular, midday and night. In 1957 it was estimated that nonagricultural workers worked 306 days a year, with days off occurring on Sundays or other days and seven national festivals. Actually, in many instances more hours are worked than the standard hours in response to special situations such as the end of a plan period, or during emulation campaigns or plant political or production meetings. Workers whose immediate families live a considerable distance from the job site are entitled to annual home leave. Pressure has sometimes been put on such workers to forego their leave rights, reducing time off averages.[25]

The safety and sanitary conditions under which workers labor are salient elements of the total work situation. (We touched on these in chapter 5.) There is great difficulty in taking the measure of the degree to which workers are in jeopardy from their work environment, since we do not have at hand the kinds of statistics which allow some meaningful overall evaluation. Some official data indicate general improvement in safety and health conditions. One recent visitor to Chinese industrial plants, however, has questioned the adequacy of safety and health arrangements in the locations he surveyed. Reporting that workers now have a greater voice in the running of factories and may criticize conditions and recommend changes, this observer has also pinpointed dangerous circumstances: the absence of eye goggles to protect against flying metal or sparks, inadequate covering of pipes which carry noxious gases, and the heavy odor of ammonia in plant dormitories. Other visitors have reported generally healthful and safe working conditions. This writer saw evidence of attention to safety and health needs in factories he visited.[26]

How representative are the conditions which the critical visitor saw is not known. But the avowed concern of responsible officials and agencies is well documented, and periodic national conferences and "labor protection" campaigns attest to widespread attempts to heighten the concern of the worker for an effective implementation of regulations. In these endeavors the ministries of labor and health have collaborated with the ACFTU to promulgate regulations and administrative stipulations on health and safety procedures, for example, stopping coal-tar poisoning, controlling temperatures, preventing fires, making safety-in-production inspections, and providing special clothing and safety devices. Periodically, mass campaigns to indoctrinate and train workers in safety and health measures have been launched, sometimes as emulative contests.[27]

The social insurance system which covers workers in units employing at least 100, discussed in chapter 4, is an important psychological and material consideration affecting workers' feelings toward the job situation. It includes benefits for disability, illness, childbearing, retirement, and death for workers and members of the immediate family. Though unemployment is not insured in the same systematic way, financial provisions have been made to relieve its impact. Development of and nationwide publicity on new surgical techniques helps reassure workers who may be subject to accidents and loss of limbs. For most workers and their families these protections against major hazards of life symbolize a sharp break with the more uncertain past when the advent of any of these events signalled personal and familial tragedy.[28]

The state of public health is another significant dimension of each person's quality of life, including that of the workers. Here, too, its quantitative measure does not yield the full reality. Even if all the relevant statistical indicators were at hand, the full sense of how good public health is would still hinge on important qualitative evidence. We review below some of the data, of both types, to gain a first approximation of the general level of public health in China.

The vital statistics in table 6.7 below are one student's estimation of the changing patterns of births and deaths throughout China and provide a somewhat tenuous quantitative basis for analyzing public health in China. The estimates must be viewed carefully, since they are based more on the good sense of one who has studied these problems for many years than on a highly reliable set of data.

The rates in cities are undoubtedly lower for both deaths and births where medical facilities have been considerably superior to those in the countryside, and where urban living patterns militate against the large families found in rural areas. The reduction in the death rate to roughly half of its 1949 level is a significant achievement bringing that indicator in China's cities within striking distance of rates in advanced industrial societies which fall near 10 per 1000. The decline in the birth rate by 25 percent in little over twenty years to 32 per thousand for the whole country, and perhaps to 27 per 1000 in the cities, places the latter rate close to the 25 per 1000 rate which obtained in the United States during the 1950s. Reducing the birth rate markedly was aided by birth control campaigns in the middle 1950s and 1960s which carried over to the 1970s.[29]

The indicated rate of natural increase in population, ranging between 1.1 and 1.8 percent per annum, represents an important achievement over the natural pressures in developing countries for growth rates to border on the explosive. The rate is close to those of many advanced industrial societies in recent decades, including the United States. Continued containment of excessive population expansion has been seen by Premier Chou En-lai as a major way to maintain and improve life's quality in China.[30]

The general improvement in public health services for workers in cities over the years has taken on several dimensions beyond that suggested by changes in the vital rates. The achievements of public health and sanitation in Chinese cities since 1949 have been quite significant: levels of public sanitation have been raised sharply, infectious diseases have been held in check, medical facilities have been expanded, and new techniques have been developed with consequent reduction in certain chronic ail-

Table 6.7

Estimated Vital Rates in China,
1949–1970
(Rates per 1000 Population)

Year	Births	Deaths	Natural Increase
1949	43	32	11
1950	43	32	11
1951	43	31	12
1952	43	30	13
1953	43	29	14
1954	43	28	15
1955	42	26	16
1956	41	24	17
1957	40	22	18
1958	39	22	17
1959	38	23	15
1960	38	25	13
1961	38	25	13
1962	38	24	14
1963	37	23	14
1964	36	22	14
1965	35	21	14
1966	34	20	14
1967	34	20	14
1968	33	19	14
1969	33	18	15
1970	32	17	15

Source: Orleans, "Propheteering: The Population of Communist China," p. 17.

ments. Public health research has grown. Mosquitoes, flies, rats, bedbugs, cockroaches, and other harmful insects have been eliminated or brought under effective control. Cleanliness levels in cities have been raised: handling of food and water has approached standards in advanced societies. Mass inoculation programs have reduced the incidence of certain infectious diseases drastically. Malaria is now less widespread through effective mosquito control. The latest common parasitic disease to be attacked with some success on a mass basis is schistosomiasis (known also as snail fever and rice farmer's disease) which has afflicted over ten million Chinese, mainly in the countryside.[31]

The marked improvement in the quality of public health and sanitation has resulted from periodic "patriotic" campaigns that have been launched to rid the environment of pests or disease. In these as in other campaigns the CCP's organizational acumen has been effectively demonstrated. People from all walks of life and of all ages have been coordinated in such campaigns which not only have specific objects for eradication but contain an important educational function. The result has been an immensely improved urban environment on which recent returning visitors to China have invariably commented favorably.[32]

Part of the growth of public health facilities includes expansion of medical and related services which was touched on earlier in this chapter. The large urban clinics and hospitals with research facilities provide arenas for development of new techniques and discoveries and reflect an important aspect of public health. Workers have benefitted from medical advances which are made available to factory or independent clinics and hospitals. Modern medical practice is combined with traditional Chinese medicine including acupuncture techniques and herbal therapy.[33]

Since the GPCR the urban public health and medical facilities have faced reallocation of staff and resources to the countryside. This reduction in the wherewithal for attending to the health needs of city workers may have meant some decline in the quality and quantity of health services. To compensate for this modified resource and personnel mix, readjustments in work schedules of medical personnel have been arranged, and workers have been assigned to short courses in medicine called Red Medical Classes. The development of such paramedical personnel trained to give first aid and inoculations and to perform a variety of other tasks is aimed at relieving physicians' burdens as their numbers diminished, a development which is analogous to the new physicians' assistants in the United States.[34]

Another important aspect of the quality of life for workers is the natural environment, specifically the air and the bodies of water. China is young enough as an industrial nation so that problems in the natural environment are far from critical, and yet she has been made enough aware of them and their implications to program new industries and communities as well as to put existing units within a coordinated control mechanism as means to prevent them. Today's smog from Shanghai's and Peking's industries symbolizes the threat to the future. So far the response to the problem has been part of a broader socioeconomic approach to the question of scarce resources and capital. Human and industrial wastes and worn-out equipment and tools have great value where capital and resources are scarce and labor is abundant. The aspect of the Maoist economic model calling for development of small and intermediate indigenous industry which would make use of readily available labor to process low-quality raw materials for relatively crude implements is easily extended to include chemical and other industrial wastes. Economic and social needs are congruent. "Self-reliance" of workers is called upon to devise smog-reducing mechanisms, more a social than economic need, and to implement recycling procedures for seemingly useless materials, equipment, and tools, which can be put to economic use. The aspect of the Maoist model calling for social welfare considerations rather than economic profit alone as the determinant of economic decisions may lead to effective institutionalization of waste recycling so that the natural environment is continually kept in good condition.[35]

An array of public services, beyond what has already been mentioned, is available to and enhances the life of the Chinese worker: educational programs, cultural and recreational facilities, developed vacation locations, and widespread sport activities for both observation and participation. These important aspects of Chinese life are paid for partially by workers who enjoy their services with a goodly portion of the cost subsidized by the state, the enterprise, or the trade-union. In recent years the state has increasingly placed the financial responsibility of such activities on the units closest to the operating level, relieving itself of some of the major capital costs of this important expanding area of workers' lives.[36]

One index of the greater availability of education is the number of students involved. By 1958 students in institutes of higher learning, technical middle schools, middle schools, and primary schools had increased since 1949 by 327, 284, 470, and 265 percents, respectively. Total student enrollments rose from just under twenty-five million in 1949, to about ninety-seven million in 1958. During the 1960s enrollments continued to rise. Spare-time education in factories and elsewhere, which was most convenient for workers, also flourished in the 1950s, starting from scratch in 1949. By 1958 over thirty-one million people were participating in such programs, and about forty million newly literate people were noted. One estimate in 1966 gauged that the over 90 percent national illiteracy rate existing for China before 1949 had been reduced to below 60 percent with urban illiteracy down to less than 20 percent.[37]

Various indicators attest to the burgeoning of cultural and recreational facilities which workers and their families have at their disposal. The growing number of lectures, exhibitions, film and lantern slide shows, cultural halls, parks, public libraries, museums, cinemas, theaters, dramatic groups, newspapers, journals, books, radio stations, and physical culture programs during the 1950s has been impressive. The tripling of the number of cultural halls from 896 to 2,616 from 1949 to 1958 was at the low end of the range of growth of cultural activity and facilities. Public libraries grew in number from 55 in 1949 to 922 in 1958, a rise of over 1,400 percent. Radio stations increased in number from 8 in 1949 to 6,772 in 1958, and the number of public loudspeakers rose from 500 to just over 3 million. Afforestation and urban planning have extended park areas greatly. The continued growth of these activities and facilities during the 1960s was also robust and played an important communications role in the GPCR. In 1964 there were 11,975 radio stations, and public loudspeakers totaled 6 million for all China; while in 1970 the loudspeaker total for Shantung province's countryside alone exceeded 5 million. This development of communications for the people continues into the 1970s.[38]

Another important condition of workers' lives which the regime has attempted to foster has been the development of mutual aid among workers to improve further their day-to-day existence. Self-reliance is put forth as a powerful tool for realizing objectives without direction from and involvement of the state or other agencies. This contributes, of course, to the cultivation of Communist consciousness as existential problems are overcome through group cooperation. Such activities include helping the sick at home through preparing medicinal herbs, washing clothes and cooking; tending the ill while family breadwinners are at work; minding children; repairing houses for the needy; assisting at marriages, funerals, etcetera; helping to settle disputes in families or among neighbors. To these ends as well as others, the widespread establishment of "mutual-help teams" have been set up in industrial and mining enterprises, among others, and their national development has been encouraged.[39]

One important aspect of Mao's egalitarian thrust not yet revealed in our review of workers is the concerted effort to achieve equality of the sexes. The data and analysis of the earlier chapters throw no light on how women workers have fared vis-à-vis men. Today in China two facts are clear: women have advanced significantly along the road to equality, but a long way has to be traveled to reach the goal, and resistant factors still slow the forward movement.

The official CCP position on women's liberation has always been positive, and over the years much progress toward equality has been made. In

Mixed train crew (China Pictorial, *3, 1972, p. 31*)

Workers and technicians make their own processing equipment (China Pictorial, *4, 1973, p. 31*)

the 1950s Chairman Mao related such progress to the socialization process: "Genuine equality between the sexes can only be realized in the process of the socialist transformation of society as a whole." [40] With the GPCR, however, the pace of progress was accelerated so that in the last few years as the socialization of the people's consciousness has been stepped up, so has the advance of women toward liberation.

The progress by 1965, the eve of the GPCR, was noteworthy. In the Third National People's Congress almost 18 percent of the deputies were women. In education and scholarship higher ratios obtained: 45 percent among secondary school faculties, 25 percent of the students in colleges, and 20 percent of Academy of Sciences staff. In Peking the percentage of women functionaries was 35 percent, having risen by 9 percent since 1956. For all China, women functionaries rose by 100 percent from 1957. [41]

In the CCP itself women have done less well, though since the GPCR there has been noticeable improvement. In 1965 there were no women on the Politburo, at the peak of CCP structure, and only four regular members and four alternates on the Central Committee. In 1969 the situation changed markedly: two women were elected to the Politburo, and thirteen regular members and ten alternates were chosen for the Central Committee; in 1973 the numbers were twenty regular members and twenty-one alternates. In the latter year thirty-two of the 148 members of the presidium were women. Women also held a variety of positions in municipal and provincial CCP bodies. Among party secretaries for such units less than 4 percent were women, but their proportion among lower level CCP positions was much higher, exceeding one third in a Kwangsi *hsien*. [42]

Resistance to equal treatment of women has continued in economic and political areas. The party dictum, enunciated by Mao, that "men and women must receive equal pay for equal work in production" still is violated throughout the country; probably more widely in the countryside than in the cities. Women are often denied membership in the CCP with some men maintaining that "women cannot play much of a role anymore after they marry." Official reaction to such hostility is swift and unequivocal. [43]

Women workers today are found in a wide variety of occupations in increasing numbers: Chairman Mao's assertion that "whatever men comrades can accomplish, women comrades can too," is more and more being realized as women electricians, construction workers, lathe operators, prospectors, pilots, navigators, scientists, cadres, surgeons, engineers, and plant directors distinguish themselves. The PLA and the people's militia also have considerable numbers of women in their ranks. And yet official recognition is made of the need to fight against traditional views of women still held by both men and women. Especially in rural areas are women occasionally ill treated as in the old society. The Federation of Women has been reactivated to help accelerate the movement toward sexual equality.[44]

This advance toward sexual equality is an important and dramatic indicator of the direction and pace of China's socialization process. It is all the more remarkable, as much of China's recent progress is, when one reflects on the very low status of women in China over the millennia and well into the twentieth century.

Seven

Conclusion

In looking at the Chinese worker today one generalization emerges quite clearly: the industrial revolution which is shaping her or his being is radically different from its counterpart in advanced capitalist or East European countries. This was not yet true at the outset in the 1950s, and its continued reality is not assured, but the Maoist strategy for lifting China into the twentieth century unmistakably is moving her workers and peasants into a new society whose existential realities will differ significantly from those which define industrial societies today.

The Maoists have realized, in their early efforts to modernize-industrialize and to socialize Chinese society, that they were accepting definitions of these processes that mainly continued old institutional meanings and forms in both capitalist and socialist countries. To the extent that modernization-industrialization along Soviet lines conflicted with the socialization of the means of production and of the consciousness of the work force, and to the extent that that conflict was resolved in favor of industrialization, or "production in command," effective socialization and building of socialist consciousness was frustrated, and the ultimate Communist goals were put in doubt. Thus the Maoist realization matured to the view that modernization-industrialization and socialization had to be molded in an opposite way to the Soviet practice, and socialization took priority for the time. The GPCR meant that until a socialist superstructure was firmly established, to proceed single-mindedly to modernize-industrialize would be to wind up on the return voyage to capitalism.

For the Chinese worker this has meant that his or her conditions of life and labor have for some years been shaped by a radical redefinition of modern socialist society in transition toward communism. Not only have Chinese workers been pushed more toward development of group or social consciousness, but they have also found themselves in a work milieu quite different from their counterparts in the USSR and the United States. The technical and mechanical setup in a modern machine tool plant in any of the three countries will be fundamentally the same; but the social realities of organization, management, decision making, variety of work tasks, motivational configuration, and human interaction will be different in important ways in the Chinese plant.

Throughout this book we have seen varied and changing aspects of the life and labor of Chinese workers: the occupations they fill, the way they are trained and allocated for jobs, the role of wages and other material and nonmaterial emoluments, the management of workers with and without trade-unions, how conflicts between workers and their managers arise and are dealt with, and the level of living they enjoy. This account documented to some extent the remolding of the Chinese worker in the new industrial revolution unfolding in Maoist China. Here, at the end, we restate what this signifies for the worker and society, focusing on the two interrelated objectives that have delimited the CCP's strategy, modernization-industrialization and socialization of the means of production and human consciousness.

These two objectives merge with one another in many ways and thus cannot be kept quite distinct. Our intention is to concentrate on social aspects in dealing with modernization-industrialization and to confine ourselves mainly to the economic in commenting on the recent role of socialization in the Maoist redefinition of modern socialist society.

The evolving Maoist process of modernization-industrialization is already changing the life and labor of workers both in their immediate existence and in their relationship to peasants and professionals. The CCP's ideological goal of revolutionary egalitarianism envisioning a classless society in the not-too-distant future is a major determinant of the Chinese meaning of modernization. In their thinking, to modernize in the essential fashion of the USSR and Eastern Europe is to abandon the revolution.

The egalitarian bent of the party is revealed in varied facets of its current and long-range program to shape an advanced socialist industrial society. Industry itself is to be developed dualistically with modern technology and indigenous techniques to be pushed simultaneously with the gap being reduced as the country's technological wherewithal and work force mature. One role of workers in modern industry is to cooperate with their more backward counterparts in indigenous industry to help accelerate the rate of progress.

This linking of modern to indigenous development is an important part of the long-run aim of erasing the difference between town and country which extends, of course, beyond industrial to agricultural activity and workers. Bridging the gap between town and country includes rejection of

Conclusion
181

the urbanization model developed in advanced industrial societies. The Maoist idea is to develop China's technological and capital thrust mainly in the countryside. The influx of people from the country into the city, a vexing phenomenon of the 1950s and early 1960s with attendant urban unemployment, has been stopped and reversed. The attempt to keep Chinese cities from swelling in size and generating an array of forbidding existential problems involves a drastic transformation of rural areas, mainly through the commune, into well-rounded, relatively self-sufficient units organismically functioning in economic, cultural, educational, recreational, administrative, military, and other ways. In the cities, where industry predominates, nurturing of agricultural along with other activities essential to integrated living contributes to the containment of viable rather than exploding concentrations of people, a major consideration for a population approaching 800 million.

For the worker, in town or country, successful attainment of these objectives means much the same array of services and opportunities. For the worker vis-à-vis the peasant, the long-range goal is to raise the peasant's material level to that of the worker. This is to be accomplished not only in income, which already is moving up toward that of the industrial and professional worker, but also in working conditions. The ultimate mechanization of agriculture and the already existing variation in work tasks beyond the agricultural to the industrial and service sectors on communes as well as the introduction of workers from town and country into that unit foreshadow the final eradication of major differences of labor and life between peasants and workers in the distant future.

The gaps in the living and working conditions of workers and professionals likewise are slated for narrowing and have already been brought closer together. One aspect of work differences is the mental labor-physical labor dichotomy which is already being limited. This is being achieved in two particular ways: professional workers (managerial, engineering, technical) are required to engage in productive (physical) labor periodically, sometimes being sent to the countryside on this stint; and other workers (who are engaged mainly in physical labor) are involved in professional (mental) labor through innovation and design campaigns, group decision making, group problem solving, and representation on revolutionary committees running factories. In material terms, as we have seen in chapters 4 and 6, professional workers are not doing so well as formerly, while other workers have enjoyed rising levels of living. Professional workers' salaries in many units have been reduced, especially after the GPCR, to new lower maxima which are only 10 to 30 percent above the maxima for the highest skilled worker and about four times the minimum wage in the same unit. In the 1950s the wage-salary spread was considerably wider: sometimes it exceeded the maximum skilled worker wage by twice or more and was greater by six or more times than the minimum wage in the plant. Furthermore, preferential claims of professional workers to plant housing facilities have been abolished in many places.

The training of workers, a significant factor shaping their lives, has also been radically modified in the Maoist redefinition of modernization. Here the CCP, especially after the GPCR, has stressed Mao's notion of "linking theory and practice" and "proletarianizing" education by combining classroom learning and shop and farm work problems and integrating students with workers or peasants. Faced with a growing predominance of students from nonworker and nonpeasant families, the Maoists have reversed this trend by fundamentally changing admissions procedures and curricula. Admission to universities and institutes comes after several years of work in factories or on farms during which the worker or peasant excels so that she or he is recommended for further education in appropriate institutions. Qualifications include outstanding work performance and exemplary social and political behavior. The curriculum is shortened and contains most of the traditional "theoretical" subjects plus courses in applied problems in the factory or on the commune. School extends to plant and farm. Plant extends to school. The worker or peasant maintains his or her link to the work unit which may be involved in the curriculum, and she or he usually returns to the unit after formal education is completed.

Under these conditions the workers' chances of advanced formal training are increased if their civic and work performance meet required standards. For those workers who do not go on to universities and institutes, but who wish to advance their education there are other routes. Spare-time education is provided through factories, mines, and offices for both general and technical training. Many enterprises also offer work-study arrangements through which workers can advance their learning. Other educational facilities in cities, outside the factory (e.g., trade-unions), minister to the educational needs of workers.

The CCP's efforts to develop sexual equality among workers at all levels has had considerable success in the cities and less success in the countryside. The movement toward equal pay for equal work as applied to women has been one aspect of that success, the other being the admission of women to a wide variety of occupational choices heretofore restricted to men. During and after the GPCR the pace toward equality

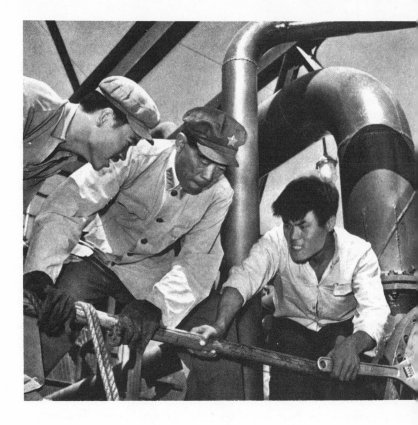

Cadre participation in labor, Peking (China Pictorial, *1, 1972, p. 26*)

quickened, but still there is recognition that a long road remains to be trod before full equality is attained.

In their recently stepped-up drive to develop a one-class or classless society, the CCP has subjected workers as well as peasants to ceaseless ideological remolding. The constant class struggle that Mao called for involves reshaping the thought processes and attitudes of workers to eradicate "bourgeois" mentality and to sensitize individual workers and groups to the negative effects of such thinking and behaving. Pursuing economic gain for self alone and ignoring the interest of one's work or neighborhood group are considered the worst kind of social sins. Using the dialectical process in struggle-criticism-transformation, cadres and workers are expected to put all ideas and mechanisms to the test. Model groups such as the PLA, which started its own cultural revolution early in the 1960s, and the Tach'ing oil workers are constantly held up as exemplars to be emulated.

Whatever cost these ideological talk sessions place on workers, one fact stands out: Chinese workers are continuously confronted with the problems of living, on the job and off. They are left little leeway to escape from the realities that modernizing and industrializing thrust upon them. They are expected to and pressured to take seriously questions of production, organization, and management, as well as those of health care, education, cultural and recreational activity, and civic responsibility. The Maoist redefinition of modernization-industrialization demands that workers as well as other citizens play an active and continuing role in the functioning of factory and neighborhood.

The goal of modernization-industrialization has been linked by the CCP, as we have reiterated, with another goal, socialization of the means of production and of the consciousness of the work force. This latter goal, more heavily stressed by Mao in recent years, impinges on important economic institutions that greatly affect the lives of workers and others. In advancing toward this goal the Maoists have veered away from certain institutions imbedded in the conventional economic wisdom not only in capitalist countries but in Soviet types of economies. They have questioned the assumptions behind principal economic institutions and mechanisms at a time when more and more economists and social critics in the United States are themselves looking more skeptically at how the capitalist market economy operates.

Fundamentally, the Maoist prescription for developing a revolutionary socialism rejects the traditional market mechanism in which prices (including wages) serve to allocate all or some factors of production. Socialization of the means of production *à la Russe* is merely a beginning. For the Maoists socialization of the classical market, which is a highly individualistic, atomistic mechanism, must be pressed, otherwise the old market institutions and mechanisms will reinforce individualistic traits and practices even though enterprises are run by the state. Social ownership of the means of production has to be buttressed with institutions and arrangements which nurture socialist consciousness through new kinds of social relations in which cooperation and group consciousness, rather than individual asocial considerations, contribute to optimum working conditions and output.[1]

The allocative function of the price-market system has to be carried out. The socialization rather than atomization of that function is at the heart of the Maoist model for development. Socioeconomic planning, in which the fundamental strategy and goals for society are determined at the center of party and government, is implemented tactically by the operating units under decentralized supervising units. This is the Maoist framework for allocation, production, distribution, and development. The basic differences between such planning in China and that in the USSR are that the Chinese have begun socializing more of the allocative and related mechanisms as well as the consciousness of workers and peasants, and planning in China gives an important role to operating units in its implementation. For example, in the USSR labor is still allocated mainly through price (wage) differentials. In egalitarian China wage differentials have been increasingly contracted, and wages are not used as tools for allocation.

The consequences of the Maoist socialization of institutions and people affect greatly the lives of workers and others. Interestingly, Maoist arrangements seem to violate or modify drastically important economic principles accepted generally in advanced industrial societies. Along with the implicit questioning of the significance of allocative efficiency as a touchstone to economic development, there is skepticism about the unadulterated acceptance of conventional wisdom on the role and importance of mobility and specialization of labor, motivation, organization, and management of work units, and the pattern of economic development. Looking at how workers have been affected by the Maoists' broad socialization drive reveals some of the radical economics of China.

Chinese workers have been much affected by the Maoist attempt to substitute broad social welfare considerations for the narrower criterion of allocative optimization (what they call "the law of value" which is a profit index of efficiency). Instead of workers choosing occupational specialities, job and living locations, and what amount of input they will contribute and attention they will give to work mainly on the grounds of differential money rewards, they have been expected to move themselves physically and psychically, as has the whole economy, in response to socially determined priorities and values. Specifically, advanced occupational training, beyond high school, depends on the availability of openings in colleges, universities, and institutes (a function of national labor force needs), the individual's interest (affected by societal value emphasis in the mass media), and his or her ability to be recommended by peers for admission to school. As already noted, opportunities for further training are open in individual mines and factories.

But the mobility, specialization, and motivation configuration is such that new, flexible, and open situations are developing. Geographic and horizontal mobility are achieved by administrative assignment, and huge numbers of workers have been moved this way. Individuals may request specific assignments which are granted if they are not in conflict with labor allocation requirements. Individual roaming about to find jobs is illegal, though it exists and probably is not consistently restrained. The unemployment problem in the cities appears to have been solved by massive reassignments to the countryside.

Vertical mobility within work units is relatively flexible, the opportunities being a function of the number and variety of operations in the unit and the extent to which advanced workers and professionals are assigned to newly opened work areas or to other units. The breaking down of rigid and extreme specialization for workers and even for plants themselves (so that steel plants may also make different types of machinery) offers further opportunity for workers to move into new jobs, but perhaps even more significantly, such varied activity in which workers are called upon to do things beside their specialties may reduce greatly alienation and boredom and stimulate self-reliance and greater productivity.

The restriction on individual horizontal mobility, diminished somewhat if operating units are large, and the deemphasis on extreme worker specialization fly in the face of certain accepted economic principles. Yet in our own country there is more and more evidence developing that allocative efficiency, which effective mobility and specialization contribute to, is not as important as organizational and motivational factors.[2] Growing disillusionment with the unquantified costs of growing gross national product is making those economic frameworks more fashionable which take into account broad social welfare considerations instead of narrower economic parameters. Japan's experience with labor mobility, which is quite restricted for large industrial units, shows that rapid growth can occur in spite of the absence of mobile labor.

Chinese socialization of motivation and organization and management of work in factories, mines, and other units has also had an important impact on workers and may in the long run be a major force in her development. The deemphasis of individual material incentives, the development of group-linked incentives, and the reorganization of operating units so that workers are integrally involved in more than their own special assembly-line stint are fundamental elements of the Chinese model. Mao maintains that in the last analysis the human element is the most vital, and that if it be properly nurtured it could deliver unimagined performance. The implementation of this transitional policy while material incentives still operate is part of the effort to transform workers' consciousness into a new socialist mold. For workers it means constant ideological pressure to see their self-interest as imbedded in that of the group, the work unit, the factory, the community, or the society. Paralleling the ideological indoctrination are the socializing mechanisms: group-linked wages, struggle sessions, involvement in emulation campaigns, meetings to deal with specific work problems as well as plant policy, setting of work norms, choice of revolutionary committee representatives, exchange of work teams with other plants, and so on. The constant involvement of workers in many facets of plant operation defines their jobs in much broader terms than either the occupational specialty or the job function so that the effective operation of the whole rather than each worker's part becomes the continuing work focus. The narrowing wage differences between skilled and professional workers as well as the policy of involving all workers in design, innovation, and problem solving facilitate flexible in-plant functional movement and return to earlier job posts.[3]

Maoist motivational policy, while clearly aimed at the ultimate goal of the Communist ideal—from each according to his or her ability, to each according to his or her need—has and will vary. The pendulum swinging from stress on material and individual incentives to emphasis on nonmaterial and group motivation will continue. This transitional dialectic in which the pendulum will not return to its exact earlier opposite is considered an essential means for transforming bourgeois mechanisms into socialist and then Communist ones, not in one giant step but in a series of swings each arc of which becomes more socialistic and communistic in its sweep.

The Maoist view that economic development should be proportionate rather than disproportionate, that agriculture should have highest priority, and that industry and agriculture must be developed simultaneously has resulted in a variety of policies affecting favorably the material well-being of workers and peasants. The overall growth strategy has included greater emphasis on consumer goods and services in the countryside as well as in the cities. Capital formation has not been neglected, but its growth has been handled dualistically: agriculture and indigenous industry have been provided with pools of labor from among the urban unemployed to develop capital locally while modern industry has generated the capital for its further growth in its own sector.

For workers in general the more measured and balanced industrial growth has meant rising consumer goods and services. Though consumer goods output has risen only modestly in the modern sector, a variety of services has developed more robustly. Education, cultural and recreational activity, public sanitation, and health care services have grown substantially since 1949, contributing to an improved quality of life going beyond the material. Housing, which has been tight over much of the last twenty years, has probably eased somewhat recently with expanded construction and the mass transfer of people to the countryside during and after the GPCR. Workers in the cities may have lately suffered some decline in these services as teachers, artists, and health-care personnel were sent in large numbers from the cities, though compensatory training of city-dwellers to replace transferred health-care personnel and others may have held any such decline in check. Workers in the countryside undoubtedly have enjoyed marked rises in these services as the underdeveloped areas of health, education, and culture were given a solid boost since the GPCR. As for consumer goods in the countryside, they have been increased in number greatly in communes and for workers in county and provincial industries.

Interestingly, this significant shift from the older policy and practice of squeezing savings for capital formation from agriculture and consumer industries comes in China at a time when Western economists have been developing the notion of investing in human capital. The idea of such human investment, paralleling capital formation in the form of machinery, roads, canals, etcetera, is not necessarily in conflict with conventional economic thinking. Research on the effects of such investment in the past on our own economic development supports the general idea that providing human beings with more and better education, health care, nutrition, recreation, and the like, contributes to more efficient work input. In China the idea of leading to greater output through serving the basic needs of the people conforms to this economic thinking.[4]

Another economic aspect of the Maoist model which seems to fly in the face of conventional wisdom is its emphasis on a degree of autarkic development in many parts of the economy. This policy has both economic and military elements that are interrelated. The economic rationale is linked to the idea of simultaneous development of indigenous and modern industry with autarky more prominent in the former sector as it struggles to grow rapidly. Furthermore, self-sufficient or self-reliant communes, counties, and provinces save considerable capital in minimizing the development of modern transportation and communications; local extension of educational, cultural, recreational, health care, and other human services by localities also reduces greatly capital expenditure by the modern sector.

The existence of 50,000 self-sufficient communes as well as numerous independent county and provincial economic units provides, in the Maoist view, an excellent grass-roots base for defensive military activity in the event of sudden nuclear or other attack. The shaping of the PLA itself, over its entire history, as a multifaceted unit, military, economic, political, and social, reflects the guerrilla psychology, the Yenan Spirit, which informs the strategic development of China even after guerrilla warfare has long ceased.[5]

The functioning of self-sufficient economic units among large numbers of people also gives very wide play to the cultivation of individual and group self-reliance which is a salient element in Maoist political economy, impinging on the area of revolutionary motivation. In the framework of communes, where an extensive variety of economic work roles has to be carried out, autarkic activity allows greater vertical and horizontal mobility within the unit, calls for specialists to engage in other activities using slack periods productively, and affords more opportunity for group-oriented projects reinforcing social incentives.

In plants and mines, especially in the modern sector of industry, there has been some movement in an autarkic direction as the policy of "comprehensive" or "multipurpose utilization" has been expanded. This policy calls for production of many items other than the specialized activity of a brewery, paper, or textile plant to serve their own needs or that of nearby agricultural units and to utilize unused labor capacity, waste materials, and plant capacity. Some industrial plants have been engaged in agricultural cultivation to meet certain food needs of the plants' workers. This variety of worker activity, as already suggested above, sets up a more attractive situation for workers, is expected to unleash greater worker inputs, and substitutes responsive planning for dictates of a market mechanism.[6]

Thus we see that the Chinese worker is, along with the peasant, in the midst of a revolutionary modernization process aimed at uniting the earlier dual objectives, modernization-industrialization and socialization (which in the 1950s and early 1960s often were in conflict) toward the end of a Communist human being whose commitment and self-fulfillment will sustain an ever-expanding egalitarian economy and society. Modernization moves toward greater human control over the natural environment and culture, including technology; socialization shapes institutions and people to achieve that control through new modes and formats more clearly suited to a socialist society and qualitatively different from those shaped by earlier market-oriented travellers on the modernization trail. Revolutionary modernization thus calls for sharp breaks with the past in which modernization and socialization mutually reinforce one another in molding a new society, a new worker, a new peasant.[7]

For the Maoists the new society, if it is to fulfill Marxist-Leninist ideals, must put technology in the service of man and woman rather than cast them in the roles of alienated actors directed and used by a bureaucratic technocracy. Such a classless society by definition must be distinguished by the absence of institutional exploitation, deprivation, and alienation. Society's fundamental legitimation must rest on a decentralized hierarchy, a leadership in which the ability to relate effectively to and to galvanize others to work cooperatively toward joint goals is cultivated. For the worker, the Maoist vision predicts, alienation is erased by group identification, development of self-reliance and creativity of individuals and groups, and personal fulfillment and satisfaction through functional participation in numerous facets of daily economic, social, political life.

For China as well as the outside world the above Maoist agenda for effective continuing revolution until the essentials of a classless society are molded holds momentous import. If the social order is lifted and transformed by all people raising their consciousness rather than an elite achieving those same ends, a new era will unfold. If, on the other hand, the Chinese are forced to return to elitist or traditional mechanisms and relationships, conventional wisdom informed by the Chinese experiment will be reinforced in many of its aspects. Whatever the outcome China's vast Maoist essay in social and human transformation cannot help but affect all peoples.

Notes

The following periodicals which are cited throughout the notes are described briefly here.

Current Background is a translation series which is published occasionally by the United States Consultate in Hong Kong.

China Quarterly is published in London.

China Reconstructs is a monthly periodical published in Peking.

Current Scene is published twice a month in Hong Kong.

Far Eastern Economic Review is published weekly in Hong Kong.

Hung-ch'i [Red flag] is published semi-monthly in Peking.

Jen-min jih-pao [People's daily] is published in Peking.

Kung-jen jih-pao [Workers daily] is published in Peking.

Kuang-ming jih-pao [Kuangming daily] is published in Peking.

Lao-tung [Labor] was published monthly in Peking.

Peking Review is published weekly in Peking.

T'ung-chi kung-tso [Statistical work] was published semi-monthly in Peking.

T'ung-chi kung-tso t'ung-hsün [Statistical work bulletin] was published in Peking semi-monthly.

Ta kung pao [Impartial daily] is published in Peking.

Chapter 1. Introduction

1. Alexander Eckstein et al., eds., *Economic trends in Communist China* (Chicago: Aldine, 1968), p. 580; and N. R. Chen, ed., *Chinese Economic Statistics* (Chicago: Aldine, 1967), p. 187.

2. *Peking Review,* 6 January 1961, p. 8.

3. See Leo A. Orleans, "Propheteering: The Population of Communist China," *Current Scene,* 15 December 1969, pp. 13–19.

4. Jo Shui, "Jen k'ou ho jen shou" [Mouths and hands], *Jen-min jih-pao,* 15 April 1959, p. 7; and Leo A. Orleans, "Evidence from Chinese Medical Journals on Current Population Policy," *China Quarterly,* October–December 1969, pp. 137–46.

5. See Dwight H. Perkins, "Mao Tse-Tung's Goals and China's Economic Performance," *Current Scene,* 7 January 1971, pp. 10–13.

6. "Politics Is In Command," *Peking Review,* 25 July 1969, pp. 6–7.

7. "The Road to China's Socialist Industrialization," *Hung-ch'i,* no. 10 (September

1969), translated in U.S. Consulate, Hong Kong, *Selections from China Mainland Magazines,* 31 October 1969, p. 14 (hereafter cited as SCMM). Cf. Stuart R. Schram, "Mao Tse-tung and the search for a 'Chinese Road' to Socialism" (address to the Royal Central Asian Society, 24 July 1968).

8. *The Red Book and the Great Wall* (New York: Farrar, Straus & Giroux, 1968), pp. 50, 86.

9. "Socialist Construction and Class Struggle in the Field of Economics," *Ta kung pao,* 19–25 February 1970 (abridged from *Hung–ch'i,* no. 2 [1970], p. 7).

10. Ibid., p. 6 (emphasis added). Chinese planning involves considerably fewer global targets than are found in Soviet plans.

11. See Dwight H. Perkins, *Market Control and Planning in Communist China* (Cambridge: Harvard University Press, 1966), passim.

12. "Resolutely Defend the Party Principle of Democratic Centralism," *Peking Review,* 19 April 1968, pp. 20–22; also article in *Jen-min jih-pao,* reported in U.S. Foreign Broadcast Information Service, *Daily Report: Communist China,* 22 July 1970, pp. B6–B7 (hereafter cited as FBIS-1).

13. New China News Agency release, "PLA Party Committee Stresses Democratic Centralism," 13 June 1970, reported in FBIS-1, 15 June 1970, p. B6. See also "The Road to China's Socialist Industrialization," *Hung-ch'i,* no. 10 (1969), translated in SCMM 666, 31 October 1969, pp. 15–17. (Emphasis added. New China News Agency hereafter cited as NCNA.)

14. See "Socialist Construction and Class Struggle."

15. Jack Gray, in Bulletin of the Atomic Scientists, *China After the Cultural Revolution* (New York: Random House, 1969), pp. 140–42.

16. Mao Tse-tung, "On the Question of Agricultural Co-operation," in *Selected Readings from the Works of Mao Tse-Tung* (Peking: Foreign Languages Press, 1967), pp. 329, 331, 332, 335. The views of Eric Axilrod, director of the Economic Research Centre at The Chinese University of Hong Kong, have also helped inform my perception of the Maoist-Liuist strategic conflict.

17. "The Road to China's Socialist Industrialization," SCMM, 30 September 1969, pp. 14–15.

18. NCNA release, "Achieve Greater, Faster, Better, and More Economical Results in Developing Local Industries," Peking broadcast, reported in FBIS-1, 12 June 1970, pp. B1–B10.

19. Ibid.

20. Leo A. Orleans and Richard P. Suttmeier, "The Mao Ethic and Environmental Quality," *Science,* 11 December 1970, pp. 1173–76; NCNA release, "Something New in Industry's Support to Agriculture," Peking broadcast, 30 November 1970, reported in FBIS-1, 2 December 1970, p. B7; NCNA release, "Concentrate on Production in Breadth and Depth," Peking broadcast, 1 December 1970, ibid., pp. B4–B7; Changsha Hunan provincial broadcast, "Hunan Municipality Utilizes Industrial Wastes," 11 December 1970, reported in FBIS-1, 16 December 1970, pp. D4–D5; Peking broadcast, "Industrial Waste Recovery," reported in British Broadcasting Corporation, *Summary of World Broadcasts,* pt. 3, "The Far East,: 29 September 1971, FE/W641/A/4-A/5; also reported in *New York Times,* 18 September 1971, p. 9. (*Summary of World Broadcasts* will be cited hereafter as SWB.)

21. John G. Gurley, "Capitalist and Maoist Economic Development," in E. Friedman and M. Selden, eds., *America's Asia* (New York: Vintage, 1971), p. 339.

22. *China Pictorial*, no. 5 (1970), p. 1.

23. "Vigorously Constitute Socialist Cooperation," *Jen-min jih-pao*, 18 May 1970, reprinted in U.S. Consulate, Hong Kong, *Survey of China Mainland Press*, 28 May 1970, p. 98 (hereafter cited as SCMP).

24. Martin King Whyte, "The Tachai Brigade and Incentives for the Peasant," *Current Scene*, 15 August 1969, pp. 1–13.

25. "Socialist Construction and Class Struggle in the Field of Economics," *Ta kung pao*, 19–25 February 1970, p. 7; "Notes on the Taching Oilfield," *China Reconstructs*, December 1968, pp. 38–41; and "Across the Land," *Peking Review*, 1 November 1968, pp. 29–30.

26. See NCNA, "Liaoning Stresses Role of Man in Production," Peking broadcast, 11 June 1970, reported in FBIS-1, 23 June 1970, p. G12; "Lay Emphasis on One Thing and Engage in Diversified Operations," Peking broadcast, 14 November 1970, reported in FBIS-1, 24 November 1970, pp. B1–B2; and "Nanking Plants Promote Multipurpose Utilization," Peking broadcast, 27 August 1971, reported in FBIS-1, 1 September 1970, pp. C2–C3.

27. NCNA, "Communists Should Be Advanced Elements of Proletariat," 30 June 1970, reprinted in SCMP, 10 July 1970, pp. 219–22; and *The Constitution of the Communist Party of China* in *China Reconstructs*, July 1969, p. 33.

28. Ibid.

Chapter 2. Employing the Chinese Worker

1. John Philip Emerson, *Nonagricultural Employment in Mainland China: 1949–1958* (Washington, D.C.: Government Printing Office, 1965), pp. 45–52. (U.S. Bureau of the Census, International Population Statistics Reports, series P-90, no. 21).

2. See John S. Aird, *The Size, Composition, and Growth of the Population of Mainland China* (Washington, D.C.: U.S. Government Printing Office, 1961), p. 83 (U.S. Bureau of the Census, International Population Statistics Reports, series P-90).

3. Ibid.

4. See Christopher Howe, *Employment and Economic Growth in Urban China: 1949–1957* (Cambridge: Cambridge University Press, 1971), p. 61.

5. See People's Republic of China, State Statistical Bureau, *Ten Great Years* (Peking: Foreign Languages Press, 1960), p. 16.

6. A. Donnithorne, *China's Economic System* (New York: Praeger, 1967), p. 184.

7. Peter Schran, "Handicrafts in Communist China," in C. M. Li, ed., *Industrial Development in Communist China* (New York: Praeger, 1964), pp. 151–73. By 1961 millions of workers were still working on handicrafts in communes and elsewhere. See also *Kuang-ming jih-pao* 19 October 1964, p. 1, reported in U.S. Joint Publications Research Service, 29 January 1965, p. 92 (hereafter cited as JPRS).

8. Ralph C. Croizier, *Traditional Medicine in Modern China* (Cambridge: Harvard University Press, 1968), pp. 167–68, 184–85; and Emerson, *Nonagricultural Employment in Mainland China*, p. 155.

9. Emerson, *Nonagricultural Employment in Mainland China*, p. 154.

10. Ibid.

11. Ibid., pp. 153–54.

12. Ibid., pp. 156–57.

13. Ibid., pp. 146–53, 162–63, 165.

14. Robert M. Field, "Industrial Production in Communist China: 1957–1968," *China Quarterly,* April-June 1970, p. 47; and S. Swami amd S. J. Burki, "Foodgrains Output in the People's Republic of China, 1958–65," *China Quarterly,* January-March 1970, pp. 58–63.

15. R. Field, "Industrial Production in Communist China," p. 47; Barry Richman, *Industrial Society in Communist China* (New York: Random House, 1969), p. 600; and John Philip Emerson, "Employment in Mainland China: Problems and Prospects," in U.S. Congress, Joint Economic Committee, *An Economic Profile of Mainland China* (Washington, D.C.: U.S. Government Printing Office, 1967), 2:445, 460.

16. See "Full Employment Stable Prices and Self-Sufficiency in Grain," SWB, 19 September 1971, FE/3791/C/1-C/2; and *New York Times,* 21 September 1971, p. 11 and 10 December 1972, p. 11.

17. Emerson, *Nonagricultural Employment in Mainland China,* pp. 445, 460; Field, "Industrial Production in Communist China," p. 610; Donnithorne, *China's Economic System,* p. 185.

18. Field, "Industrial Production in Communist China," p. 56; and Richman, *Industrial Society in Community China,* pp. 600–602.

19. *China News Summary,* no. 455, 15 February 1973.

20. Field, "Industrial Production in Communist China," p. 56.

21. C. Y. Cheng, "Growth and Structural Change in the Chinese Machine Building Industry, 1952–66," *China Quarterly,* January-March 1970, pp. 26–57.

22. John Philip Emerson, *Administrative and Technical Manpower in the People's Republic of China,* International Population Reports, series P-65, no. 72 (Washington, D.C.: U.S. Department of Commerce, 1973), p. 37.

23. Quote cited in Wang Ya-nan, "The Marxist Population Theory and China's Population Problem," *K'o-hsueh ch'u pan-she* (Peking, 1956); translated in *Chinese Economic Studies* 2, nos. 3–4 (Spring-Summer 1969):82. See also *Hsueh-hsi* [Study], no. 114 (18 June 1957), translated in *Union Research Service* 8, no. 21 (10 September 1957):363, for another clear-cut expression of the expectation that unemployment would be around for a long time. In this extended discussion the author proposed, in a neoclassical attitude, that "when formulating wage policy, consideration should be given to the lowering of wages in order to create more jobs" (p. 369).

24. Donnithorne, *China's Economic System,* p. 184.

25. Chi-ming Hou, "Manpower, Employment, and Unemployment," in Alexander Eckstein et al., eds., *Economic Trends in Communist China* (Chicago: Aldine, 1968), pp. 370–71. See also, e.g., William C. Thiesenhusen, "Latin America's Employment Problem," *Science,* 5 March 1971, 868–74.

26. Donnithorne, *China's Economic System,* p. 184; *Chinese Workers March Towards Socialism* (Peking: Foreign Languages Press, 1956), p. 79; *Lao Tung,* 3 November 1957, translated in *Union Research Service* 10, no. 3 (10 January 1958):45; and Christopher Howe, *Employment and Economic Growth,* pp. 107–37.

27. *Chinese Workers March Towards Socialism,* pp. 80–81.

28. On relief see Christopher Howe, *Employment and Economic Growth,* p. 93–97.

29. Alexander Eckstein, *The National Income of Communist China* (New York: Free Press of Glencoe, 1961), p. 150; and Donnithorne, *China's Economic System,* p. 387. See also directives and regulations on various aspects of the unemployment question. For example, "General Regulations on the Establishment of City Employment Agencies," issued by the Labor Ministry in May 1950 in *Chung yang ts'ai ching cheng ts'e fa ling hui pien* [Collections of laws and regulations on financial and economic policies of the Central Government], pp. 773–74; and "Directive on the Method of Collecting and Distributing Relief Contribution Funds for Unemployed Workers," issued by the All-China Federation of Trade-Unions in May 1950, which is also in *Collections of Laws and Regulations,* pp. 769–70.

30. Richman, *Industrial Society in Communist China,* p. 216.

31. Donnithorne, *China's Economic System,* pp. 184–87 and Howe, *Employment and Economic Growth,* pp. 116–17.

32. For discussion of the various factors giving rise to unemployment see *Hsueh-hsi* [Study], no. 114 (18 June 1957), and *Heilungkiang Jih-pao* [Heilungkiang Daily], 4 June 1957 (extracts from a speech by Chang Ming-lun) which are both translated in *Union Research Service* 8, no. 21 (10 September 1957): 362–70 and 370–77; and *Honan Jih-pao,* 26 March 1957 in SCMP, 21 May 1957, pp. 27–29.

33. "Peking's Program to Move Human and Material Resources to the Countryside," *Current Scene,* 15 September 1969, pp. 1–17.

34. *New York Times,* 18 January 1971; p. 46; Edgar Snow, "The Open Door," *New Republic,* 27 March 1971, p. 21; and SWB, 19 September 1971, FE/3791/C1-C2.

35. People's Republic of China, *Ten Great Years,* p. 110.

36. Ibid., and Robert M. Field, "Industrial Production in Communist China," p. 637.

37. People's Republic of China, *Ten Great Years,* p. 110.

Chapter 3. Allocating Workers

1. Christopher Howe, *Employment and Economic Growth in Urban China: 1949–1959* (Cambridge: Cambridge University Press, 1971), pp. 107–17, for a discussion of allocation problems during the FFYP.

2. *New York Times,* 18 January 1971, p. 46

3. *Important Labour Laws and Regulations of the People's Republic of China* (Peking: Foreign Languages Press, 1961), p. 11.

4. See "Provisional Regulations on Apprenticeship of the State Council, 16 November 1957," in Chao Kuo-Chun, *Economic Planning and Organization in Mainland China* (Cambridge: Center for East Asian Studies, 1960) 2: 103–107; and NCNA, "State Council Notification Calls for Extension of the Period of Apprenticeship," Peking, 9 May 1957, reported in SCMP 1537, 24 May 1957, 1–2

5. Cf. *Labor War Bulletin,* translated in *Chinese Sociology and Anthropology* 1, no. 4 (Summer 1969); "Sources of Labor Discontent in China," *Current Scene,* 15 March 1968, pp. 49–60.

6. See "Sources of Labor Discontent in China," *Current Scene*, 15 March 1968; and Jerome A. Cohen, *The Criminal Process in the People's Republic of China* (Cambridge: Harvard, 1968), Chapters 4 and 11.

7. "Sources of Labor Discontent in China," pp. 49–60.

8. "Yen-ko chih chih szu chih chao-shou lin-shih-kung" [Employing temporary workers privately is strictly prohibited], *Anhwei jih-pao*, 18 December 1957; and "Hunan People's Council Adopts Resolution on Employment of Workers" *Hsin Hunan Pao*, 5 January 1957 in SCMP, 28 January 1957, pp. 25–26.

9. *Labor War Bulletin, ibid.; Current Scene,* and NCNA, "Colliery in Shansi Makes Use of Surplus Agricultural Labor," Taiyuan broadcast, 1 November 1964 in SCMP, 16 November 1964, pp. 16–17.

10. "Sources of Labor Discontent in China," *Current Scene,* 15 March 1968, pp. 7–14.

11. "Representative and Contract Labor in Maintaining Roads," *Kung-lu* [Roads], no. 4 (20 April 1965), pp. 7–9, in JPRS, 30 August 1965, pp. 5–7 and *Current Scene,* 15 March 1968, pp. 6–7.

12. "Superiority of Contract Labor in Highway Construction," *Kung-lu,* no. 4 (20 April 1965), pp. 6–7 in JPRS 31, 759, 30 August 1965, pp. 1–4.

13. *Labor War Bulletin,* pp. 54–60; and "Sources of Labor Discontent in China," pp. 8–12.

14. Barry Richman, *Industrial Society in Communist China* (New York: Random House, 1969), pp. 306–307.

15. A. Donnithorne, *China's Economic System* (New York: Praeger, 1967), pp. 98–99; Taipei Institute for the Study of Chinese Communist Problems, *1969 chung-kung nien-pao* [1969 yearbook on Chinese Communism], pp. 85–86; and *New York Times,* 18 January 1971, p. 46.

16. Donnithorne, *China's Economic System,* pp. 97–99, 106, 151; and "Soldiers in Work Clothes," *China Reconstructs,* May 1970, pp. 16–18.

17. Richman, *Industrial Society in Communist China,* pp. 292–306 and my own personal inquiries in China.

18. On examples of educational reform related to vocational needs and the "educational revolution" see NCNA, "Investigation Report: Shanghai Worker-Technicians Mature," Shanghai broadcast, 29 July 1969, in SCMP, 6 August 1969, pp. 16–19; NCNA, "Report on New-Type Shanghai Workers College," Peking broadcast, 28 September 1969, cited in FBIS-1, 29 September 1969, pp. C5–C7; "Wuhan University Personnel Reeducated in factories," Wuhan Hupeh radio broadcast, 6 June 1970, cited in FBIS-1, 8 June 1970, p. D4; Wang Hsueh-wen, "An Analytical Study of the Chinese Communist 'Educational Revolution,' " *Issues & Studies,* April 1968, pp. 24–36; "Brilliant 'May 7 Directive' Is Guideline for Running Socialist Engineering College Well," *Kuang-ming jih-pao,* 7 May 1970, in SCMP 4660 (20 May 1970):74–81; and Ross Terrill, "Tomorrow's China," *Observer Review,* 9 January 1972.

19. Richman, *Industrial Society in Communist China,* pp. 126–28. For a specific description of Chinese educational institutions, see Stewart E. Fraser, ed., *Education and Communism in China* (Hong Kong: International Studies Group, 1969).

20. Richman, *Industrial Society in Communist China,* pp. 126–28.

21. See Terrill, "Tomorrow's China"; Ethan Signer and Arthur W. Galston, "Education and Science in China," *Science,* 7 January 1972, pp. 15–23; and Jen Wen,

"Road of Training Technicians from Among the Workers," *Peking Review,* 6 August 1971, pp. 12–15.

22. Quoted in Shenyang Liaoning provincial radio service, "Acting on Chairman Mao's Instructions Means Victory," 26 July 1970, cited in FBIS-1, 31 July 1971, p. G4.

23. Quote from *Educational Revolution,* no. 20, cited in *Issues & Studies,* October 1970, p. 13.

24. *Issues & Studies,* October 1970, p. 13; Shanghai radio broadcast, 24 July 1970, cited in FBIS-1, 30 July 1970, p. C2; and Changsha radio broadcast, ibid., 26 August 1971, p. D3.

25. *Peking Review,* no. 31, 31 July 1970, p. 5.

26. "Strive to Build a Socialist University of Science and Engineering," (originally in *Hung-ch'i,* no. 8, 1970) *Peking Review,* 5 August 1971, pp. 5–15.

27. See Terrill, "Tomorrow's China"; Ethan Signer and Arthur W. Galston, "Education and Science in China," *Science,* 7 January 1972, pp. 15–23; and Jen Wen, "Road of Training Technicians from Among the Workers," *Peking Review,* 6 August 1971, pp. 12–15; "Building a Socialist University of Science and Engineering," *China Reconstructs,* January 1971, pp. 2–6, 9–10; and "Anhwei Colleges Open Doors, List Admission Procedures," Hofei radio broadcast, 21 February 1972, cited in U.S. Foreign Broadcast Information Service, *Daily Report: People's Republic of China,* 23 February 1972, pp. C7–C9 (after 2 August 1972, the title of *Daily Report: Communist China* [FBIS-1] was changed to *Daily Report: People's Republic of China,* which hereafter will be cited FBIS-2).

28. See, e.g., "Nanking Agricultural College Creates County College," Nanking radio broadcast, 11 May 1970, cited in FBIS-1, 20 May 1970, pp. C9–C10; "Study Once Again While Doing Mass Work," *Jen-min jih-pao,* 2 June 1970, in SCMP 4, 678, 17 June 1970, pp. 79–83; and Committee of Concerned Asian Scholars, *China! Inside the People's Republic* (New York: Bantam, 1972), pp. 99–102.

29. Richman, *Industrial Society in Communist China,* p. 134; and "Decision of the Central Committee of the Chinese Communist Party Concerning the Great Proletarian Cultural Revolution" (adopted 8 August 1966), in *Chinese Communist Party Documents of the Great Proletarian Cultural Revolution, 1966–1967* (Hong Kong: Union Research Institute, 1968), pp. 50–51.

30. Richman, *Industrial Society in Communist China,* pp. 126–28, 302; C. Y. Cheng, *Scientific and Engineering Manpower in Communist China 1949–1963,* (Washington D.C.: National Science Foundation, 1965) p. 61; and "Do a Good Job in Operating Short-Term Workers' Training Classes," *Jen-min jih-pao,* 12 October 1971, cited in FBIS-2, 9 November 1971, pp. B3–B4.

31. NCNA, "Report of New-Type Shanghai Workers College," cited in FBIS-1, 28 September 1970, pp. C5–C7. See also "A Hsien-Operated New-Type Socialist College," *Kuang-ming jih-pao,* 6 May 1970, in SCMP 4, 658, 18 May 1970, pp. 1–7.

32. Richman, *Industrial Society in Communist China,* pp. 126–28.

33. Cheng, *Scientific and Engineering Manpower,* pp. 176–77; Chou En-lai, *Report on the Question of Intellectuals* (Peking: Foreign Languages Press, 1956), pp. 16–17.

34. Ministry of Labor, "Temporary Regulations on Employment of Workers from Other Areas," in *Chung Yang Ts'ai Ching Cheng Ts'e Fa Ling Hui Pien* [Collections of the laws and regulations of financial and economic policies of the Central Government] (Peking: Hsin Hua Bookstore, 1952), p. 1066.

35. Personnel Bureau, State Council, "Notice Concerning the Correct Handling of Resignations of Government Workers and Staff" issued 4 September 1957.

36. "Decisions of Employment of the Government Administration Council," (25 July 1952), in *Labour Laws and Regulations of the People's Republic of China* (Peking: Foreign Languages Press, 1956), pp. 65–80.

37. "State Council Directive Concerning Preventing Country People from Drifting into the Cities," (30 December 1956), in *Collections of Laws and Regulations of the People's Republic of China* (Peking: Law Press, 1956), pp. 225–26; and NCNA, "State Council Decides to Stop Increase of Government Organs," 16 November 1956, in SCMP 1, 415, 21 November 1956, p. 5.

38. For a variety of actions on the problem of uncontrolled movement, see NCNA, "Resettlers Settled Down Well in Heilungkiang," 22 December 1956, in SCMP, 14 January 1957, p. 17; NCNA, "725,000 Persons Resettled for Reclamation in Country in 1956," 27 December 1956, in SCMP, 17 January 1957, pp. 8–9; "Hunan People's Council Adopts Resolution on Employment of Workers by Organs, Enterprises," Changsha, *Hsin Hunan Pao*, 5 January 1957, in SCMP, 28 January 1957, pp. 25–26; "Shanghai Takes Steps to Prevent Infiltration of People into City from Outside," Shanghai *Hsin Wen Jih-pao*, 8 January 1957, in SCMP, 21 February 1957, pp. 13–15; "Canton Organs Prepare for Retrenchment," *Nan-fang Jih-pao*, 10 January 1957, in SCMP, 28 January 1957, pp. 26–27; "About the Problem of Resettlement and Reclamation," *Kuang-ming Jih-pao*, 15 January 1957, in SCMP, 7 February 1957, pp. 6–8; "Direct Employment of Members of Agricultural Cooperatives Is Not Permitted," *Tsitsihar Jih-pao*, 15 January 1957, in SCMP, 28 February 1957, p. 29; "Peasants Blindly Infiltrate into Amoy," *Amoy Jih-pao*, 22 January 1957, in SCMP, Honan Provincial People's Council, 21 February 1957, p. 15; "A Directive on Preventing Country People from Drifting to the Cities," Chengchow *Honan Jih-pao*, 26 March 1957, in SCMP, 21 May 1957, pp. 27–29; and "Tens of Thousands of Peasants Flow into Cities," Peking, *Takung pao*, 3 June 1957, in SCMP, 24 June 1957, p. 23.

39. Ibid.; and "Report of the Ministry of Internal Affairs on the Situation and Opinion of the Handling of Peasants in Famine Areas Infiltrating the Cities," (30 April 1957), in *Collections of Laws and Regulations of the People's Republic of China* (Peking: Law Press, 1958), pp. 107–11.

40. *Employing Temporary Workers Privately Strictly Prohibited*, in *Anhwei Jih-pao*, 18 December 1957 (Union Research Institute Microfilm Files, 1957) Carton B29, 141344.

41. Richman, *Industrial Society in Communist China*, pp. 374–80.

42. Donnithorne, *China's Economic System*, p. 183.

43. Ibid., pp. 183, 311.

44. "The Road to China's Socialist Industrialization," *Hung-ch'i*, no. 10, 30 September 1970, in SCMM, 31 October 1970, pp. 18–19. On Mao's program to move tens of millions of people to the countryside, see "Peking's Program to Move Human and Material Resources to the Countryside," *Current Scene*, 15 September 1969, pp. 1–17.

45. The primary sources are replete with descriptions and analyses of a wide array of labor activities in indigenous sectors of the economy. The following samples reflect that array: "Way of Development for Local Small Industries," *Jen-min jih-pao*, 28 May 1970, in SCMP, 9 June 1970, pp. 1–12; "Combine One Main Industry with Multiple Undertakings," *Jen-min jih-pao*, 23 November 1970, pp. 18–22;

"Wholeheartedly Serving the Poor and Lower-Middle Peasants," *Jen-min jih-pao,* 7 November 1970, in SCMP, 1 December 1970; "College Graduates Reeducated on Canton PLA Farms," Canton City Service radio broadcast, 4 May 1970, cited in FBIS-1, 5 May 1970, p. D5; "Sinkiang Youths Reeducated by Peasants, Herdsmen," Urumchi Sinkiang radio broadcast, 4 May 1970, cited in FBIS-1, 6 May 1970, pp. H4–H5; "Advance Along the Brilliant Road of '7 May,' " Nanchang Kiangsi radio broadcast, 6 May 1970, cited in FBIS-1, 18 May 1970, pp. C8–C9; NCNA, "Industry Must Give Vigorous Support to Agriculture," Peking radio broadcast, 3 June 1970, cited in FBIS-1, 5 June 1970, pp. B1–B6, NCNA, "Achieve Greater, Faster, Better, and More Economical Results in Developing Local Industries," Peking radio broadcast, 8 June 1970, cited in FBIS-1, 12 June 1970, pp. B1–B10; "Commentary on Resettled Intellectuals 'Growing Rusty,' " *Jen-min jih-pao,* 7 June 1970, p. 2, cited in FBIS-1, 19 June 1970, p. B1; "Heilungkiang Improves Medical, Health Service," Harbin Heilungkiang radio broadcast, 24 June 1970, cited in FBIS-1, 26 June 1970, pp. G1–G2; and NCNA, "Everyone Give a Hand, Rely on Your Own Efforts . . . in the Renovation of Industrial Equipment," Peking radio broadcast, 9 July 1970, cited in FBIS-1, 14 July 1970, pp. B1–B6. See also, Charles Snyder, "Tomorrow's Challenge," *Far Eastern Economic Review,* 31 October 1970, pp. 43–44, on pollution and waste problems.

Chapter 4. Motivating Workers

1. See Charles Hoffmann, *Work Incentive Practices and Policies in the People's Republic of China 1953–1965* (Albany: State University of New York Press, 1967) for a comprehensive review of work incentives to the eve of the GPCR. For a comparative view of incentives in another Communist country see, Robert M. Bernardo, *The Theory of Moral Incentives in Cuba* (University, Alabama: University of Alabama Press, 1971) and Carmelo Mesa-Lago, *The Labor Sector and Socialist Distribution in Cuba,* (New York: Praeger, 1968).

2. I am indebted to Carl Riskin for some of these ideas. They have come from discussions with him and from a fine paper, "Homo Economicus vs. Homo Sinicus: A Discussion of Work Motivation in China," which he presented at the Conference on New Perspectives for the Study of Contemporary China, Montreal, September 1971, and which will be published in a book not yet titled by Pantheon in 1973 or 1974.

3. See Peter Schran, "The Structure of Income in Communist China" (Ph.D. diss., University of California, Berkeley, 1961), pp. 249–252, for a review of these problems.

4. See, e.g., "Even if Pay According to Work is Bourgeois, It Helps Socialist Construction," *Ta kung pao,* 15 October 1963, in JPRS, 6 February 1964, pp. 36–38; and Yuan Fang, "The Ratio of Increase Between Labor Productivity and Wages," *Hsin chien-she,* 3 December 1956, in U.S. Consulate, Hong Kong, *Extracts from China Mainland Magazines* no. 71, 25 February 1957, pp. 10–18 (hereafter cited as ECMM).

5. The account of changing incentive policy is based on Hoffmann, *Work Incentive Practices,* ch. 5. See also E. L. Wheelwright and B. McFarlane, *The Chinese Road to Socialism* (New York and London: Monthly Review Press, 1970), chapter 8, for an insightful discussion of incentives.

6. See *China Topics,* YB547 (Economic-32), 28 April 1970, p. 11.

7. For some actual scales in different branches see *Lao-tung* [Labor], no. 7 (3 April 1957); no. 8, (18 April 1957); no. 10 (18 May 1957) in JPRS, 14 October 1958, pp. 16–23. Reports in 1964 indicate that mechanisms were much as depicted in the model wage grade pattern above. See Dick Wilson *Far Eastern Economic Review,* 4 June 1964, pp. 502–503 and 18 June 1964, pp. 595–97. For the 1965 situation see "Ta lu kung jen ti kung tzu ho shang huo" [The wages and living of the workers in mainland China], *Chin-jih shih-chieh* [World today], no. 316, (May 1965), p. 8. In 1972 the Shenyang No. 1 Lathe Factory had an eight-grade wage scale much the same as some spelled out above. Wages started in Grade 1 at ¥ 33 a month and rose to ¥ 104 for Grade 8. For details on workers' welfare in this factory see *China Now,* no. 31, (April-May 1973), pp. 1–4. The scales for the Peking Machine Tools Plant were obtained personally by the author during a visit to the plant on July 9, 1973.

8. *Chin-jih shih-chieh,* no. 316, p. 8.

9. "Notification on the Issuance of a Program of Wage Scales for the Workers on State Organs" (State Council no. Hsi-54, 1956), in *Compilation of the Laws and Regulations of Financial Administration of the Central Government* (Peking: 1956), pp. 226–247, translated in JPRS 35, no. 455, (11 May 1966): 25, 38.

10. Ibid., pp. 15–18; Barry Richman *Industrial Society in Communist China* (New York: Random House, 1969), pp. 799–803; Abram Bergson, *The Structure of Soviet Wages* (Cambridge: Harvard University Press, 1954), passim.; and "Talking about wages," *China Now,* July 1971, pp. 2–3. The diary of Bruce McFarlane, an Australian academic who visited Chinese plants in 1968, confirms the narrowing of the wage spread between directors, engineers, and other managers and regular industrial workers. The recent data on senior professors' salaries were obtained personally by the author in visits to universities during July 1973. Copies of the diary are in the possession of Columbia University's East Asian Institute. There are exceptions to the ¥ 400 maximum cited in the text, including wages for workers with great seniority, foreign workers, etcetera. An interesting one is that of United States expatriates working in Chinese publishing, broadcasting, and industry. Their monthly pay ranges from ¥ 300 to ¥ 800 (see *New York Times,* 17 March 1972, p. 10). Interestingly, servants still exist, at least for foreign diplomats, and these amahs, cooks, and waiters average about ¥ 100 a month (see *San Francisco Chronicle,* 14 June 1970, p. 7 [Sunday Punch].

11. See *Lao-tung,* numbers cited in JPRS, October 1958, pp. 16–23.

12. *T'ung-chi kung-tso,* no. 7, 14 April 1957, in JPRS, 14 October 1958, pp. 16–23; and J. G. Gliksman, *The Control of the Industrial Labor Force in the Soviet Union* (Santa Monica, California: RAND Corporation, 1960), pp. 33, 60. For a general survey of different types of wage systems see Lin Fang, "A Discussion on the Forms of Wages," *Jen-min jih-pao,* 28 October 1961, in JPRS, 25 April 1962, pp. 79–93.

13. "Discussion on Progress of the Piece-Work System," *Lao-tung,* no. 3, 3 February 1962, in JPRS, 14 December 1962, pp. 70–74.

14. "Conditions for the Enforcement of the Piece Wage System," *Ta kung-pao* 2 November 1962, p. 3, in JPRS, 17 December 1962, pp. 50–51; and Gliksman, *Control of the Industrial Labor Force,* p. 28.

15. "A Study of the System of Piece Work Incentive Awards," *Lao-tung,* no. 23, 3 December 1959, pp. 24–27, in JPRS, 1 June 1960, pp. 9–16; and Gliksman, *Control of the Industrial Labor Force,* p. 19.

16. *Lao-tung,* no. 8 (18 April 1957), in JPRS, no. 754, 14 October 1958, pp. 16–23.

17. *Lao-tung,* no. 23 (3 December 1959), pp. 27–28, in JPRS, 1 June 1960, pp. 17–20.

18. *Lao-tung,* no. 7 (3 April 1957), pp. 13–14, in JPRS, 14 October 1958, pp. 16–23.

19. See "tui mu ch'ien shou kung yeh ho tso she chi chien kung tzu wen t'i shang ch'ueh" [Problems of the piece work system at the present stage of handicraft cooperatives] *Lao-tung,* no. 3 (18 March 1964).

20. *Lao-tung,* no. 5 (3 March 1957); no. 10 (18 May 1957), in JPRS, pp. 39–42; and Gliksman, *Control of the Industrial Labor Force,* p. 31. Special bonuses are occasionally bestowed. For example, a bonus of ¥ 30,000 was given to Chief Engineer Yin Chun-tien and others under him for the successful production of China's first 6000 KW steam turbine at the Shanghai State Steam Turbine Plant in 1956. See NCNA Shanghai, May 8, 1956, in SCMP, 11 May 1956, p. 16.

21. *Lao-tung,* no. 196 (18 May 1962), pp. 31–33, in JPRS, 16 April 1963, p. 23.

22. Ibid., pp. 25–26.

23. "Provisional Regulations on the Composition of the Total Amount of Wages" (approved by the State Council 21 May 1955). See *T'ung-chi Kung-tso t'ung-hsin,* no. 1 (January 1956), pp. 7–8.

24. Wheelwright and McFarlane, *The Chinese Road to Socialism,* pp. 134–36, 141 and author's personal observations and discussion in China during July 1973.

25. *Labour Laws and Regulations of the People's Republic of China* (Peking: Foreign Languages Press, 1956), pp. 54–64; "Regulations Governing Awards for Inventions," and "Regulations Governing Awards for Technical Improvements," *Jen-min jih-pao,* 2 December 1963, in JPRS, 6 February 1964, pp. 13–21; and Margaret Dewar, *Labour Policy in the U.S.S.R. 1917–1928* (New York and London: Royal Institute of International Affairs, 1956), pp. 128, 157, 251, 259, 267.

26. See "Regulations Governing Awards for Inventions" and "Regulations Governing Awards for Technical Improvements," pp. 13–21.

27. See *Labour Insurance in New China* (Peking: Foreign Languages Press, 1953), pp. 1–8; *Labour Laws and Regulations,* pp. 31–36; State Statistical Bureau, *Ten Great Years,* p. 218; Gliksman, *The Control of the Industrial Labor Force,* pp. 67–72, *Union Research Service* (Union Research Institute, Hong Kong) 35, no. 21 (12 June 1964):335; and Joyce Kallgren, "Social Welfare and China's Industrial Workers," in A. Doak Barnett, ed., *Chinese Communist Politics in Action* (Seattle: University of Washington Press, 1969), p. 541.

28. *Labour Laws and Regulations,* pp. 41–47, and Joyce Kallgren, *Chinese Communist Politics in Action,* pp. 546–47.

29. Shen Liao-chin, "Politics Is the Life-Line of All Economic Activities," *Jen-min jih-pao,* 6 June 1960, p. 6, in JPRS, 8 August 1960, pp. 9–20 and *Peking Review,* 20 February 1970, p. 15.

30. The transmission belt technique, originally defined by Lenin, extends to many activities, not just emulations and mass movements. For an interesting comment by a foreign visitor on this role of trade unions, see Bruno Di Pol, "Chinese Trade Unions as 'Transmission Belt'," *Avanti,* no. 279 (November 1960), p. 3, in JPRS, 19 January 1961, pp. 103.

31. For examples of such campaigns see *Peking Review,* 1 November 1968, pp. 29–30; and "Hupeh Provincial Revolutionary Committee and PLA . . . Accelerate

Struggle-Criticism-Transformation," *Jen-min jih-pao,* 21 June 1970, in SCMP, July 1970 pp. 212–18.

32. For a discussion of the Goals of such incentives see *The National Conference of Outstanding Groups and Workers in Socialist Construction in Industry, Communications and Transport, Capital Construction, Finance and Trade* (Peking: Foreign Languages Press, 1960), pp. 15, 32–37, 54–57.

33. Lin Hai, "How to Handle Labor Models Correctly," *Shih-shih shou-ts'e* [Current events], no. 22 (November 1961), in SCMM, 15 January 1962, pp. 22–23; and "Model Worker on Te-hua," *Kung-jen jih pao,* 16 May 1962, p. 1, in JPRS, 2 July 1962, pp. 18–21. Peking broadcast, 26 March 1973 cited in FBIS-2, 28 March 1973, p. B1. See also Dewar, *Labor Policy in the U.S.S.R. 1917–1928,* pp. 128–129; and "Veteran Worker Tireless in Building Socialism," *China Reconstructs,* (May 1973), pp. 35–37.

34. See, e.g., NCNA, Taiyuan, 19 January 1953, in SCMP, 22 January 1953, pp. 11–12; and ibid., Peking, 20 January 1955, in SCMP, 21 January 1955, p. 20. See also G. Bienstock et al., *Management in Russian Industry and Agriculture* (Ithaca: Cornell University Press, 1948), pp. 169–170.

35. Liu Chien-kuo, "Contest Between Red Banner Sections and 'Six Good Workers,' " *Kung-jen jih pao,* 27 May 1961, p. 2, in JPRS, 31 August 1961, pp. 1–5. Money Awards were also given with the three classes.

36. NCNA, Wusih, 17 April 1953, in SCMP, 18–20 April 1953, p. 33; and NCNA, Shanghai, 30 April 1953, in SCMP, 7 May 1953, pp. 19–20.

37. For a sense of this experience, see *The National Conference of Outstanding Groups and Individuals in Socialist Construction in Education, Culture, Health, Physical Culture and Journalism* (Peking: Foreign Languages Press, 1960), passim.

38. See Gliksman, *The Control of the Industrial Labor Force,* pp. 77–78.

39. "Tsinan Sets Performance Standards for Train Crews," *Tieh-tao Chou-kan,* no. 2 (January 1960), p. 15.

40. Liu Pang-chieh, "Family Emulation Drive," *China Reconstructs,* October 1961, pp. 17–18.

41. "A Glimpse of the Emulation Movement in Industry," *Peking Review,* 22 May 1964, pp. 15–16; and "Shantung Spreads the 'Red Flag Furnace' Steel Refinery Movement," *Kung-jen jih pao,* 20 October 1960, p. 2, in JPRS, 16 December 1960, 3–4. See also David Granick, *Management of the Industrial Firm in the U.S.S.R.* (New York: Columbia University Press, 1954), pp. 152, 192.

42. "Give Prominence to Proletarian Politics and Carry Out the Socialist Revolutionary Emulation Drive," broadcast, Peking, 20 January 1970, in FBIS-1, 22 January 1970, pp. F6–F7.

43. "Shanghai Workers Learn From Peking Workers," broadcast, Shanghai, 23 September 1969, in FBIS-1, 2 October 1969, pp. C6–C8; and *China News Summary,* no. 447, 7 December 1972, pp. 1–4.

44. For examples of mass participation, see *China's Big Leap in Water Conservancy* (Peking: Foreign Languages Press, 1958), passim; and "The Technical Cooperation Activities in Tientsin and Other Areas," *Kung-jen jih pao,* 17 May 1964, p. 2, in JPRS, 22 June 1964, pp. 22–24. See also Granick, *Management of the Industrial Firm in the U.S.S.R.,* pp. 232–243.

45. Contemporary psychology's attempts to deal with alienation through behavior

therapy, as one major thrust; a configuration of technique aimed at closer group identification through confrontation (T-group sensitivity training, etcetera); and other approaches, all seem to point in the direction of greater group involvement. Even where approaches are individual, the effort toward group identification is clear. For the behavior orientation and some suggestive bibliography, see Leonard Krasner, "Behavior Therapy," *Annual Review of Psychology* 22 (1971): 483–532. Subsequent notes cite other sources of the T-group variety.

46. For a contemporary social psychological theory delineating basic interpersonal needs, see William C. Schutz, *FIRO: A Three Dimensional Theory of Interpersonal Behavior* (New York: Rinehart, 1959). The movement in the United States to raise labor productivity through enhanced psychic conditions started years ago under Elton Mayo. More recently attempts have been made, applying social psychological concepts in small group sessions (T-groups) in industry to achieve the end. See, e.g., Chris Argyris, *Interpersonal Competence and Organizational Effectiveness* (London: Tavistock, 1962), especially part 3; and *Integrating the Individual and the Organization* (New York: Wiley, 1964), pp. 249–60.

47. For some suggestive material see Harvey Leibenstein, "Allocative Efficiency vs. X-Efficiency," *American Economic Review,* June 1966, pp. 392–415; Richard B. Goode, "Adding to the Stock of Physical and Human Capital," ibid., May 1959, pp. 146–55; and Theodore W. Schultz, "Investment in Human Capital," ibid., March 1961, pp. 1–17.

48. "Ideological Education Aids Tsu-Hsing Mining Bureau to Increase Production," *Jen-min jih-pao,* 25 February 1961, p. 2, in JPRS, 12 July 1961, pp. 4–5. See also Bienstock et al., *Management in Russian Industry and Agriculture,* pp. 44–46.

49. H. F. Schurmann, "Organization and Response in Communist China," *The Annals of the American Academy of Political and Social Science,* January 1959, pp. 51–61; and "The Mass Discussion Meeting in the Number 2 Converter Workshop of the Number 3 Shanghai Steel Plant," *Kung-jen jih-pao,* 18 December 1960, p. 2, in JPRS, 1 September 1961, pp. 33–37. The ideological rationale for criticism and self-criticism is outlined in Mao Tse-tung, *On the Correct Handling of Contradictions among the People* (Peking: Foreign Languages Press, 1960), pp. 16–27.

50. H. F. Schurmann, "The Dialectic in Action—Vicissitudes in Industrial Management in China," *Asian Survey,* May 1961, pp. 3–18; and Schurmann, "China's 'New Economic Policy'—Transition or Beginning," *China Quarterly,* January–March 1964, pp. 76–77. See Gliksman, *The Control of the Industrial Labor Force,* pp. 140–48.

51. See, e.g., "Popularize the Experiences of Outstanding Work Shifts and Crews . . ," *Kung jen jih pao,* 5 November 1960, p. 2, in JPRS, 8 March 1961, pp. 81–84; "New State in China's Mass Movement in Industry," *Peking Review,* 22 May 1964, pp. 11–14; and ibid. 1 January 1970, p. 8.

52. Ibid.; and "Develop the 'Compare, Learn, Overtake and Help' Movement . . ," *Jen-min jih pao,* 6 March 1964.

53. "Notes on the Taching Oilfield," *China Reconstructs,* December 1968, pp. 38–41.

54. "Sun Yeh-fang's Economic Theory Criticized," *Ta kung pao,* 19–25 February 1970, pp. 6–7; and "Criticizing and Repudiating Sun Yeh-fang's Reactionary Fallacy, 'Political Work in the Service of Production,' " *Kuang-ming jih-pao,* 1 February

1970, in *Current Background* 905, 29 April 1970, 1–7. See also "Taching—Banner in China's Industrial Progress," *China Reconstructs*, June 1971, pp. 17–20 and "At the Taching Oilfield," Peking review, 23 July 1971, pp. 9–12.

55. See "Hupeh Provincial Revolutionary Committee and PLA . . . Committee. Accelerate Struggle-Criticism-Transformation Campaign," *Jen-min jih-pao*, 21 June 1970, in SCMP, 10 July 1970, pp. 212–18.

Chapter 5. Organizing and Managing Workers

1. "Tang wei hui tseng yang chia ch'ang tui kung hui ti ling tao" (How does the Party Committee exercise strong leadership over the trade-union?), *Kung-jen jih pao*, 19 September 1961, p. 1. On trade-union functions see Article 9 of the Trade-Union Law of the People's Republic of China, in *Labour Laws and Regulations of the People's Republic of China*, p. 8.

2. On the 1955–1957 period see Lai Jo-yu, in NCNA, "Strengthen Trade Union Construction and Improve Connections Between Trade Unions and the Masses in the Struggle for Fulfilling the First Five-Year Plan," 30 August 1955, in *Current Background* 363, 14 October 1955, as an example of the rising importance of political education despite strong efforts to raise productions through material incentive.

3. ACFTU, *Eighth All-China Congress of the Trade-Unions* (Peking: Foreign Languages Press, 1958), p. 44.

4. Thomas T. Hammond, *Lenin on Trade Unions and Revolution 1893–1917* (New York: Columbia University Press, 1957), chapter 1.

5. Isaac Deutscher, *Soviet Trade Unions* (New York: Oxford University Press, 1950), pp. 52–58.

6. Mao Tse-tung, *On the Correct Handling of Contradictions among the People*, (Peking: Foreign Languages Press, 1960), pp. 10, 16; and Stuart R. Schram, *The Political Thought of Mao Tse-tung* (New York: Praeger, 1970), pp. 84–100. For an excellent review of the relationship between the party and the trade-unions see Paul Harper, "The Party and the Unions in Communist China," *China Quarterly*, January–March 1969, pp. 84–119.

7. *Constitution of the People's Republic of China* (Peking: Foreign Languages Press, 1961), pp. 9, 13, 40–41, 42.

8. *Labour Laws and Regulations of the People's Republic of China*, pp. 16–18.

9. "Militant Role of China's Trade Unions," *Peking Review*, 14 May 1965, pp. 26–29.

10. Ibid., 30 April 1965, pp. 22–25; ACFTU, *Eighth All-China Congress*, pp. 115–16; and Don Fletcher, "Trade Unions in Communist China," unpublished ms., pp. 7–8. See also, on management organization, Franz Schurmann, *Ideology and Organization in Communist China* (Berkeley: University of California Press, 1966, 1968), ch. 4.

11. ACFTU, *Eighth All-China Congress*, pp. 120–22.

12. Ibid., pp. 123–24.

13. *Labour Laws and Regulations of the People's Republic of China*, pp. 10–11.

14. Ibid., pp. 12–13.

15. Ibid., pp. 14–15; and ACFTU, *Eighth All-China Congress*, pp. 124–25.

16. *Peking Review,* 30 April 1965, p. 24.

17. Ibid., pp. 23–24 and ACFTU, *Eighth All-China Congress,* pp. 117–18.

18. ACFTU, *Eighth All-China Congress,* pp. 119–20.

19. *Labour Laws and Regulations of the People's Republic of China,* p. 9.

20. ACFTU, *Eighth All-China Congress,* pp. 115–16; and *New York Times,* 8 December 1966.

21. ACFTU, *Eighth All-China Congress,* pp. 115–20.

22. On the trade-union role in the GPCR, see Fletcher, "Trade Unions in Communist China," pp. 58–63; and *China Reporting Service,* 11 March 1969.

23. The development of workers' congresses is documented by numerous radio broadcasts. See, e.g., a sampling of these reported in *China Notes* 258 (4 April 1968), and 289 (21 November 1968).

24. Broadcasts cited in *China News Summary* 355 (4 February 1971): A1, and 404 (27 January 1972): A1–A4, and 462 (5 April 1973): 1–4. See also *Current Scene,* 7 April 1971, pp. 17–18; *Peking Review,* 27 April 1973, pp. 13–15; and FBIS-2, 24 April 1973, pp. C5–C7.

25. Peking broadcast, 24 April 1973, cited in FBIS-2, 24 April 1973, pp. B1–B4.

26. "Hold High the Red Banner of the Thought of Mao Tse-tung, Develop the Fighting Role of the Trade-Union," *Kung-jen jih pao,* 30 April 1965, in JPRS, 22 April 1966, pp. 78–81.

27. *Labour Laws and Regulations* of the *People's Republic of China,* p. 8.

28. A. Donnithorne, *China's Economic System* (New York: Praeger, 1967), pp. 189–92.

29. "Depend on Activists in Doing Trade Union Work With Success," *Kung-jen jih pao,* 16 February 1962, in SCMP, 8 March 1962, pp. 14–16.

30. *Jen-min jih-pao,* 17 June 1971, Peking broadcast, 17 June 1971, cited in FBIS-1, 17 June 1971, p. B1.

31. "People Are the Decisive Factor," *Peking Review,* 26 June 1970, p. 26; and *China Notes* 289 (21 November 1968).

32. *China Notes* 289 (21 November 1968); and "Thoroughly Criticize and Repudiate China's Khrushchov's Counter-Revolutionary Revisionist Line in the Workers' Movement Based on 'Three Kinds of Trade Unions and One Syndicalism,' " *Jen-min jih-pao,* 27 May 1968, in SCMP, 10 July 1968, pp. 1–9.

33. "Shanghai Workers Learn from Peking Workers," *Wen Hui Pao,* 24 September 1969, p. 2, cited in FBIS-1, 2 October 1969, pp. C6–C8; and "Peking Steelworkers Set Off Nationwide Emulation Drive," *China Reconstructs,* January 1970, pp 2–7.

34. For a sketch of trade-union functions, see "China's Trade Unions," *Peking Review,* 30 April 1965, pp. 22–25.

35. See *Labour Protection in New China* (Peking: Foreign Languages Press, 1960), p. 22; and "Safe Coal Production," *China Reconstructs,* January 1971, 26–28.

36. Ibid.; and *Compendium of Laws and Regulations of the People's Republic of China* III, 447–49 and IX, 295–302, in JPRS, 13 July 1962, and JPRS [7.62]. One group of visitors to China in 1971 reported their favorable impressions of safety conditions. See Committee of Concerned Asian Scholars, *China! Inside the People's Republic* (New York: Bantam, 1972), pp. 187–90.

37. "Workers' Health and Safety Improved," *Chung-kuo hsin-wen,* 2 April 1966, in JPRS, 15 August 1966, p. 108.

38. *Important Labour Laws and Regulations in the People's Republic of China,*

pp. 34–71; *Compendium of Laws* IX; and "Labor Protection, Benefits and Retirement," *Kuang-ming jih-pao*, 28 April 1964, p. 2, in JPRS, 15 June 1964, p. 32–33.

39. *Labour Protection in New China*, pp. 9–38; *First Five-Year Plan for Development of the National Economy of the People's Republic of China in 1953–1957* (Peking: Foreign Languages Press, 1956); *Compendium of Laws* III and IX, passim; NCNA "Further Measures Protecting Industrial Workers Decided On," Peking, 30 January 1953, in SCMP, 31 January–2 February 1953, pp. 15–16; and *Wall Street Journal*, 2 July 1971, p. 12.

40. *Labour Insurance in New China* (Peking: Foreign Languages Press, 1953), pp. 3–8; and "The System of Wage Allowances Should Be Radically Reformed," *Chi-hua Ching-Chi*, no. 5 (May 1958), in ECMM, 14 July 1958, pp. 29–32.

41. *Labor Insurance*, pp. 18–21 and "The System of Wage Allowances."

42. Ibid., and "China's Trade Unions," *Peking Review*, 30 April 1965, p. 24.

43. *Labour Insurance*, pp. 29–32.

44. "The System of Wage Allowances," pp. 29–32.

45. "China's Trade Unions," p. 24.

46. V. I. Lenin, *Collected Works* (New York: International Publishers, 1927–1945), 27: 149.

47. "What Is the Fundamental Cause Behind the Trade Union Work 'Crisis'?", *Kung-jen jih-pao*, 21 May 1957, in SCMP, 17 June 1957, p. 16; and "How Contradictions Within the Ranks of the People Are Handled by the Trade Unions," *Kung-jen jih-pao*, 9 May 1957, in SCMP, 22 May 1957, pp. 8–11.

48. Mao Tse-tung, *On the Correct Handling of Contradictions*, p. 59; and *Jen-min jih-pao*, 13 May 1957, in SCMP, 23 May 1957, p. 1.

Strikes and other labor disputes occurred in China before 1956 to 1957 and after, though they were not always publicly acknowledged. Officially unacknowledged strikes in the early 1950s were reported in Hong Kong. During the GPCR officially reported strikes of railway and dock workers in Shanghai were part of the struggle between Maoists and anti-Maoists. See *Review of the Hong Kong Chinese Press* 146/53, 7 August 1953, p. 3; and 29/54, 13–14 February 1954, p. 4 for examples of early strikes. On the GPCR, see Peking Wall Poster, "Message to Worker Comrades Who Have Left Their Production Posts," 15 January 1967, in JPRS Special, 1 August 1967; "Message to All Shanghai People," *Peking Review*, 13 January 1967, pp. 5–7, published 5 January by Shanghai Workers' Revolutionary Rebel General Headquarters and ten other groups; and "The Great 'January Revolution' in Shanghai" and "Storm in the Port of Shanghai," *China Reconstructs*, April 1967, pp. 8–13 and 29–31, respectively.

49. Mao Tse-tung, *On the Correct Handling of Contradictions*, pp. 9–10. See also Stuart R. Schram, "Mao Tse-tung and the search for a 'Chinese Road' to Socialism," address to the Royal Central Asian Society, 24 July 1968, pp. 84–100.

50. Edgar Snow, *The Other Side of the River* (New York: Random House, 1961), pp. 234–36, 240–41; and Roderick MacFarquhar, *The Hundred Flowers Campaign and the Chinese Intellectuals* (New York: Praeger, 1960), p. 241.

51. *Kwang-chou jih-pao*, 12 May 1957, in SCMP 1569 (15 July 1957): 28–30.

52. Ibid.

53. Ibid.

54. Ibid.; and *Jen-min jih-pao*, 13 May 1957, in SCMP 1536 (23 May 1957): 1.

55. Mao Tse-tung, *On the Correct Handling of Contradictions*, pp. 59–61.

56. *Kwang-chou jih-pao*, 12 May 1957, in SCMP 1569 (15 July 1957): 28–30.

Chapter 6. Workers' Welfare

1. See "Talking About Wages," *China Now,* July 1971, pp. 2–3.

2. See, e.g., *New York Times,* 21 September 1971, p. 11, for official data on wages, rents, and prices.

3. Visits of Barry Richman and Bruce McFarlane during the GPCR, and, more recently, correspondents Edgar Snow, Tilman Durdin and Seymour Topping of the *New York Times,* and Robert Keatley of the *Wall Street Journal* have provided interesting spot quantitative information. See, e.g., Richman, *Industrial Society in Communist China* (New York: Random House, 1969); E. L. Wheelwright and Bruce McFarlane, *The Chinese Road to Socialism* (New York and London: Monthly Review Press, 1970); Bruce McFarlane's three-volume diary, East Asian Institute, Columbia University; Edgar Snow, "Reports from Red China" in *The New Republic* starting 27 March 1971; *New York Times,* April–June 1971; and *Wall Street Journal,* 30 June 1971.

4. See Charles Hoffmann, *Work Incentive Practices and Policies in the People's Republic of China 1953–1965* (Albany: State University of New York Press, 1967), pp. 118–19, for data on salary scales for staff employees. Table 4.3 in chapter 4 parallels the wage-grade scale for certain blue-collar workers.

5. See Barry Richman, "Ideology and Management: The Chinese Oscillate," *Columbia Journal of World Business,* January–February 1971, pp. 23–32.

6. Ibid.

7. Robert Michael Field, "Industrial Production in Communist China: 1957–1968," *China Quarterly,* April–June 1970, p. 47.

8. *Wall Street Journal,* 30 June 1971, p. 1; and *New York Times,* 22 May 1971, p. 7, 31 May 1971, p. 2, 17 June 1971, p. 20, and 21 September 1971, p. 11. See also Committee of Concerned Asian Scholars, *China! Inside the People's Republic* (New York: Bantam, 1972), p. 189; and *China Now,* no. 24 (August–September 1972), pp. 2–3.

9. SWB, 19 September 1971, FE/3791/ C1–C2; People's Republic of China, State Statistical Bureau, *Ten Great Years* (Peking: Foreign Languages Press, 1960), pp. 172–216; and *New York Times,* 21 September 1971, p. 11.

10. Richman, *Industrial Society in Communist China,* pp. 804–805, and SWB, 19 September 1971, FE/3791/ C1–C2.

11. Richman, "Ideology and Management: Communism and Compromise," *Columbia Journal of World Business,* May–June 1971, pp. 45–58.

12. *New York Times,* 13 March 1971, p. 3; *Jen-min jih-pao,* 1 January 1972; and *Peking Review,* 14 January 1972, pp. 7–8.

13. *Wall Street Journal,* 30 June 1971, p. 1; *New York Times,* 13 March 1971, p. 3; and SWB, 22 April 1971, FE/3791/C1–C2.

14. See Kang Chao, *Agriculture Production in Communist China* (Madison: University of Wisconsin Press, 1970), pp. 261–65, for information of "technical" crops including peanuts, rapeseed, sesame, tobacco, sugar cane, and sugar beets. More equal food distribution today means higher levels of food consumption for more people.

15. Kang Chao, *The Rate and Pattern of Industrial Growth in Communist China* (Ann Arbor; University of Michigan Press, 1965), p. 96

16. Field, "Industrial Production in Communist China," p. 47.

17. Ibid.

18. Ibid. Reports from various sources support the claim to continued industrial expansion and adequate availability of consumer goods. See, e.g., *Current Scene*, 7 February 1971, pp. 1–4; *Wall Street Journal*, 30 June 1971, pp. 1, 17; and *New York Times*, 22 April 1971, pp. 1–8, 22 May 1971, p. 7, 31 May 1971, p. 2, and 27 June 1971, p. 20. In August 1969 a rollback of 37 percent in the prices of many vaccines, pharmaceuticals, and drugs helped raise workers' living levels. See "Public Health Developments—Continued Focus on the Farms," *Current Scene*, 15 December 1969, p. 2. On improving quantity and quality of consumer goods, see Emile Van Heuval, "China's New Mood—Relaxation, Self-Confidence," *New York Times Magazine*, 25 July 1971, pp. 10–11, 47–52.

19. Richman, *Industrial Society in Communist China*, pp. 806–807; and *New York Times*, 27 June 1971, p. 20.

20. *New York Times*, 31 May 1971, p. 2.

21. *Current Scene*, 1 May 1968, p. 1, and 15 June 1969, p. 6.

22. Ibid., 15 June 1969, p. 12.

23. Ibid.

24. See *New York Times*, 1 May 1971, p. 2, for reports on clean streets.

25. A. Donnithorne, *China's Economic System* (New York: Praeger, 1967); pp. 214–15 and *China Now*, no. 31 (April–May 1973), pp. 1–4.

26. *Wall Street Journal*, 2 July 1971, p. 12; and Committee of Concerned Asian Scholars, *China! Inside the People's Republic*, pp. 187–90. See also Donnithorne, *China's Economic System*, pp. 214–15; and *Labour Protection in New China*, chapter 3.

27. On laws, regulations, campaigns concerning health and safety see *Compendium of the Laws and Regulations of the People's Republic of China* (1956), III, in JPRS, 31 July 1962, pp. 447–96 and (1959), IX, in JPRS, n.d. (7.62), pp. 295–308; *Important Labour Laws and Regulations of the People's Republic of China*, pp. 34–71; NCNA, "Further Measures Protecting Industrial Workers Decided On," Peking, 30 June 1957, in SCMP, 5 July 1957, p. 4; "Labor Protection Benefits and Retirement," *Kuang-ming jih pao*, 28 April 1964, p. 2, in JPRS, 15 June 1964, pp. 31–34; "Freely Mobilize the Masses to Grasp Safety in Production Well," *Jen-min jih-pao*, 20 November 1970, in SCMP, 7 December 1970; "Safe Coal Production," *China Reconstructs*, January 1971, pp. 26–28; *Union Research Service* 37, no. 19 (December 1964), pp. 280 ff; and Peking radio broadcast, 27 April 1973, cited in FBIS-2, 27 April 1973, pp. F3–F4.

28. See, e.g., *New York Times*, 23 April 1971, pp. 1, 13, for limb saving surgical development.

29. Leo Orleans, "Propheteering: The Population of Communist China," *Current Scene*, 15 December 1969, p. 17; and *New York Times*, 21 April 1971, pp. 1–8, and 6 May 1973, p. 5.

30. *New York Times*, 10 August 1971, pp. 14–15.

31. "Public Health Developments—Continued Focus on the Farms," *Current Scene*, 15 December 1969, pp. 1–12; and *New York Times*, 28 March 1971, p. 25.

32. Ibid.; "Sinkiang: Circular on Launching Summer Health Campaigns," radio broadcast from Urumchi Sinkiang, 26 June 1971, cited in FBIS-1, 2 July 1971, pp. H3–H4; and *New York Times*, 24 April 1971, p. 7, 1 May 1971, p. 2, 22 May 1971, p. 7.

33. Richman, *Industrial Society in Communist China*, pp. 551–54; and *New York*

Times, 23 April 1971, pp. 1,13, 24 May 1971, p. 10, 4 July 1971, p. 3, and 6 May 1973, p. 7.

34. "Public Health Developments—Continued Focus on the Farms," pp. 10–11. A fascinating, first-hand account of the quality of Chinese medical care, combining modern and indigenous medical practice (including herbal and acupuncture therapy) is given by James Reston, renowned correspondent and vice-president of the *New York Times,* who underwent an emergency appendectomy while visiting Peking. See *New York Times,* 26 July 1971, p. 1.

35. Van Heuvel, "China's New Mood—Relaxation, Self-Confidence," pp. 10–11, 47–52; *New York Times,* 27 June 1971, pp. 1, 20; NCNA, "Shenyang Utilizes Industrial Waste, Reduces Pollution," Peking broadcast, 15 May 1971, cited in FBIS-1, 18 May 1971, pp. G1–G2; Leo Orleans and Richard P. Suttmeier, "The Mao Ethic and Environmental Quality," *Science,* 11 December 1970, pp. 1173–76; and "Multipurpose Utilization of Materials is Good," Peking broadcast, cited in FBIS-2, 14 March 1972, pp. B3–B5.

36. See, e.g., the policy on installation of radio loudspeakers in the countryside, "Kiangsi Achieves Successes in Broadcasting Network," Nanchang Kiangsi radio broadcast, 28 January 1971, cited in FBIS-1, 5 February 1971, pp. C1–C2.

37. Richman, *Industrial Society in Communist China,* p. 134; and State Statistical Bureau, *Ten Great Years,* pp. 192–93, 198.

38. Alan P.L. Liu, "Mass Media in the Cultural Revolution," *Current Scene,* 20 April 1969, p. 7; State Statistical Bureau, *Ten Great Years,* p. 208; and "Shantung Wired Broadcast Network Continues to Expand," Tsinan Shantung radio broadcast, 28 December 1970, cited in FBIS-1, 6 January 1971, pp. C7–C8.

39. *Union Research Service* 41, no. 11 (November 5, 1965), pp. 145–60.

40. *Quotations from Chairman Mao Tse-Tung* (Peking: Foreign Languages Press, 1967), p. 297.

41. Joan M. Maloney, "Chinese Women and Party Leadership: Impact of the Cultural Revolution," *Current Scene,* 10 April 1972, pp. 10–15. Some recent publications covering women in China include *Chinese Women in the Great Leap Forward* (Peking: Foreign Languages Press, 1960); Committee of Concerned Asian Scholars, *China! Inside the People's Republic;* Christopher Lucas, *Women of China* (Hong Kong: Dragonfly, 1965); Helen Foster Snow, *Women in Modern China* (Hague: Mouton, 1967); and Margaret Wylie, *Children of China* (Hong Kong: Dragonfly, 1965).

42. Maloney, "Chinese Women and Party Leadership," pp. 10–15 and *Peking Review,* 7 September 1973, pp. 8–10.

43. Ibid.; and *Quotations from Chairman Mao Tse-Tung,* p. 297.

44. Peking radio broadcast, 4 March 1973, cited in FBIS-2, 5 March 1973, pp. B4–B5; *New York Times,* 27 May 1973, p. 3; and *China Now,* no. 31 (April–May 1973), pp. 1–4.

Chapter 7. Conclusion

1. For a comparison of the Maoist and capitalist models see John G. Gurley, "Capitalist and Maoist Economic Development," in Edward Friedman and Mark Selden, eds., *America's Asia: Dissenting Essays on Asian-American Relations* (New York: Vintage, 1971), pp. 324–56.

2. See, e.g., Harvey Leibenstein, "Allocative Efficiency vs. 'X-Efficiency,'" *American Economic Review,* June 1966, pp. 392–415; and "Notes on X-Efficiency and Technical Progress," discussion paper no. 162, January 1971, Harvard Institute of Economic Research, pp. 1–32.

3. Mao Tse-tung, *On the Correct Handling of Contradictions Among the People* (Peking: Foreign Languages Press, 1960), p. 67.

4. On human capital investment see, e.g., T.W. Schultz, "Investment in Human Capital," *American Economic Review,* March 1961; Gary S. Becker, *Human Capital* (New York: National Bureau of Economic Research, 1964); Frederick Harbison and Charles A. Myers, *Education, Manpower and Economic Growth* (New York: McGraw-Hill, 1964); "Symposium on the Rates of Return to Investment in Education," *Journal of Human Resources,* Summer 1967, pp. 291–374; and Arnold C. Harberger, "Investment in Man Versus Investment in Machines: The Case in India," in C.A. Anderson and M.J. Bowman, eds., *Education and Economic Development* (Chicago: Aldine, 1965).

5. For an excellent study of the Yenan period see Mark Selden, *The Yenan Way in Revolutionary China* (Cambridge: Harvard University Press, 1971).

6. See, e.g., "Regional Self-Sufficiency," *China News Summary,* no. 392 (28 October 1971); and "Shantung Light Industry Rushes Multipurpose Utilization," Tsinan radio broadcast, 10 March 1972, cited in FBIS-2, 17 March 1972, pp. C1–C2.

7. For a perceptive view of revolutionary modernization in China, see Stephen Andors, "Revolution and Modernization: Man and Machine in Industrializing Society, The Chinese Case," in Friedman and Selden, eds., *America's Asia,* pp. 393–444.

Appendixes

Appendix A
Workers' Wage Scales in State Enterprises

Table A.1

Wage Scale for the Workers of State Organs (1) (July 1956)

Levels	Wage Scales, Unit: Yuan/Month									
	1	2	3	4	5	6	7	8	9	10
1	290	298.5	307.5	316.0	325.0	333.5	312.0	351.0	359.5	368.5
2	250	257.5	265.0	272.5	280.0	287.5	295.0	302.5	310.0	317.5
3	215	221.5	228.0	234.5	241.0	247.5	253.5	260.0	266.5	273.0
4	185	190.5	196.0	201.5	207.0	213.0	218.5	224.0	229.5	235.0
5	159	164.0	168.5	173.5	178.0	183.0	187.5	192.5	197.0	202.0
6	137	141.0	145.0	149.5	153.5	157.5	161.5	166.0	170.0	174.0
7	118	121.5	125.0	128.5	132.0	135.5	139.0	143.0	146.5	150.0
8	102	105.0	108.0	111.0	114.0	117.5	120.5	123.5	126.5	129.5
9	89	91.5	94.5	97.0	99.5	102.5	105.0	107.5	110.5	113.0
10	77	79.5	81.5	84.0	86.0	88.5	91.0	93.0	95.5	98.0
11	65	67.0	69.0	71.0	73.0	75.0	76.5	78.5	80.5	82.5
12	54	55.5	57.0	59.0	60.5	62.0	63.5	65.5	67.0	68.5
13	48	49.5	51.0	52.5	54.0	55.0	56.5	58.0	59.5	61.0
14	42	43.5	44.5	46.0	47.0	48.5	49.5	51.0	52.0	53.5
15	37	38.0	39.0	40.5	41.5	42.5	43.5	45.0	46.0	47.0
16	32	33.0	34.0	35.0	36.0	37.0	38.0	38.5	39.5	40.5
17	27	28.0	28.5	29.5	30.0	31.0	32.0	32.5	33.5	34.5
18	24	24.5	25.5	26.0	27.0	27.5	28.5	29.0	30.0	30.5

Source: State Council, "Notification on the Issuance of a Program of Wage Scales for the Worke
State Organs," no. HSI-54, 1956, in *Compilation of the Laws and Regulations of Financial Admin
tration of the Central Government* (Peking: 1956), pp. 226–47. This was also printed in U.S. Joint
Publications Research Service, No. 35,455 *Translations on Communist China's Management,
Trade, and Finance,* no. 79 (11 May 1966), pp. 1–55.

Notes: This table is applicable to the steel and iron, coal mining, nonferrous machine-producin
logical, and aircraft industries.

The wage scales listed above are of eleven kinds. In accordance with the commodity prices and
ing standards in various localities, individual wage scales are provided for execution in these lo
ties. In localities where commodity prices are exceedingly high, subsidies for living expenses ar
added. Details of wage scales applicable to various localities and proportions of subsidies for li
expenses are in the wage scales applicable to various localities and subsidies for living expenses

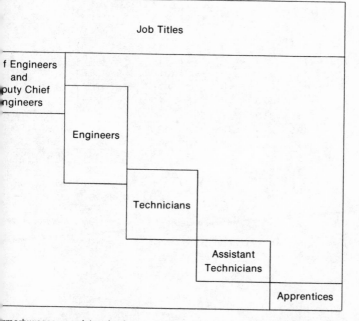

Job Titles

f Engineers and puty Chief ngineers

Engineers

Technicians

Assistant Technicians

Apprentices

rmerly wages were determined according to technical capabilities. The foregoing table is a
*thod by which wages are determined according to the technicians' duties. Each title consists of
veral wage levels. In determining the technicians' wages, however, the principle which combines
ties with virtues and talents with due regard for experience is also applicable.

ose titles which are not listed above may be evaluated and determined according to the equiva-
t titles listed above.

e wage scales for graduates of higher schools who have worked six months on technical jobs are
nerally evaluated and determined as follows: the wage scales for those who accomplished four
ive years of nigher school education may be determined at the level of Grade 14; those who
iduated from professional schools may be given Grade 18; those who graduated from middle or
ecial schools and have worked six months may be evaluated and determined according to the
os for assistant technicians.

Table A.2
Wage Scale for the Workers of State Organs (2) (July 1956)

Levels	Wage Scales, Unit: Yuan/Month									
	1	2	3	4	5	6	7	8	9	10
1	285	293.5	302.0	310.5	319.0	328.0	336.5	345.0	353.5	362.0
2	246	253.5	261.0	268.0	275.5	283.0	290.5	297.5	305.0	312.5
3	212	218.5	224.5	231.0	237.5	244.0	250.0	256.5	263.0	269.0
4	183	188.5	194.0	199.5	205.0	210.5	216.0	221.5	227.0	232.5
5	158	162.5	167.5	172.0	177.0	181.5	186.5	191.0	196.0	200.5
6	136	140.0	144.0	148.0	152.5	156.5	160.5	164.5	168.5	172.5
7	117	120.6	124.0	127.5	131.0	134.5	138.0	141.5	145.0	148.5
8	101	104.0	107.0	110.0	113.0	116.0	119.0	122.0	125.0	128.5
9	88	90.5	93.5	96.0	98.5	101.0	104.0	106.5	109.0	112.0
10	76	78.5	80.5	83.0	85.0	87.5	89.5	92.0	94.0	96.5
11	65	67.0	69.0	71.0	73.0	75.0	76.5	78.5	80.5	82.5
12	54	55.5	57.0	59.0	60.5	62.0	63.5	65.5	67.0	68.5
13	48	49.5	51.0	52.5	54.0	55.0	56.5	58.0	59.5	61.9
14	42	43.5	44.5	46.0	47.0	48.5	49.5	51.0	52.0	53.5
15	37	38.0	39.0	40.5	41.5	42.5	43.5	45.0	46.0	47.0
16	32	33.0	34.0	35.0	36.0	37.0	38.0	38.5	39.5	40.5
17	27	28.0	28.5	29.5	30.0	31.0	32.0	32.5	33.5	34.5
18	24	24.5	25.5	26.0	27.0	27.5	28.5	29.0	30.0	30.5

Source: State Council, "Notification on the Issuance of a Program of Wage Scales," pp. 226

Note: This table is applicable to the electric power, petroleum processing, machine-building, h chemical, and lumber industries.

Job Titles

Engineers
and
uty Chief
gineers

Engineers

Technicians

Assistant
Technicians

Apprentices

Wage Scale for the Workers of State Organs (3) *(July 1956)*

Levels	Wage Scales, Unit: Yuan/Month										
	1	2	3	4	5	6	7	8	9	10	
1	280	288.5	297.0	305.0	313.5	322.0	330.5	339.0	347.0	355.5	3
2	242	249.5	256.5	264.0	271.0	278.5	285.5	293.0	300.0	307.5	3
3	299	215.5	221.5	228.0	234.0	240.5	246.5	253.0	259.0	265.5	2
4	180	185.5	191.0	196.0	201.5	207.0	212.5	218.0	223.0	228.5	2
5	155	159.5	164.5	169.0	173.5	178.5	183.0	187.5	192.0	197.0	2
6	134	138.0	142.0	146.0	150.0	154.0	158.0	162.0	166.0	170.0	1
7	116	119.5	123.0	126.5	130.0	133.5	137.0	140.5	144.0	147.5	1
8	100	103.0	106.0	109.0	112.0	115.0	118.0	121.0	124.0	127.0	1
9	87	89.5	92.0	95.0	97.5	100.0	102.5	105.5	108.0	110.5	1
10	75	77.5	79.5	82.0	84.0	86.5	88.5	91.0	93.0	95.5	
11	64	66.0	68.0	70.0	71.5	73.5	75.5	77.5	79.5	81.5	
12	54	55.5	57.0	59.0	60.5	62.0	63.5	65.5	67.0	68.5	
13	48	49.5	51.0	52.5	54.0	55.0	56.5	58.0	59.5	61.0	
14	42	43.5	44.5	46.0	47.0	48.5	49.5	51.0	52.0	53.5	
15	37	38.0	39.0	40.5	41.5	42.5	43.5	45.0	46.0	47.0	
16	32	33.0	34.0	35.0	36.0	37.0	38.0	38.5	39.5	40.5	
17	27	28.0	28.5	29.5	30.0	31.0	32.0	32.5	33.5	34.5	
18	24	24.5	25.5	26.0	27.0	27.5	28.5	29.0	30.0	30.5	

Source: State Council, "Notification on the Issuance of a Program of Wage Scales," pp. 226–

Note: This table is applicable to construction, railroad, tele-communications, highways, agricultu forestry, water conservancy, and weather.

Job Titles					
Engineering Technicians			Agricultural Technicians		
f Engineers and puty Chief ngineers			Chief Agri. Technicians and Deputy Chief Agri. Tech.		
	Engineers			Agricultural Technicians	
		Technicians			Technicians
	Assistant Technicians			Assistant Technicians	
		Apprentices			Apprentices

Table A.4
Wage Scale for the Workers of State Organs (4) *(July 1956)*

Levels	Wage Scales, Unit: Yuan/Month										
	1	2	3	4	5	6	7	8	9	10	1
1	275	283.5	291.5	300.0	308.0	316.5	324.5	333.0	341.0	349.5	35
2	237	244.0	251.0	258.5	265.5	272.5	279.5	287.0	294.0	301.0	30
3	205	211.0	217.5	223.5	229.5	236.0	242.0	248.0	254.0	260.5	26
4	177	182.5	187.5	193.0	198.0	203.5	209.0	214.0	219.5	225.0	23
5	153	157.5	162.0	167.0	171.5	176.0	180.5	185.0	189.5	194.5	19
6	132	136.0	140.0	144.0	148.0	152.0	156.0	159.5	163.5	167.5	17
7	114	117.5	121.0	124.5	127.5	131.0	134.5	138.0	141.5	145.0	14
8	99	102.0	105.0	108.0	111.0	114.0	117.0	120.0	123.0	125.5	12
9	86	88.5	91.0	93.5	96.5	99.0	101.5	104.0	106.5	109.0	11
10	74	76.0	78.5	80.5	83.0	85.0	87.5	89.5	92.0	94.0	9
11	63	65.0	67.0	68.5	70.5	72.5	74.5	76.0	78.0	80.0	8
12	54	55.5	57.0	59.0	60.5	62.0	63.5	65.5	67.0	68.5	7
13	48	49.5	51.0	52.5	54.0	55.0	56.5	58.0	59.5	61.0	6
14	42	43.5	44.5	46.0	47.0	48.5	49.5	51.0	52.0	53.5	5
15	37	38.0	39.0	40.5	41.5	42.5	43.5	45.0	46.0	47.0	4
16	32	33.0	34.0	35.0	36.0	37.0	38.0	38.5	39.5	40.5	4
17	27	28.0	28.5	29.5	30.0	31.0	32.0	32.5	33.5	34.5	3
18	24	24.5	25.5	26.0	27.0	27.5	28.5	29.0	30.0	30.5	3

Source: State Council, "Notification on the Issuance of a Program of Wage Scales," pp. 226–47

Note: This table is applicable to industries of textile, papermaking, drug-making, printing, oil stuffs rubber, and measurement.

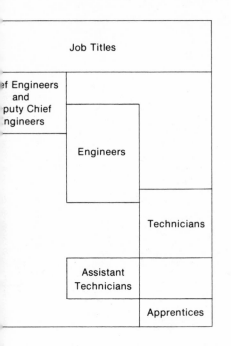

Job Titles

ef Engineers
and
puty Chief
ngineers

Engineers

Technicians

Assistant
Technicians

Apprentices

Table A.5
Wage Scale for the Workers of State Organs (5) (July 1956)

Levels	Wage Scales, Unit: Yuan/Month										
	1	2	3	4	5	6	7	8	9	10	1
1	270	278.0	286.0	294.5	302.5	310.5	318.5	326.5	335.0	343.0	35
2	233	240.0	247.0	254.0	261.0	268.0	275.0	282.0	289.0	296.0	30
3	201	207.0	213.0	219.0	225.0	231.0	237.0	243.0	249.0	255.5	26
4	174	179.0	184.5	189.5	195.0	200.0	205.5	210.5	216.0	221.0	22
5	150	154.5	159.0	163.5	168.0	172.5	177.0	181.5	186.0	190.5	19
6	130	134.0	138.0	141.5	145.5	149.5	153.5	157.5	161.0	165.0	16
7	113	116.5	120.0	123.0	126.5	130.0	133.5	136.5	140.0	143.5	14
8	98	101.0	104.0	107.0	110.0	112.5	115.5	118.5	121.5	124.5	12
9	85	87.5	90.0	92.5	95.0	98.0	100.5	103.0	105.5	108.0	11
10	73	75.0	77.5	79.5	82.0	84.0	86.0	88.5	90.5	92.5	9
11	63	65.0	67.0	68.5	70.5	72.5	74.5	76.0	78.0	80.0	8
12	54	55.5	57.0	59.0	60.5	62.0	63.5	65.5	67.0	68.5	7
13	48	49.5	51.0	52.5	54.0	55.0	56.5	58.0	59.5	61.0	6
14	42	43.5	44.5	46.0	47.0	48.5	49.5	51.0	52.0	53.5	5
15	37	38.0	39.0	40.5	41.5	42.5	43.5	45.0	46.0	47.0	4
16	32	33.0	34.0	35.0	36.0	37.0	38.0	38.5	39.5	40.5	4
17	27	28.0	28.5	29.5	30.0	31.0	32.0	32.5	33.5	34.5	3
18	24	24.5	25.5	26.0	27.0	27.5	28.5	29.0	30.0	30.5	3

Source: State Council, "Notification on the Issuance of a Program of Wage Scales," pp. 226–47

Note: This table is applicable to flour, match, tobacco and food industries.

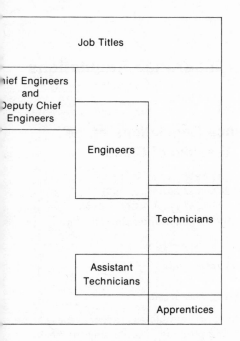

Job Titles
Chief Engineers and Deputy Chief Engineers
Engineers
Technicians
Assistant Technicians
Apprentices

Appendix B Labor Insurance Regulations

Labour Insurance Regulations of the People's Republic of China *

(First promulgated on February 26, 1951 by the Government Administration Council)
(Promulgated as amended on January 2, 1953 by the Government Administration Council)

Chapter One

GENERAL PRINCIPLES

Article 1   The present Regulations are formulated in accordance with the present economic conditions for the purpose of protecting the health of workers and staff members and alleviating difficulties in their livelihood.

Article 2   In carrying out the present Regulations, the method of gradual extension to include more and more enterprises shall be adopted. At present, the scope within which the Regulations are to be applied shall be temporarily confined to the following enterprises:

    (a) State, joint state-private, private, or co-operative-owned factories and mines, employing 100 or more workers and staff members, and their ancillary units;

    (b) Railway, water and air transport, post and telecommunication enterprises and their ancillary units;

    (c) Capital construction units of factories, mines, and transport enterprises;

    (d) State-owned building companies.

---

* *Important Labour Laws and Regulations of the People's Republic of China* (Enlarged Edition) (Peking: Foreign Languages Press, 1961), pp. 11–31.

Suggestions concerning further extension of the scope of application of the present Regulations should be submitted at the opportune time according to actual circumstances by the Ministry of Labour of the Central People's Government to the Government Administration Council of the Central People's Government for decision.

Article 3   Matters relating to labour insurance in enterprises which do not fall within the scope of the present Regulations and in enterprises of a seasonal character may be settled through the conclusion of collective agreements after consultation between the managements or the owners of such enterprises or of the industries or trades to which such enterprises belong and their trade union organizations, by taking into consideration the principles as laid down in the Regulations and the actual conditions in such enterprises, industries, or trades.

Article 4   The present Regulations apply to all workers and staff members (including apprentices) who are employed in enterprises which provide labour insurance, regardless of their nationality, age, sex or citizenship. Persons deprived of political rights, however, are excluded.

Article 5   Provisions governing labour insurance for temporary workers, seasonal workers, and persons on probation working in enterprises which provide labour insurance are separately made in the Detailed Rules for Carrying Out the Labour Insurance Regulations of the People's Republic of China.

Article 6   Enterprises within the scope of the present Regulations which, due to special financial stringencies, find it difficult to continue operations or which have not yet formally opened business operations, may temporarily put off the carrying out of the present Regulations after agreement has been reached through consultation between the managements or the owners of the enterprises and the primary trade union committees and after approval of the labour administration organ of the local people's government has been obtained.

Chapter Two

COLLECTION AND CUSTODY OF LABOUR
INSURANCE FUNDS

Article 7   The various labour insurance expenses as stipulated in the present Regulations shall be borne in full by the managements or owners of enterprises which provide labour insurance; a part of such expenses shall be disbursed directly by the managements or owners of such enterprises, while the other part shall be paid by the managements or owners of such enterprises in the form of a labour insurance fund to be managed by the trade union organizations.

Article 8   The managements or owners of enterprises which provide labour insurance in accordance with the present Regulations shall pay to the labour insurance fund each month a sum equal to 3 per cent of the total pay-roll of all workers and staff members in the enterprises concerned. This labour insurance fund shall not be deducted from the wages of the workers and staff members, nor shall it otherwise be collected from the workers and staff members.

Article 9   The methods of collection and custody of labour insurance funds shall be as follows:
(a) The managements or owners of enterprises shall, within the period from the first to the tenth day of each month, pay in a lump sum to the state bank designated by the All-China Federation of Trade Unions, the monthly amount due to the labour insurance fund, calculated according to the total pay-roll for the preceding month.
(b) In the first two months of the enforcement of labour insurance, the monthly sum to be paid by the managements or owners of enterprises to the labour insurance fund shall be deposited in full into the account of the All-China Federation of Trade Unions as the general labour insurance fund to be used for financing collective labour insurance undertakings. Counting from the third month, 30 per cent of the monthly sum due to the labour insurance fund shall be deposited into the account of the All-China Federation of Trade Unions as the general labour insurance fund; 70 per cent shall be deposited into the accounts of the respective primary trade union committees of the enterprises concerned as labour insurance funds for paying pensions, allowances, and relief benefits to workers and staff members in accordance with the present Regulations.

Article 10   The managements or owners of enterprises which fail to meet their payments to the labour insurance fund when due, or which do not pay to the funds in full, shall for each day overdue pay an additional amount equivalent to one per cent of the sum overdue. In the case of state enterprises either under the central or local authorities, or joint state-private enterprises or co-operative-owned enterprises, if the payments are

20 days overdue, the primary trade union committees shall notify the local branch of the state bank to deduct the amount due from the accounts of the enterprises concerned. In the case of private enterprises the primary trade union committees shall report the matter to the labour administration department of the local people's government in order that the latter may take the matter up with the owners of the enterprises concerned.

Article 11   The People's Bank of China shall be entrusted by the All-China Federation of Trade Unions to take custody of labour insurance funds.

Chapter Three

PROVISIONS FOR VARIOUS LABOUR INSURANCE BENEFITS

Article 12   The following provisions shall apply in the case of injury or disablement sustained while at work:

(a) Workers and staff members injured while at work shall be treated at the clinic or hospital of the enterprise concerned or at a hospital designated by the enterprise. If the clinic or hospital of the enterprise or the designated hospital is unable to provide the required treatment, the management or owner shall send the patient to another hospital for treatment. The total expenses for treatment, medicines, hospitalization and meals at the hospital, and travelling expenses involved shall be borne by the management or owner of the enterprise. Wages must be paid in full throughout the period of treatment.

(b) Workers and staff members who are disabled as a result of injuries sustained while at work shall be paid monthly invalid pensions or allowances from the labour insurance fund in accordance with the following conditions:

(1) A worker or staff member who has to retire from work due to complete disablement and who needs other people to take care of him, shall receive an invalid pension for life amounting to 75 per cent of his wages.

(2) A worker or staff member who has to retire from work due to complete disablement but who is not in need of other people to take care of him, shall receive an invalid pension amounting to 60 per cent of his wages until such time as he regains his ability to work or

until his death. On recovery, he shall be given suitable work by the management or owner of the enterprise.

(3) A worker or staff member who is partially disabled and is still able to work, shall be given suitable work by the management or owner of the enterprise. He shall be paid an invalid allowance from the labour insurance fund according to the degree of disablement. The amount paid shall be between 10–30 per cent of his wages prior to being disabled; but this sum, together with his wages after resuming work, shall not exceed his wages prior to being disabled. Provisions covering such cases are made in the Detailed Rules for Carrying Out the Labour Insurance Regulations of the People's Republic of China.

(c) The degree of disablement of workers and staff members injured at work, or any change in it, is to be assessed by a committee to investigate disablement. Provisions dealing with such cases are made in the Detailed Rules for Carrying Out the Labour Insurance Regulations of the People's Republic of China.

Article 13   The following provisions shall apply in cases of sickness, injuries or disablement not sustained at work:

(a) In cases of sickness or injuries not sustained at work to be treated at the clinic or hospital of the enterprise, in a designated hospital, or by designated doctors of traditional Chinese or Western school, all expenses for treatment, operations, hospitalization and ordinary medicines shall be paid by the management or owner of the enterprise; the total cost of expensive medicines, expenses for meals at the hospital and travelling expenses involved shall be borne by the patient. If he is in financial straits, he may obtain an allowance from the labour insurance fund according to his actual circumstances. In the case of sickness or injuries not sustained at work, it is all for the hospital to decide whether the patient should be hospitalized, or sent to another hospital for treatment and when he should be discharged from the hospital.

(b) A worker or staff member who is absent from work to receive medical treatment for sickness or injury not sustained at work shall, according to the length of time he has been employed in the enterprise, be paid sick or injury leave wages equivalent to 60–100 per cent of his original wages by the management or owner of the enterprise, provided the period of absence does not exceed 6 consecutive months. When such period of absence exceeds 6 consecutive months he shall receive relief benefits for sickness or injury not sustained at work, which shall be paid to him monthly from the labour insurance fund at the rate of 40–60 per cent of his wages until he resumes work, or until he is classified as disabled, or until his death. Provisions dealing with such cases are made in the Detailed Rules for Carrying Out the Labour Insurance Regulations of the People's Republic of China.

(c) In the case of a worker or staff member who is obliged to retire from work after his complete disablement is established while receiving treatment for sickness or injury not sustained at work, the payment of sick leave or injury wages or relief benefits for sickness or injury not sustained at work shall be suspended. He shall be paid relief benefits for disablement not sustained at work from the labour insurance fund. The amount shall be determined according to the following conditions: if he needs other people to take care of him, he receives 50 per cent of his wages; if he does not need such help, he receives 40 per cent. This sum shall be paid until he resumes work or until his death. A partially disabled worker or staff member who can still work, is not entitled to this benefit. The degree of disablement or any change in it shall be assessed according to the provisions as stipulated in *Clause C* of *Article 12*.

(d) Workers or staff members who fall ill, or who sustain injury or disablement not at work shall be given suitable work by the management or owner of the enterprise when they have recovered and are certified fit for work by the medical institution concerned.

(e) When a lineal dependent of a worker or staff member falls ill, he or she may receive free treatment at the clinic or hospital of the enterprise, at a designated hospital, or from designated doctors of traditional Chinese or Western school. The operation fees and the cost of ordinary medicines shall be paid in half by the management or owner of the enterprise; expensive medicines, travelling expenses involved, hospitalization, meals at the hospital and all other expenses shall be paid by the patient.

Article 14 Provisions for death benefits for workers and staff members and their lineal dependents:

(a) Funeral expenses shall be paid by the management or owner of the enterprise concerned in the event of the death of a worker or staff member while at work. The amount of such benefit shall be equivalent to 3 months' wages based upon the average wages of workers and staff members in the enterprise. In addition, the lineal dependents of the deceased shall receive from the labour insurance fund a monthly pension which shall be based upon their number. The amount of such a pension shall be 25–50 per cent of the wages of the deceased and shall be paid until such a time when the dependents no longer have the status of dependents. Provisions dealing with such cases are made in the Detailed Rules for Carrying Out the Labour Insurance Regulations of the People's Republic of China.

(b) A funeral allowance equivalent to 2 months' wages based on the average wages of workers and staff members in the enterprise, shall be paid from the labour insurance fund in the case of the death of a worker or staff member from sickness or injury not sustained at work. In addition, a relief benefit shall be paid from the labour insurance fund to the lineal dependents of the deceased which shall be equivalent to 6–12 months' wages of the deceased according to the number of his dependents. Provisions dealing with such cases are dealt with in the Detailed Rules for Carrying Out the Labour Insurance Regulations of the People's Republic of China.

(c) Funeral expenses and a pension for lineal dependents shall be paid in accordance with *Clause A* of this Article in the case of a worker or staff member who dies after retirement because complete disablement resulting from injury sustained at work. A funeral allowance and a relief benefit for lineal dependents as stipulated in *Clause B* of this Article shall be paid in the case of a worker or staff member who dies after his old-age retirement or who dies after retirement because of complete disablement resulting from injury not sustained at work.

(d) A funeral allowance shall be paid from the labour insurance fund in the case of the death of a lineal dependent of a worker or staff member. The amount shall be equivalent to one half of the monthly average wages of workers and staff members in the enterprise if the deceased is 10 years of age or more; one-third of the monthly average wages, if the deceased is between 1 and 10 years of age; no allowance shall be paid if the deceased is under one year of age.

Article 15 Provisions for old-age pensions:

(a) A male worker or staff member, upon attaining the age of 60, who has worked for 25 years, including 5 years in the enterprise concerned, is entitled to old-age retirement from work. He shall receive a monthly old-age pension upon retirement from the labour insurance fund until his death. The amount, to be calculated on the basis of the number of years he has worked in the enterprise concerned, shall range from 50 to 70 per cent of his wages. If the interest of the enterprise calls for his staying on the job, even though he is qualified to old-age retirement, he shall receive, in addition to his original wages, a monthly old-age work pension from the labour insurance fund according to the number of years he has worked in the enterprise concerned. This pension shall be equivalent to 10–20 per cent of his wages. Provisions dealing with such cases are made in the Detailed Rules for Carrying Out the Labour Insurance Regulations of the People's Republic of China.

(b) A woman worker or staff member, upon attaining the age of 50, who has worked for 20 years, including 5 years in the enterprise concerned, shall receive an old-age pension as stipulated in *Clause A* of this Article.

(c) Male workers and staff members, upon attaining the age of 55, and women workers and staff members, upon attaining the age of 45, who work in mines or in places which are constantly at a temperature below 32° F. or at 100° F. or above, shall receive old-age pensions as stipulated in *Clause A* of this Article. However, in calculating the number of years of employment, including those in the enterprise concerned, one year's work under such conditions shall be counted as one year and three months.

(d) Male workers and staff members, upon attaining the age of 55, and women workers and staff members, upon attaining the age of 45, who are directly engaged in work detrimental to health in industries extracting or manufacturing lead, mercury, arsenic, phosphorus, and acids or in other chemical and armament industries, shall receive old-age pensions as stipulated in *Clause A* of this Article. However, in calculating the number of years of employment, including those in the enterprise concerned, one year's work in such places shall be counted as one year and six months.

Article 16 Provisions for maternity benefits:

(a) Women workers and staff members are entitled to a total of 56 days' leave of absence from work before and after confinement. Wages shall be paid in full during maternity leave.

(b) Women workers and staff members are entitled up to 30 days' leave, as prescribed by the doctor, in cases of miscarriage during the first 7 months of pregnancy. Full wages shall be paid during such leave.

(c) In cases of difficult delivery or the birth of twins, women workers and staff members are entitled to an additional 14-day leave during which wages shall be paid in full.

(d) Expenses for pre-natal examinations and child delivery of pregnant women workers and staff members at the enterprise's clinic or hospital, or at a designated hospital, shall be paid by the management or owner of the enterprise. Other expenses shall be paid in accordance with *Clause A* of *Article 13.*

(e) In the case of a woman worker or staff member medically certified, at the end of maternity or miscarriage leave, if unfit to resume work, she is entitled to the benefits as for the sick stipulated in *Article 13.*

(f) In the case of child-birth, a woman worker or staff member or the wife of a male worker or staff member shall receive a maternity benefit of 40,000 yuan,[1] from the labour insurance fund.

Article 17   Provisions for collective labour insurance undertakings:

(a) All workers and staff members working in the enterprises which provide labour insurance are entitled to benefits from the collective labour insurance undertakings. Provisions are to be worked out by the All-China Federation of Trade Unions.

(b) The primary trade union committee of an enterprise, together with the management or owner, shall undertake to run collective labour insurance undertakings such as sanatoria, spare-time sanatoria, and nurseries according to the financial conditions of the enterprise and the needs of the workers and staff members. Provisions are made in the Detailed Rules for Carrying Out the Labour Insurance Regulations of the People's Republic of China.

(c) The All-China Federation of Trade Unions may run, or entrust various local trade union organizations or industrial unions with the task of running, the following collective labour insurance undertakings:
   (1) Sanatoria;
   (2) Rest homes;
   (3) Homes for the aged;
   (4) Orphanages;
   (5) Homes for the disabled;
   (6) Others.

[1] Referring to the old people's currency of the People's Republic of China. A new people's currency was introduced as of March 1, 1955; the rate of exchange was set at 1 yuan (new currency) to 10,000 yuan (old currency).—*Translator.*

Article 18 Workers and staff members who work in enterprises which provide labour insurance but who are not trade union members shall, according to the provisions of the present Regulations, receive benefits in cases of injury, disablement, or death sustained while at work, as well as child-birth, medical care for sickness or injury not sustained at work and medical care for their lineal dependents. They are entitled, however, to only half the amount prescribed of wages and relief benefit during the period of medical treatment in cases of sickness or injuries not sustained at work, relief benefit for disablement not sustained at work, relief benefit for their lineal dependents, old-age pensions, and funeral allowances.

Chapter Four

PROVISIONS FOR PREFERENTIAL LABOUR INSURANCE BENEFITS

Article 19 All model workers or model staff members who have made outstanding contributions to the enterprise concerned, and demobilized army combat heroes working in the enterprise concerned, are entitled to the following preferential labour insurance benefits when so recommended by the primary trade union committees and approved by provincial or municipal trade union organizations or the national committees of the industrial unions concerned:

(a) The cost of expensive medicines, travelling expenses involved, and meals at the hospital during treatment for sickness or injury not sustained at work shall be borne by the management or owner of the enterprise concerned.

(b) When undergoing medical treatment for sickness or injury not sustained at work, wages are to be paid in full during the first six months. Relief benefit for sickness, for injury or disablement not sustained at work shall be at a rate of 60 per cent of the wages of the person concerned. Invalid pension for disablement sustained at work shall be equivalent to the full amount of the wages of the person concerned. Allowances for disablement sustained at work shall be equivalent to the difference between the wages received by the person concerned prior to the disablement and the wages received after resuming work. In the case of death being incurred while at work the lineal dependents shall receive a pension equivalent to 30–60 per cent of the wages of the deceased. Old-age pensions upon retirement shall be 60–80 per cent of the wages of the person concerned. Old-age pensions for persons continuing to work beyond the age limit shall be 20–30 per cent of the wages of the person concerned. Provisions for dealing with such matters are made in the Detailed Rules for Carrying Out the Labour Insurance Regulations of the People's Republic of China.

(c) The right to priority in receiving benefits from the collective labour insurance undertakings.

Article 20   Disabled ex-servicemen working in enterprises shall be paid full wages during the first six months of their absence from work to receive medical treatment for sickness or injury not sustained at work, regardless of the length of time they have worked in the enterprise concerned. After six months such matters shall be dealt with according to the provisions of *Clause B* of *Article 13*.

Chapter Five

ALLOCATION OF LABOUR INSURANCE FUNDS

Article 21   Provisions for the allocation of labour insurance funds shall be as follows:

(a) The general labour insurance fund shall be used by the All-China Federation of Trade Unions to run collective labour insurance undertakings.

(b) Labour insurance funds are to be used by primary trade union committees to pay various pensions, allowances and relief benefits, and allowances for the collective labour insurance undertakings run by the enterprise concerned. Balance sheets are to be drawn up each month. Funds left in hand shall be turned over in full to the accounts of the provincial or municipal trade union organizations or of the national committees of industrial unions to serve as an adjustment fund for labour insurance (hereafter referred to as "adjustment fund").

(c) The adjustment fund shall be used by the provincial or municipal trade union organizations or the national committees of industrial unions to subsidize their affiliated primary trade union committees which are found to be short of labour insurance funds, or to run collective labour insurance undertakings. National committees of industrial unions may authorize their local organizations to manage the allocation of the adjustment fund. The All-China Federation of Trade Unions has the right to over-all management and allocation of the adjustment funds of the various provincial and municipal trade union organizations and of the national committees of industrial unions, and it may use such funds to run collective labour insurance undertakings. In the case of shortage of adjustment funds, the provincial or municipal trade union organizations or the national committees of industrial unions may apply to the All-China Federation of Trade Unions for subsidies.

Article 22 Labour insurance funds are not to be expended for any purpose other than that of labour insurance undertakings.

Article 23 The accounting departments of all enterprises concerned shall open separate accounts for the receipt and expenditure of the labour insurance fund. The accounting system for labour insurance fund shall be worked out by the Ministry of Labour of the Central People's Government in conjunction with the All-China Federation of Trade Unions.

Article 24 The receipt and disbursement of the adjustment fund for labour insurance shall be administered by the finance departments of trade union organizations at various levels in accordance with the regulations drawn up by the All-China Federation of Trade Unions.

Chapter Six

ADMINISTRATION AND SUPERVISION OF LABOUR
INSURANCE

Article 25 The primary trade union committees shall be the basic units in the administration of labour insurance, whose chief tasks shall be: to supervise the payment of labour insurance funds; decide on payments from labour insurance funds; supervise the various expenses from the fund directly paid by the managements or owners of enterprises as stipulated in the present Regulations; urge the enterprises to improve the management of the collective labour insurance undertakings and public health services; attend to all practical matters relating to labour insurance; compile monthly reports on labour insurance funds, and annual budgets, financial reports, plans of work, and reports on work to be submitted to the provincial or municipal trade union organizations or the national committees of industrial unions, as well as to the labour administration organs of the local people's governments; and to report on their work to the general membership meetings or to congresses of trade unions.

Article 26   The auditing commissions of the various primary trade union committees shall each month audit and make public the accounts of the labour insurance fund and of the various expenses paid directly by the managements or owners of enterprises as stipulated in the present Regulations.

Article 27   The provincial and municipal trade union organizations and the national or regional committees of industrial unions shall be responsible for directing and supervising their affiliated primary trade union committees in administering the labour insurance. They shall audit the monthly balance sheets, budgets, and financial reports of the labour insurance funds, and determine whether there are errors in the receipts and disbursements of these funds, receive complaints from workers and staff members on matters relating to labour insurance, and draw up monthly reports on the state of the labour insurance funds and adjustment funds, and annual budgets, financial reports, plans of work and reports on work. Reporting in this respect shall be made according to the following procedure:
- (a) The provincial and municipal trade union organizations shall report to the labour administration organs of the local people's governments and to the trade union organizations of the Greater Administrative Areas.
- (b) The national committees of industrial unions shall report to the All-China Federation of Trade Unions and to the Ministry of Labour of the Central People's Government.

Article 28   The trade union organizations in the Greater Administrative Areas shall be responsible for directing and supervising the labour insurance work of their affiliated provincial and municipal trade union organizations and the industrial trade union organizations in their respective areas. They shall audit the monthly balance sheets, budgets, and financial reports of the labour insurance funds and adjustment funds, plans of work, and reports on work submitted by the provincial and municipal trade union organizations. They shall draw up quarterly financial reports on the collection and expenditure of labour insurance funds, annual budgets, financial reports, plans of work, and reports on work, and submit such reports to the departments of labour of the people's governments in the Greater Administrative Areas concerned, to the Ministry of Labour of the

Central People's Government and to the All-China Federation of Trade Unions.

Article 29   The All-China Federation of Trade Unions is the highest leading organ for directing the labour insurance work throughout the country. It shall administer in a unified manner the operation of labour insurance undertakings throughout the country, supervise and guide the carrying out of labour insurance work by the local trade union organizations and the industrial union organizations. It shall audit and compile financial reports on labour insurance funds and general labour insurance funds. It shall draw up annual budgets and financial reports of labour insurance funds, plans of work, and reports on work and send such reports to the Ministries of Labour and of Finance of the Central People's Government for reference.

Article 30   Labour administration organs of the people's governments at all levels shall supervise the payment of labour insurance funds, inspect the carrying out of labour insurance work and deal with complaints relating to labour insurance.

Article 31   The Ministry of Labour of the Central People's Government is the highest supervisory organ for labour insurance throughout the country. It shall be responsible for the thorough enforcement of the Labour Insurance Regulations and shall inspect the fulfilment of labour insurance work throughout the country. The rules governing such inspection shall be drawn up separately.

Chapter Seven

SUPPLEMENTARY PROVISIONS

Article 32   The present Regulations shall come into effect upon adoption and promulgation by the Government Administration Council of the Central People's Government. In amending these Regulations the same procedure shall apply.

Appendix C   Reform through Labor in China

In China, correctional labor is the most severe punitive measure, excepting the death penalty, which hangs over workers whose violations of labor discipline are most flagrant and protracted.[1] Aimed at "reactionary" and "counterrevolutionary" individuals and groups convicted of specific violations of the Constitution and legal statutes, correctional labor sentences are meted out to workers whose negative behavior is labeled antisocial or treasonable.

The ideological basis for such labor has been set forth by Mao Tse-tung:

> As for the members of the reactionary classes and individual reactionaries, so long as they do not rebel, sabotage or create trouble,
> . . . land and work will be given to them . . . to allow them to live and remould themselves through labour into new people. If they are not willing to work, the people's state will compel them to work. Propaganda and educational work will be done among them too. . . .[2]

The legal basis for correctional labor is defined in the Constitution of the People's Republic, where "reform through labour" is the means by which "landlords and capitalists" reeducate themselves and become good citizens (Article 19). All workers are required to "observe labour discipline" (Article 100). Thus, workers who are egregious violators of work performance norms may be treated as enemies of the state requiring rectification through labor.[3]

The structure of correctional labor in China has been clearly set forth by the CCP and the government in regulations and editorials and other commentaries so that its meaning and the means for its implementation are quite evident. Compulsory labor (as distinct from labor elicited by the usual material or nonmaterial mechanisms) is of two kinds: (1) that noncompensated labor which is a punishment together with deprivation of freedom given to persons convicted of specific crimes (*reform and rehabilitation through labor*); and (2) that compensated labor which is required of persons who have committed antisocial acts or violated security measures and who have not been indicted, tried, and convicted but who persist in "antisocial behavior" (*labor reeducation*).[4]

Reform through labor is carried out through four types of institutions. The first is the *detention house* which is mainly for people awaiting trial but also domiciles convicts serving terms of up to two years. All inmates are required to engage in labor service for reform. Second is the *prison* which is for criminals whose violations have been very serious (e.g., those with life sentences) and for whom outside labor service is carried out within the institution's walls. A third type of institution in which reform through labor is prescribed is the *juvenile delinquents' institutes* for those between thirteen and eighteen years of age. While inmates are exposed to education in cultural subjects, politics, the socialist moral code, and industrial production techniques, they are also required to perform "light labor service." The fourth and most important type of reform through labor, the *labor service for reform corps,* is what is usually thought of when correctional labor is mentioned. This corps is responsible for "the custody of convicted counterrevolutionary criminals and other criminals suited for labor service in the open." It is structured to carry out planned production in the various sectors of the economy and is expected to coordinate such work with ideological education. The criminals are organized into work groups pyramided into a general corps paralleling the hierarchic arrangement in factories and rural communes.[5]

Labor reeducation arrangements are made for those not covered by reform through labor institutions. Such labor reform is under joint jurisdiction and operations of civil administrations and public security agencies and is required of antisocial elements who are expected to live by their own work, for which they are compensated, and to rectify their behavior so that public order is better maintained. Included in this category are: (1) those who have records as vagrants or petty thieves and refuse to change despite reeducative efforts; (2) "counterrevolutionaries" and "antisocialist reactionaries" who commit minor offenses or have no means of livelihood; (3) those who though capable of working have refused to do so, or those who violate standards of public order and have no visible means of livelihood; and (4) those who refuse to take on work assigned to them or to follow out arrangements for their transfer or "make trouble for no reasons" or "hinder the transaction of official business." These last infractions apparently include violations of labor discipline.[6]

Individuals required to submit to labor reeducation live in freer conditions than those undergoing correctional labor reform in organized institutions. They are to receive compensation commensurate with the quantity and quality of their work, and other awards are scheduled for the outstanding performers. Some may even have their "counterrevolutionary" status annulled. Provision is made for money to be deducted and transmitted for family maintenance. They are not confined to a jail or to some such institution but live in or near the special work project to which they have been assigned. They are subject to heavy political education along with their mandated work stints and labor custody disciplinary restrictions. The actual framework within which they work and live varies according to local conditions and requirements. Sometimes reform is combined with resettlement or other economic or social programs.[7]

Although many details about correctional labor in China are relatively easy to come by, getting the measure of its quantitative dimensions is a more difficult task. Discussion of the question of correctional labor, its regulation, and its institutional arrangement has been freely carried on in the Chinese press and by officials. Even the location and estimated population of correctional labor units have been published in new reports and analyses.[8] Given such data, some have tried to construct a total figure. For example, the Nationalist government on Taiwan has submitted an estimate of over 25 million in its report on forced labor to the United Nations in 1955. This estimate was based on actual figures gleaned from the Chinese press on correctional labor in a province or in particular units. Then taking all the known labor units, the authors made assumptions about relative size and number by province and aggregated these to yield the 25-million result.[9]

An estimate of this sort is fraught with many pitfalls, since the location and population of correctional labor units change frequently, and some may go out of existence while new ones emerge. In a country of China's vast population, 25-million people seems to be a small enough number, though in my view it is a quite exaggerated estimate. And yet in the middle 1950s it represented 15 percent of all males between the ages of 15 and 55. Qualitative evidence suggests that correctional labor is not a very significant factor in China's overall labor picture. Its significance was greatest in the early 1950s when repression of landlords and other "class enemies" was widespread. By 1957 when collectivization had been fully achieved in agriculture, there was less evidence of the widespread use of correctional labor, and public attention was focused on the "labor custody" aspects of reform of antisocial individuals and groups. The Chinese reliance on internal pressures to exact desired behavior contrasted with Soviet imposition of external pressures suggests less need for repression once basic organizational units (such as the commune) were set up and stabilized. Since the late 1950s less and less attention has been given to correctional labor both in the official press and in hostile newspapers in Hong Kong. It seems that whatever the role of correctional labor was in the middle 1950s, it is much less prominent today.[10]

Appendix C. Reform through Labor in China

1. For a survey of labor reform see Y. L. Wu, *An Economic Survey of Communist China* (New York: Bookman, 1956), 9; and Edgar Snow, *The Other Side of the River* (New York: Random House, 1961), chapters 47–48.

2. Mao Tse-tung, "On the People's Democratic Dictatorship," in *Selected Works of Mao Tse-tung* (Peking: Foreign Languages Press, 1961), 4:419.

3. *Constitution of the People's Republic of China* (Peking: Foreign Languages Press), 1961, pp. 13–14, 42.

4. Cf. Martin King Whyte, "Corrective Labor Camps in China," *Asian Survey* 13 (March 1973): 253–69. See "Reform through Labor of Criminals in Communist China," in *Current Background,* 15 September 1954, pp. 1–2; "State Council's Decision on Question of Labor Custody," *Jen-min jih-pao,* 4 August 1957, in SCMP, 13 August 1957, pp. 1–2; and "Labor Custody: An Effective Measure to Handle Depraved Elements," *Shih-shih Shou-ts'e* [Current events], no. 16 (August 1957), in SCMM, 28 October 1957, pp. 5–7 for the overall view.

5. NCNA, "Regulations Governing Labor Service for Reform of the People's Republic of China," Peking, 15 September 1954, in *Current Background* 293 (15 September 1954):3–7.

6. "State Council's Decree Relating to Labor Custody," *Jen-min jih-pao,* 4 August 1957, in SCMP, 13 August 1957, pp. 1–2. See also "Changchow Takes over Undesirable Characters for Labor Custody," *Honan jih-pao,* 8 October 1957, in SCMP, 4 November 1957, pp. 12–13; and "Decision of the State Council of the PRC Relating to Problems of Rehabilitation Through Labor" (Approved at the 78th meeting of the Standing Committee of the National People's Congress, 1 August 1957; promulgated by the State Council, 3 August 1957), cited in Jerome Alan Cohen, *The Criminal Process in the People's Republic of China* (Cambridge: Harvard University Press, 1968), pp. 249–50.

7. Ibid. See also "Shanghai Vagrants Become New Men Through Labor Reform," *Chieh-fang jih-pao* (Shanghai), 6 September 1956, in SCMP, 4 December 1956, p. 18; and NCNA, "Counter-revolutionary Status of Group Annulled in Soochow," Nanking, 3 May 1957, in SCMP, 14 May 1957, pp. 26 –27.

8. See, e.g., Meng Chao-liang, "Basic Conditions of Labor Reform Work During the Past Nine Years," *Cheng-fa Yen-chiu,* no. 5 (October 1958), in SCMM, 22 December 1958, pp. 11–18.

9. United Nations Economic and Social Council, *Forced Labour.* Report by the secretary-general of the United Nations and the director-general of the International Labour Office, 15 December 1955.

10. John S. Aird, *The Size, Composition and Growth of the Population of Mainland China,* International Population Statistics Reports, Series p-90, No. 15 (Washington, D.C.: Government Printing Office, 1961), p. 81, provides the population data upon which the 15 percent estimate is based. See "I Was A Slave Laborer in Fat Shan Airfield," *Chung-nan jih-pao* (Hong Kong), 28 March 1954, in RHKCP 60/54, 31 March 1954, pp. 4–6 for an example of external reports on correctional labor.

Appendix D Income and Expenditure of the All-China Federation of Trade-Unions

Table D.1

Income and Expenditure of the ACFTU
(1953–1956)

Income

Members' fees	¥ 94,275,000.00
From the administrations of enterprises, government organs, and schools	363,486,000.00
From activities of culture, education, and athletics	5,637,000.00
Government subsidy	24,793,000.00
Others	30,461,000.00
Total	¥ 518,652,000.00

Expenditure

Cultural, educational, and athletic affairs (including ¥23,191,000.00 for capital construction)	¥ 105,842,000.00
Cadre training (including ¥ 16,316,000.00 for CCP)	46,268,000.00
Administration (including ¥ 11,187,000.00 for capital construction)	202,349,000.00
Subsidy to the basic trade-union units	15,362,000.00
Expenditures of the basic organs of five national trade-unions (railway, post, and	

Expenditure

communication; seaman; 2d machinery workers; salt industry) and the general trade-union of Hunan province	52,880,000.00
International activities	4,874,000.00
Others	5,969,000.00
Total	¥ 433,544,000.00
Surplus:	¥ 85,108,000.00

Source: Li Tsai-Wan, "Report on the Financial Work," *The Important Documents of the 8th Congress of ACFTU* (Chung Kuo Kung Hui Ti Pa Tzu Ch'uan Kuo Tai Piao Ta Hui Tsu Yao Wen Chien) (Peking, 1958).

Note: There was still ¥ 81,086,000.00 of surplus from the years prior to 1952. Besides the expenditures mentioned above, ¥ 56,160,000.00 of the members' fees was spent as a welfare subsidy for needy members.

Name Index

Subject Index

Ideology, 13, 15-17, 30, 81, 110-11,
116-17, 125-27, 144-45. *See also*
Mao Tsetung thought.
Incentives, 93-122, 188. *See also* Emulation; Wages.
—competitive, 112-16
—cooperative, 25, 117-22
—material, 5-6, 24-26, 94-96, 136, 188
—nonmaterial, 5-6, 94, 110-22, 188
—social, 1, 5-6, 111
Income disparity, *see* Income inequality.
Income inequality, 9, 95, 151, 181-83
Individualism, 11, 24, 26-27, 187
Indonesia, 50
Industrial disputes, *see* Strikes.
Industrialization, 1, 3, 7, 10-20, 29, 37,
181, 185, 191. *See also* Modernization; Socialization.
Industrial waste, 21. *See also* Ecology.
Industry, 3, 6, 18, 20-22, 25, 34-35, 38,
40, 57-58, 99, 101, 130, 146-47, 164-
65, 189-90. *See also* Output.
—heavy, 5, 16, 20
—indigenous, 18, 20, 174
—light, 3, 18, 95, 164-65
—local, 20-21
—modern, 22-23
Inflation, 5
Innovation, 108-9, 117
Institute of Scientific Research on
Labor Protection, 141
Inventions, *see* Innovation.
Investment, *see* Capital; Capital accumulation.
Investment in human capital, 23, 189

Jamaica, 50
Japan, 63, 188
Jen-min jih-pao (People's Daily), 133-
34, 145
Job titles, 102-3, 215, 217, 219, 221,
223
"Joining theory and practice," 23
Joint state-private enterprise, 14, 37
July 21 College, 80

Kung-jen jih-pao (Workers' Daily),
110, 132, 134
Kuomintang, 87
Kwangsi, 178

Labor, 2, 18, 22-23, 50, 55, 62, 180-81
Labor allocation, 9, 22-23, 62-92, 94,
181-83, 186-88. *See also* Labor mobility.
Labor discipline, *see* Correctional
labor.
Labor force, 2-3, 22-23, 29-92, 181-83,
186-88
Labor hero, 113. *See also* Advanced
worker; Labor models; Model.
Labor insurance regulations, 142-43,
224-37
Labor-intensive techniques, 9, 18, 21
Labor mobility, 22-23, 62-92, 94, 187-
88. *See also* Labor allocation.
—horizontal, 63-64, 66, 73-76, 187
—vertical, 63-64, 66, 76-78, 187
Labor models, 94. *See also* Advanced
worker; Labor hero; Model.
Labor productivity, 29, 55-60, 112, 148
Labor protection, *see* Safety mea-
sures.
Liberation Daily, 133
Liuists, 1, 7, 10, 17-18, 69, 97, 116
Living levels, 10, 25, 28, 151, 153-68

Mang-ya area, 100
Maoist development strategy, 7, 10-
28, 40, 54, 56, 62, 65, 75, 77, 91-93,
118, 174, 180-83, 185-86, 188-91
Maoist model, *see* Maoist develop-
ment strategy.
Maoists, 1, 10-11, 14-18, 24, 26-27, 47,
67, 69, 93-94, 96-97, 116, 122, 134-
35, 180
Mao Tsetung thought, 24, 27, 71, 79
Markets, 14, 64, 185-87
Mass decision-making, 16, 117, 119,
137
Mass meetings, 117
Mass movements, 15, 25, 75, 112-13,
117-18, 121, 139
Mass participation, 15, 117